Book Reviews

MIRRORS OF REFLECTION. By R. M. Wildego. Illustrated by Lynette Howells. East-West Publications (U.K.) Ltd., Jubilee House, Chapel Road, Hounslow, Middlesex TW3 1TX. £5.50.

This finely produced volume with its sensitive illustrations expresses a deep wisdom and inner promise which embraces one's attention, and draws out of the deep well of the heart the waters of realisation to quench the thirst of all those who search for greater truth.

In the foreword it says: "It was written out of that inner silence which throbs with the pulse of life itself, that silence which brings forth, which generates, quickens, is rich with meaning with the peace, joy and love at the root of our nature. It invites us to probe our own silence, our own fullness, wherein we learn, as the author himself has done, to distinguish the flashes of truth our soul sends forth."

The wisdom revealed within its pages, deeply reflects the beauty and guidance of that silent voice within each one of us which lovingly bids us to open the closed door of one's heart. It is full with aspects of truth which serve to awaken us to our Divine Nature and contains precious gifts of instruction which help to sustain us through the difficulties that are presented to us in our everyday lives.

Among the many passages, flames of inspiration that burn brightly through a dark night, are guidelines on: *Wonder; Service; Simplicity; Awareness; Time and Timelessness; Life; Death; Purpose; Love; Faith; The Central Point; Meditation; Self; Soul; Spirit; Destiny; Oneness; Consummation* and many more . . .

In the "mirror" of *Awareness*, the author reveals that; "To find the truth is to know the inner temple. To know the inner temple is to discover the jewel of God's gift and become as the diamond of incandescent light. To observe the flow of life is to be immersed in life and flow with it in silence. From within the hub of life we watch life pass by, but in our silence we observe all things from the centre. To observe all things with patience is to learn; the process of learning is the way to wisdom. In studying all things an open mind is needed as much as an open heart, for they who study their own ways wisely find out much about their virtues and shortcomings and they who correct their shortcomings will one day master their own destiny. . .".

This enriching volume springs forth out of the soul's own wisdom. To contemplate its contents, to ponder its truths will bring many blessings to numerous souls in need. May its essence touch you as deeply as it has touched myself. Very much recommended.

BRIAN GRAHAM

MIRRORS OF REFLECTION

MIRRORS OF REFLECTION

R. M. WILDEGO

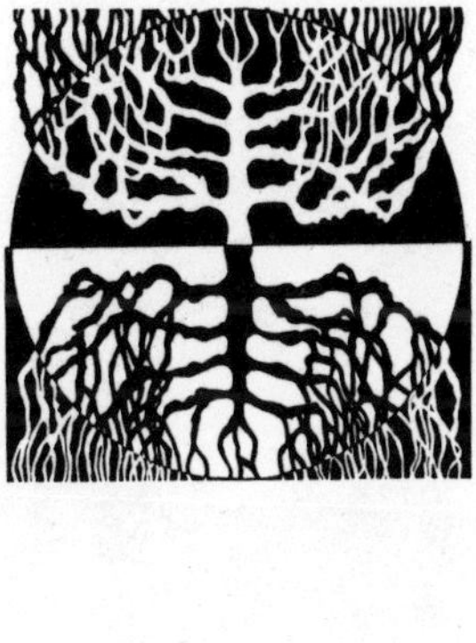

EAST·WEST PUBLICATIONS
LONDON AND THE HAGUE

East-West Publications (U.K.) Ltd.
Jubilee House, Chapel Road
Hounslow, Middlesex TW3 1TX

Printed in Great Britain by The Camelot Press, Southampton
Photoset by Tellgate Ltd, Shaftesbury, Dorset

ISBN 0 85692 090 8

Contents

Part III

Part IV

Foreword

A BOOK that expresses the flame of inspiration is a rare experience. Each its insight, its quickening throb, its very life. We, human beings, have such depths of knowledge, we need only turn inwardly to tap treasures that the universe holds in store for us.

This book is the proof and the guarantee that such a turning and such a reaping are possible; it is the promise that each one of us may find in himself a spring of infinite wisdom that can sustain us in life's daily trials with strength and serenity. It was written out of that inner silence which throbs with the pulse of life itself, that silence which brings forth, which generates, quickens, is rich with meaning, with the peace, joy and love at the root of our nature. It invites us to probe our own silence, our own fullness, wherein we learn, as the author himself has done, to distinguish the flashes of truth our soul sends forth.

If we have never entered into the silence within our heart, if we have never heard the song which the Great Heart has been chanting to the little heart of man since time was, then these aphorisms may help us to attune our whole being to the divine call; to realise that each one of us echoes in his heart the secret song of life.

This book is one such echo, one such revelation; the token of an inner listening and an inner receiving; the sharing of our most treasured heritage, our birthright, the soul's own wisdom. To pour over its contents, to ponder over its truths, is a blessing.

This book is the result of inspiration quite beyond the author's own thoughts. In its entirety, it deals with a probing search for truths that can only be realised at a level far deeper than the mind. It is not a book of step by step instruction and therefore concerns aspects of truths that only experience within the world of meditation will bring to light. Some will understand its underlying call for unity, its plea for recognition of neighbourly love; others who have sorrows may be helped in their time of turmoil. It points towards that one guiding principle of peace and good will which holds all as one and one as all and which should be the one wish of everyone who cares for humanity.

May its wisdom reach out to all those who search and thirst for truth.

J. MILLER *(Editor)*

The wondrous beauty perceived in each thing in life's passage is none other than the divine Self reflected from within.

To enter into communion with each aspect of this divine and inherent beauty, it is crucial to understand our own nature, for each thing is none other than what we are and none other than how we envisage it to be.

We are the spring from which burst forth the myriads of forms that generate the beauty therein and constitute the immortal.

PART I

Musings

WHO knows of the cosmos within the heart and of that infinite space wherein abides true being? They alone who have found the eternal *now* and dwell within the silent void of the miracle of life, know the cosmos within the heart.

The mighty oak grows from an acorn and the seed of man grows from the infinite; man finds infinity itself in his own inner silence; he becomes the might of Deity; for Deity in Its quiescence is the invisible strength within all things.

. . .

Oceans are made to be charted. Who charts the heavens knows also the sea. Who charts the God within the heart even fractionally is knowledgeable of many oceans and spaces and gradually becomes the navigator of the unknown.

The man who walks upon the fresh sod knows the feeling of it beneath his feet. Even so the fisherman feels every mood of the sea. But the man of God's handiwork knows the feeling of being elated every second.

. . .

The clouds glide freely in the sky, blown by the winds of destiny. They cannot remain forever still at one point only, but must wander on to new lands. The man born of earth wanders aimlessly betwixt heaven and earth, blown by destiny in his search for the still and peaceful, in his search for his own meaning; yet there he cannot remain until he outgrows the winds of his own restlessness and turns all his endeavours to the greater advantage of divine purpose.

. . .

The man and the spider have much in common for both rely upon the link that joins one point with another. For the spider it is the strand of finely manufactured silk; for the man it is the manufacture of the web that he weaves inwardly and joins with an inner silence.

A wise man weaves a web towards the infinite and makes faith its strength and hope its path towards salvation; as a spider collecting leaves together makes an anchor upon which to attach its thread, so a wise man attaches his thread upon the centre of the infinite.

. . .

It is impossible for an artist to paint each star in the heavens. It is unthinkable for a mathematician to count each drop of water contained in the ocean.

Even so it is foolishness for a man to conceive of fully grasping the Deity and the majestic wonder of Deity's handiwork.

As the sea expands its realms upon the shore, so the consciousness of man gains a foothold upon the destiny set out for him to follow.

All things are expansive and contractive.

An expansion of human consciousness leads to a contraction of human foolishness.

Fill and be emptied, empty and renew, search and encompass that which you seek, for the value of jewels is that of their seeking, and that of the hardships in their finding, and in their polishing.

Wonder

So many untold wonders are there locked in the heart and to be sought after; so many moments of great joy are there hidden and to be discovered, as a many faceted jewel. What is burnished into great beauty without silent wonder? Or without the hand that stirs up the pool of creation to bring forth life's true purpose?

My friend, the world you see within your heart is the world of your reality; illuminating that reality from within is the spirit; give that reality the form of your choosing, make it manifest unto your sight, make it harmonious, radiant, vibrant.

Many times have I seen that inner world beyond this one of rigid structure, and many times have I passed into its transparent sphere, neither knowing nor understanding limitations within its boundless dimensions.

Gardens and spots of magnificent splendour have I beheld there; each manifestation have I seen spring into being, slowly take form, merging into a rainbow of soft luminous colours.
That garden is attended by the most gracious and understanding of beings; they are the gate-keepers and providers.
Soft, whispering springs sing their song to all and flashes of rainbow hues dash forth from out their crystal depths.
The water is more than wine to the taste, beyond the freshness of mountain spring, beyond the likeness of any earthly drink.
Many times have I walked into this etherial kingdom, reflecting the innermost of my thoughts and many times have my questions been answered, as a mirror shot by the sun.

. . .

Give birth to the child of wonder within, and bring forth the child of innocence in all that you do, for only then can you fully know the great Parent that watches over all and brings all eventually into one home as the living body of vibrant and radiant love.

Each point of creation is lit from the void inherent within by an incandescent light that shines forth and makes it a sparkling wonder; even so each emergent dewdrop reflects the sun of a great awakening in silent wonder.

Beauty is the mirror of life as it is reflected; its essence harmony; life reflected is the veil of wonder; each being reflects the Source and the Source gives reflection to each; beauty is the breath of the Eternal that casts its light and shade upon each thing; thus the shadow must be given light and absorbed into its depth. We all are the shadows absorbing light ere we become the light in full measure. This is the wonder of creation.

Gold is burnished to give it brilliance and the diamond is polished to give it great depth and beauty. Whosoever has burnished his heart by the wonder of contemplation upon the Source has become the shining one of majestic beauty; whosoever has polished reflection upon God by acting in a similar manner with the greatest of truths has become the jewel of the temple in the mansions of the Supreme.

The ceaseless wonder of activity is the unfolding of beauty and wisdom, for there in that wonder, that blissful state of perpetuation, exists our own immortality in the balance of the Eternal.

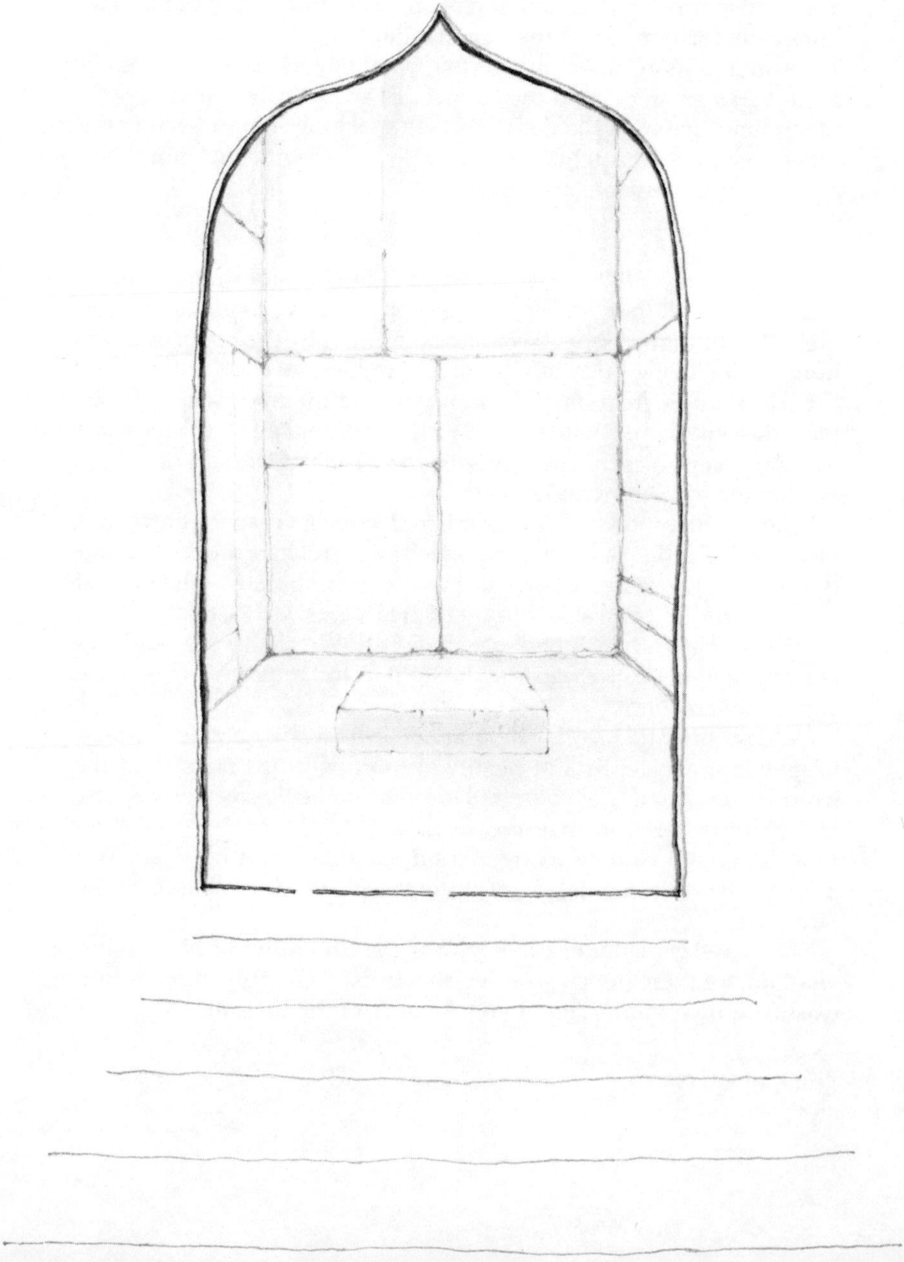

Bell Ringing

THE voice of silence beckons to all who have ears to hear – sounding as the purest of bells tolling on a clear, still night, bidding all to enter into its domain.

Hearing in silence is hearing that unstruck chord upon the soul in its purity.

Seeing is externalising that unstruck chord, and reflecting its brilliance amongst all creation.

Is it not the bellmaker that understands the tone and quality of his own making? In wisdom and in knowledge did he make its shape, with love and with care did he tend it in the crucial stages of its manufacture.

Known to him are all the blemishes within and without, as one who, loving his child, knows it by its cry.

By the experience of hand and eye he made that bell ring so pure a note, by blending the harmonies he loved together he made it sound its note of unity.

The bellmaker is the God of the universe that understands the sound of its own creation and knows its cry for truth.

The Voice

To be inspired is to wait patiently in stillness and longing, listening for a voice at the door of one's heart that that door may be opened.

The silent voice is within each one of us; all that is needed is for us to listen with an innocent mind to the one who knocks upon the door of our hearts and waits patiently for an answer.

That voice is as a visiting guest waiting recognition before entry into your home, waiting to see if it is a worthy place.

Listen carefully; only then will you hear that inner friend calling your name to tell you much about that which you have been waiting to hear.

Be patient; listen carefully; know every shade of that inner prompting that grows into a voice; for when it comes and finds that you indeed are a true friend, a listener, it will knock many times at the door of your heart and inspire you on your onward journey.

Do not lose the chance to make that visitor welcome, for he passes by but once if he finds no response; knocking at the door of each heart he brings with him riches beyond those of this world in return for a place of peace in which to stay but a short while.

Keep the door of your heart open to all; who knows which of those with whom you share bread is that traveller in disguise coming to see if you are truly worthy of his calling?

To give bread to another in your own home is to give yourself nourishment, for each one enters as the spirit of God.

Is it not wise to see all as the spirit and not as the flesh? Therefore see the inner light and not the outer manifestation, hear the inner voice and not the outer sounds.

Sowing

MANY there have been that have come as a light to this ever troublesome earth, to show its inhabitants the way towards themselves, and in doing so have been crucified or vilified by those who do not comprehend their own light of truth.

Yet they have not been crucified in vain since they have sown the seed amongst all humanity, and that seed will never die or be uprooted for no one is strong enough to uproot the truth and cast it aside.

And so is one layer of truth the very soil upon which you depend for your own bodily existence, and the resting place upon which in time to come you will rest your spirit to attain greater heights.

The knowledge of truth you impart to others is as the sower who sows good seed upon the soil of good land, knowing not whether that seed will break the surface of the soil or whether it will spring forth and be abundant within its season of harvest.

Thus will you never see the harvesting of your seeds of truth for you are but the sower and pass by to seed another field.

But the reaper shall know of your hand when he comes with the scythe to gather in that harvest, and will share your joy and speak of your deeds.

And the seeds will know not your hand but will burst forth with your truth when the next season comes, and because of you they will grow strong within their time, shedding once again a good and true seed.

All passes eternally from youth to youth, from seed to seed, from sower to sowed, and becomes the reaper of itself.

The hand that reaps knows only of its own struggle forgetting the pattern of things gone by and yet to be reborn.

The sickle is the instrument of him who comes to survive by action and yet one day will he be planted by a more gracious and knowing hand.

A word of truth and wisdom is the seed that ripens and bears fruit. An untruthful word is as the tree with no roots, dead and cut off from the substance of life, yet besides one will you find the other and know the difference.

The garden that is planted within the soul is as the hand that sows the seed upon the land, giving to life that which belongs to life, and seeding that which must be sown within its season to show fruit at the time of awakening.

Service

THE greatest task is to serve.

The task of the great servant is to become aware of God and channel that awareness towards greater heights of service.

A true master is never sure except in the service that he gives and by the service that he gives to all he is acknowledged as a master.

A true master does not acknowledge himself. Only those he serves are important and therefore he acknowledges these by being at one with them, thereby being of greater value in his knowledge towards all.

Who comes as the master disguises himself as the servant and they who listen to the servant learn much.

In service, if the service be one of unselfishness and of truth we illuminate the inner temple and thus glow with true knowledge of the Principle.

Who calls himself master is no master; who calls himself the servant of all is truly the master of himself; for humility sets a course away from the outward; and in humility lie all things simple but great.

In service there is humility, if service be in its purest form. It is therefore through service that the true master is born and raised up towards great knowledge and accomplishment.

Who serves in the ultimate is God reborn, for great service opens up the way to the greatest love.

To find the master seek out the willing servant, for there you will find the house of God.

Accomplishment

ACCOMPLISHMENT is like the seed, it grows gradually and brings forth a bountiful crop in its time of harvest. In time of famine it nourishes those who are wise enough to seek it for sustenance.

Accomplishment is one gem worth having; only those who have accomplished much through effort know the worth of the gem that they are gifted with.

Be accomplished and know the worth of accomplishment; receive of inspiration and know its full value; seek reality through illusion; thus will you grasp the purpose and the meaning of it all.

Who searches within to find a greater accomplishment is rich in all things of value and never hungers or thirsts in the ways of greater knowledge until the end.

Without effort nothing is achieved; in easy victory nothing is gained or valued.

Attainment is only gained from labour; that is the road each must travel and the gate through which each must pass to find its central state of being.

Were there no virtues, there would be no life and no joy; joy is in attaining the highest state of consciousness and in reaching out to the crown of virtues from the fragments of a confused mind.

To be accomplished is to be all, within all and without end, for this is what eternity consists of, and here lies the traveller's home of rest.

Great accomplishment is so much more than possessions; in finality, it is the letting go of all things; thus we become eternal by simplicity of being and by selflessness.

Simplicity

WHERE a still but simple heart lies, there also is the lamp of creation to warm all things and bring forth growth.

Simplicity is the most gracious and benevolent face of the Divine, complexity the most illusive. Therefore understanding is born of wisdom, simplicity and God. The simple things of life are the wisest.

Complex thoughts create greater activity than is necessary and therefore are the illusive side of man. For what is the use of being a great scholar if one lacks wisdom?

Wisdom is sought and found at the very heart of simplicity in nature.

Unfold your own simplicity and there will you find God. Become as a child and there you will find wisdom unadorned by complex thoughts. The heart of a child knows the essence that gave it birth, but the heart of man needs to find that child of God within himself.

Simplicity is the nucleus and hinging point of all else; it is the simple thoughts of the mind that are the riches of the mind.

Simplicity is created of God; complexity of man as he strives to understand the centre of the simple things where God abides.

In order to understand our higher purpose we must become a child in all that we do and cultivate simplicity through the gateway of perfect love.

Awareness

To observe carefully is to find the truth.

To find the truth is to know the inner temple.

To know the inner temple is to discover the jewel of God's gift and become as the diamond of incandescent light.

To observe the flow of life is to be immersed in life and flow with it in silence.

From within the hub of life we watch life pass by, but in our silence we observe all things from the centre.

The starting point for creative manifestations is the observation of wonder and of miracle.

That point is the creative flow observing itself and thereby being inseparable from that flow and from the Infinite, for in essence all is one. Distinction is created by an unadjusted mind in cutting off the natural within itself and superimposing the unnatural in its place.

Each point is the creative watching itself within the flow of its own life and in observing itself justly, it observes the Infinite.

In observance lies the seed of our awakening and the fruit of our greater search, for we, in observing all, know the space into which we fit and in knowing that space become complete.

In observance great truths are revealed and in truth lies our heritage and knowledge of inner being.

In observing ourselves as we truly are we observe life itself and in observing life itself we observe the principle of God at work within creation.

In true awareness there is no distinction, no human thought of deception; no form of separation; for all in true awareness is one, in love and in quality, reflecting eternally a single light from within a single point, that is itself all creation.

Awareness increases when focussed upon the point, for God is that great awareness in man and its point when his thoughts and actions serve to glorify the Principle and bring it to life through a pure and unselfish love.

To observe all things with patience is to learn; the process of learning is the way to wisdom. In studying all things an open mind is needed as much as an open heart, for they who study their own ways wisely find out much about their virtues and shortcomings and they who correct their shortcomings will one day master their own destiny.

When awareness is turned inwards to one dazzling source, and from that source reflected in true quality, God rules supreme, brings to light and bestows many great miracles.

The Temple

EACH being has light and radiance, each one has immortality and a glorious home to find; for the day is yours, also the night; death is yours, also life. The temple of eternity is yours; and so are all things to come for they belong to every aspect of creation which itself belongs to the Eternal.

If a guest is due to come to your house, do you not prepare yourself and your household to welcome him in the most pleasing way?

Even so is it with the Infinite One, that you must prepare inwardly to make both the temple and the nourishment befitting for the occasion, that communion can take place.

In a shrine we take off our shoes to show respect and to pay homage, for that is the custom. We leave, as it were, the earthly dirt at the threshold.

Then is it not also wise, when seeking the shrine of the Innermost within ourselves, that we should take off the earthly garment? The garment of desires, emotions, thoughts. These laid aside, then we enter that greater peace that abides in the depth of our shrine which shelters us from all outer storms and constitutes the threshold of a deeper communion.

The silent man is all things and yet none, is free of judgement, thus is not judged; is his own temple, thus he does not travel by foot to a distant shrine or set up an epitaph to himself, for he is God in reflective quality and God guides his footsteps wherever he goes.

True freedom is the inner communion wherein we find divine guidance and are moulded into great knowledge, for the wealth that is fashioned in the heart's temple by communion is the only true wealth of this earth that nothing can destroy.

It is unwise to keep one day holy and the other six in degrading the principle of God, when each day we can be immersed in the glorification of God's temple within by that which we do for the sake of others, by every deed performed in self oblivion.

Those knowledgeable of the inner temple are the true keepers of God's holy days; not content to spend them in rest, they find good deeds to do and carry them out wherever they are, inconspicuously and silently.

In keeping his heart open to others, man finds God and brings to life his own temple of prayer. It is in this way that he can rest from his labour and keep each day holy.

Time and Timelessness

MANY moments of measured time has the body in the sea of perpetual evolution and many times from birth to rebirth and from one level of understanding to the next. The perfect being is timeless and cannot be measured unless it be at the hands of the Divine who knows and measures all things in the scales of the Eternal.

Know then my friend and brother that through infinity you came into existence and by the laws of opposition were you moulded into unity of form.

Know also that by the same law inverted will you once more become an absolute – infinity itself – and reside therein to know its truth once more, until time beckons you towards a physical life and until infinity claims you back once again, and holds you to its bosom.

See therefore infinity in all things finite and eternity in that which passes by on your plane of consciousness.

Moments do not make eternity and are outside its realms, but omnipresent within physical activity.

Who can say that time is eternity, or that eternity comprehends time? For time is an illusion of man's choosing and the cage to which he is bound by his own consciousness; his own state of evolvement.

That which does not withstand the sands of time is unreal and illusory.

He who can step outside himself knows the unreality of time and recognises not its fleeting passage, since all is suspended in equilibrium and in a fluid state within that world, and as a dream time is forgotten in the depths of perfect silence and perfect light.

Time passes quickly on the outer plane, leaving its mark on the garment of each physical manifestation; on the inner plane, it grows and expands; the inner being remains ever youthful, the eternal is its garment for ever expressing its own essence.

If time be all we have, then we have nothing until eternity takes its place and we are fulfilled at last in the true accomplishment of God's purpose.

The road through life and its passage can only be seen in its essence by one who has overcome earthly existence and outlived time itself as timelessness.

The promise is eternity for all things; for all things change but in truth do not die.

PART II

Man

1. DUALITY

MAN is like the animal that sleeps, for in life there is illusion and illusion comes as the dark night.

But as the hours pass by and morning begins to disperse the night of illusion, both man and animal awake and face the sunlight of a new birth.

Man is what he believes himself to be, nothing more nor less, hence his understanding is the good that he has put into action amongst others and the selflessness of his own thoughts and actions. These principles give him his reward and spiritual status after his bodily death.

The tree does not master the wind, nor the man his God, for both are given strength and weakness, and both are moulded in the furnace of life by the One who gives all unto life and death, and to each its own timeless state.

Man has two aspects; the dark and the light; his physical awareness, that which he can feel, smell, touch, taste, is the reality for him, and the spiritual aspiration of each individual, is that which cannot be felt with the physical senses but which is the driving motor behind all. The more man seeks the one the less distinguishable the other becomes.

By prying into the microcosm and the macrocosm, man views himself and his activities, he pierces his own form and sees himself more clearly.

The spirit is man's microscope; the God his eye; his body the machine experiencing that which form has to offer, yet collecting each time knowledge and passing it on towards a better state of life for a higher purpose and towards a more glorious end.

. . .

2. THE BOW

Man is like the bow; he is the instrument of resilience if made from the right materials.

The string that he pulls to give flight to the arrow is drawn back in his silence, for that is where he finds his strength.

The eye with which the target is aligned is the eye of truth that he has found through wisdom.

The arrow in its swiftness and sureness is the product of his experiences matured into one pointed aspiration; thus is he sure of his mark and known for his skill.

Each new growth towards the ultimate is like the string on a bow; the further it is stretched the swifter the arrow becomes; the swifter the arrow the further its distance and the greater the impact upon its point.

If each expands and becomes taut to the voice within, then the bow becomes the object of the craftsman's hand and the arrow speeds him towards new horizons of the target set within.

. . .

3. THE VESSEL

Man is the vessel of Godly consciousness; if he restricts the creative flow within himself, then he blocks a greater understanding and sinks further into his own realm of illusion.

Man is the vessel of what he radiates, forever seeking to purify himself.

He is like the bell; when it is struck, a clear note is heard; when the note dies, its vibrations are carried to higher spheres not distinguishable to the ear but to the spirit. Man creates his own dimensions of consciousness and from that consciousness sees things from a different perspective.

The higher his evolvement the greater his inner sight; the greater his inner sight the more careful he is in his own actions and judgement towards all the aspects of life.

Action is the measure of the man for himself and what he has learned by listening to the silent thoughts within: thus the man becomes the reflector and measure of God and God similarly measures man's achievement by what he does for others.

Man's struggle is to hold the peace that he finds within, for there lie his survival, his hope and future, each being sealed in the timeless state of the now that exists eternally.

. . .

4. THE MIRROR

Man is the mirror and its image; the outer and the inner seen from one point and from that point reflected.

Man is the image of his thoughts for they are his consciousness in operation.

Man is the mould of God's making and the life-force which cannot be separated in any shape or form from that which is the God principle.

In his highest state he reflects the Godly principle; merging all his attributes into the pure oneness that is the very heart of his being, he accepts the Principle from within and thereby attains Godhood.

The greater the highlighting of his physical senses, the better receptor he becomes.

The greater his inner receptivity to God, the wiser he becomes; in his wisdom he centres himself inwards towards the Source of all.

Being centered inwards he is aware of a greater law and sense of values.

Without an inner sense man is lost, without an outer sense he cannot learn from experience and cannot radiate what lies within; he cannot progress towards the perfect expression.

All things position man for he is like the needle of a compass. If he lives in an iron cell how will he know his direction? It is what he does with his choice that binds him or sets him free in life.

Man can be likened to the camera; without a good lens he cannot focus and thus the image becomes distorted.

Without a good film the lens is useless even if it be the best.

For the film is unable to collect the image in its correct proportions, or the light in its shades and hues.

Without the two being compatible, each is incomplete and therefore incorrect.

It is therefore the body and the spirit combined in harmony that give correct understanding and unify the vital balance, thus making the being complete in knowledge and virtue.

To learn the balance between the outer and the inner, merging them together as one, is the greatest accomplishment physical man can make; therefore mastery needs much insight; its difficulty lies in the simplicity of being at peace with the self and from that point, observing all subsequent actions.

Man has to work within himself towards that expressionless Being or Essence which is his innermost Self.

Life

AT all points throbs life; in life vibrates the Eternal.

Life is not ours to take or give by judgement or other means; by divine will is it given for the purpose that it be made manifest at a point in time.

The dance of life is like the river; flowing ceaselessly it graces all; perpetually moving it expresses the immortal. Its beauty is the reflection of one Eternal face; forever shining it mirrors the truth; in its strength it is wise and in its weakness it gives to life each ceaseless wonder.

It is the mother and father of all creation; it is the generations past and yet present; it is the NOW of eternal quality; surely the river and the dance of life are the same in all things.

The quality of life depends upon what we give to each other from the heart of God within ourselves; upon what we radiate and give from ourselves to all, for all lives belong to one union and each is the nucleus of the Infinite.

Life is the flow in which all things are seen as one creative expression; thus we observe our own shadow but in that observation gaze perpetually at the progression of our own eternity.

Life for all is the medium for a greater creativity and expression towards an ultimate achievement in which the form is perfected and finally dissolved after its apex has been reached.

Life itself never ceases for it is perpetual; only those things that we do not need cease to be and are exchanged for better expressions of the true self.

Life is the wish of all, for who would suffer immortality to be torn from their breast? Even those who understand not themselves or their making and live not in brotherly love, expect the infinite to keep a covenant with them.

Life is the illusion that each grasps at to possess and hold on to, in order to make of it a reality.

If only we were to let it go by naturally and not be selfish, then in our unselfishness we would grasp the finer point of reality that lies behind life's meaning and know that reality as it truly is.

Life's illusions must give way to reality for there is the pearl of the universal oyster.

. . .

Life is not merely physical consciousness but consists of so much more, for human consciousness separates object from object and in that form of separation there can never be ultimate existence.

Physical life is the shallow reflection of spiritual life seen as pictures of experience in the framework of time; life is like the reflection on the surface of a pond that cloaks the view of its depths below and hides the truth that lies behind the form.

Who says that organisms and functions are the cause of life, knows not life itself; for both are brought into being and maturity by an unseen hand which is the very core of life, itself.

Life is the cause of organism, itself not caused by organism since the vital fire of life is that of the spirit, like to a subtle fluid, an essence, a flame.

To consider what life would be in physical form without the struggle, the lesson and the accomplishment gained from a time of ignorance to a time of knowledge, would be of little value. The value of life and its rebirth from age to age is one of greatest import and significance.

In life nothing is stable, but a creative flow in which observer and observed are one. Within that flow of creative energy the God within watches the man and the man searches for his real self.

Many are the ways and paths of life towards the ultimate, but each is attached to one thread and that one thread is God.

Unless the horizon be expanded beyond the realms of human consciousness there can be no life and no truth, for life is the ceaseless flow from one bosom and comes from one home without distinction; thus all is One and survives as One; life's purpose is One purpose and life's home is but one home.

The passages of lives are but incomplete pictures in different sequences viewed from various angles and aspects of experience towards the complete film of accomplishment.

The learning process of life is difficult and yet simple, is diverse in its application, yet unified; and is great in the path to an inner being, to an inner opening, to truth. But who are they who are wise enough to see its wisdom?

In true living the understanding of faults and the correcting of

these is the way to creating perfection; life is the medium of threading together the strands of experience into a rope that holds all through its sheer strength of unity.

Be happy in life and share in its bounties. Remould your world in unity and love for all; thus will you find that true principle of life and be loved for it; thus will you be wise in the ways of creation and be reborn knowing that wisdom.

Who breathes the air of true life knows the secret behind life itself.

If life brings forth great peace and great stillness then we have found the ultimate of life's purpose for these are the measure of understanding and insight.

Teach yourself well, my friend, and understand what you are and whence you came; pass through the eye of that needle towards life anew, unhindered by lack of understanding the principle of your own creation.

In life lies the finality of purpose. In eternity lies the touchstone of a truthful existence. The two are dissimilar yet have a common link for they are the chain welded together by God's compassion and thus are meaningful.

Does not every bird sing its love of life from the surrounding area, whatever the weather and whatever its hardship?

Relive each day in the joy of your fruitfulness that your crop be sweet and nourishing unto the body and unto the spirit; for many will pluck the fruit that you bear and many will find that fruit to taste sweeter than nectar and more palatable than the purest of wines unto the mouth.

Death

In darkness there is light and in slumber there comes a great awakening and a new horizon upon which is seen everlasting life. For in sleep there is dream and in dreams comes the message and in the message is the life of the soul.

To fear the night is not wise for the wise know that night brings silence in its finality and in that hour all illusions come to an end.

Death should not be frowned upon or mourned, for it is the illusion through which we pass again and again, and each time arise therefrom in greater understanding.

Life beyond the veil of death we have all experienced in one form or another, and many times have we seen that world; in some cases holding a vivid image of its abode, sometimes reliving that experience through a dream state, in other cases a very dim remembering, and sometimes through the medium of meditation.

Without death there can be no life, for death is the casting off of old garments in exchange for the new expression towards a greater glory of unfolding knowledge.

It is in life's true reality that we find a greater resonance and in the final hour we discover that we are in all things infinite.

No one is ever born alone, just as no one ever dies alone, since all creation survives and evolves under one law.

To die is but to return from whence we came and to step into that from which we were created, draped in spiritual vestures; and clothed with the light of our own attainment we greet that light and the beings therein, and thus we are made at home within its sanctuary.

They who fear the passage of this life into the next have not mastered their own footsteps, or paved their own road towards that inner being of the soul, and therefore they go towards the unknown with fear still in their hearts; but they who go through the passage of what is known within themselves and through their faith see the illumination of that road, they go in willingness towards a new path of light and towards a new being of contentment.

. . .

Then do not cry for me when my body is dead for I go to higher states and am in joyful bliss amongst all that is truthful and wonderful.

From the world beyond do I cast my light and will of freedom for you to gather as the flower in full bloom and give the scent of sweetness to that which has no scent.

No flower is gathered that is not of me for I inhabit all that is purposeful and all that springs forth from my expression.

Weep not and be heard not in anguish and shed not sorrow on that which is true joy. For I am the Father visited upon the son, and the Mother visited upon the daughter.

Thus am I all things of beauty that are spent within their time and thus am I the renewer of all that comes to me for eternal peace and rest.

My arms enfold all that seek me and as a bow do I draw back the strings of your longing towards my bosom, shedding them as rays of pure light unto all the trappings of creation.

No earthly eyes are there to behold the wonders of that place to which I go or return, and no earthly footsteps are there that have touched the doorstep of that mansion, or left an impression within its sanctuary.

There where all is beautiful and gracious, reflecting quality and light, is the true home of rest for the wayside traveller to cast the burden aside and partake of that which I am.

Consider then the going of my footsteps from this material plane as nothing more than an exchange of expression extending towards and encompassing all that is truly great and truly infinite; yet not being an end in itself but the beginning of a gracious and magnificent awareness of the reality that is all and one.

Thus are your tears wasted not, except in memory of that which I once was and am no longer, for they are as dew upon the soil of earthly memories, giving nourishment to the flowers of whose beauty I am the life and forever will be.

Purpose

Life is not meaningless nor death the end of life for the two begin with expression and will towards an ordained purpose that holds both in the palm of the Infinite's hand.

Therefore the processes of life and death are mere functions towards an ultimate achievement over the self, and are drawn as but a veil over that which is and remains truly immortal.

What are the years of learning in a man's life without an ultimate achievement? And what is the purpose of groping for definition and experience within that life if it is to become as dust and blows away upon the wind, scattered hither and thither as the wind sees fit?

This indeed would make a mockery of all that is held dear of creation and of God and God's wonderful works.

Thus is the soul active in life and death preparing on both planes to perfect itself in accordance with a supreme law towards ultimate perfection.

The hand that guides all from infinity back to itself gives to each a time of planting and a time of reaping, a time of sorrow and a time of joy, a time of stagnation and a time of fruition, a time of hate and a time of love within its cycle of evolution.

If we do not serve the principle of life in every aspect that confronts us, then we have failed to see our purpose and as such must stay in the cycle of human form until we become knowledgeable of ourselves.

But should one see the true purpose of life, then the journey is swift and evolvement assured, for in overcoming oneself one will be exalted and know great joy amongst the spiritual spheres.

In life lies the finality of purpose; in eternity lies the touchstone of a truthful existence. The two are dissimilar, yet have a common link for they are the chain welded together by God's compassion and thus are meaningful.

Thus do we all inwardly know and strive for a place in that sphere through experience and lives shed as skins to outgrow our very structure and immortalise the real spiritual self, outliving and outgrowing our present illusory state of being.

Life and death therefore are not the beginning and not the end, but a link in an incomplete chain towards a greater state of awareness and being.

An unused faculty is an unknown and being unused becomes atrophied, fulfilling little purpose, supplying little information until incorporated. Such is the spiritual hidden within; that which seeks or uses it not, fulfills not its intention or purpose towards achievement

Creation is all things serving towards one great purpose for the benefit of all and for the body as a whole, each stepping in the shoes of the other by evolvement towards its time of great awakening and immortality.

The plan of creation within all the manifested spheres indeed has great purpose, and each in its turn will be opened up to that purpose by outgrowing its form and restrictive abilities on this earth.

Ours is the task of completing life; of completing the work and perfecting the cycle of experience towards universal knowledge and, by the knowledge gained, so harmonise our consciousness with its supreme Source that we become immortal.

Creative Expression

THAT which cannot express cannot evolve; that which cannot evolve cannot live, since there is no instinct to survive and no will to learn through experience gained. Therefore expression is immortality on this side of manifestation since that which continues to express never dies.

The physical manifestation is the lower aspect radiated from the One Source; it is activity seeking an equilibrium; in thus seeking this it contains a flaw.

Each activity is the flaw perfecting itself; whilst the flaw exists, none is perfect; since none is perfect, inner effort is needed; since inner effort is needed a unification of experience is essential.

Whilst experience is necessary form is made manifest for each to outgrow; by outgrowing experience form is dissolved; thus in dissolving form we live: within the centre of all.

All things are the expression of a creative idea, being ever present and continually brought into existence in the now of eternity, since now is the focal point for all things.

The life that each lives is a struggle for the maintenance of harmony, a striving to be a unit of perfect oneness and know itself completely.

It is with this inherent aim in mind that each consciously or unconsciously makes its way towards the light and finally emerges Supreme.

• • •

Expression is like the flower; it unfolds in different illuminations and is seen in different states of beauty by the One who observes all life forms from within.

Expression is also like the needle: in focussing on its finer point it probes behind the shadow of life and therefore is the instrument that stitches together all truths, completing the material of universal oneness.

In new expression each changes the garment of its own life and finally becomes the tailor of itself.

To give birth to expression shows individuality, but in its ultimate form nothing remains individual but becomes immersed in the whole and God.

Expansion is life aspiring to a new and unique quality of expression; it is movement, and where there is movement there is accomplishment.

Who expands within learns to master the place of many secrets for within expansion of consciousness lies great purpose and the secret of expression.

Without expansion of consciousness what is created and how much is there gained in the ways of wisdom?

Every thing created from the initial essence of energy which is the Godhead has the inherent will of expression, and must at some stage, within its limited lifespan of physicality, express itself in its own terms towards what it feels, or inherently knows that Godhead to be.

Each is its own physician and therefore has the answer to its own state of being, thus each renews itself in the Principle or diminishes itself proportionally by what it expresses willingly.

• • •

To be is creation expressing itself naturally.

Creation is never static but perpetual.

Creation is love being extended to all things and from love is extracted the beauty of each thing; true love lies in the balance between giving and taking, between accepting and receiving, and from the unselfish heart it survives for ever. Giving and taking are the breath of life and how that life is sustained in all spheres and evolutes towards the source in its entirety.

Even if man becomes rigid to the ways of his inner God, and works against the creative, he cannot stop his own evolvement taking place.

In creativeness lies beauty, for beauty is the creative in eternal perpetuation.

Through the expression of inner creativity life is moulded anew, and the individual raised to new horizons of wonder.

It is that inner creativity that gives life beauty, and, when used in life, that enhances and guides all towards greater expression.

The world needs both the philosopher and the dreamer, for in philosophy creative activity is born and in dreaming new horizons of consciousness are reached, and thus expanded.

Consciousness

THERE are many mansions of conscious existence, each one being an extension beyond the other, but not the finality of all things, great and supreme.

Human consciousness is like the vessel that contains the essence; since it is like the vessel it restricts the flow of, and places limitations upon, the amount of essence that it can hold and shed.

If the vessel of human consciousness is put to one side even for a moment, the natural flow is unrestricted and we become that flow itself and aware of levels beyond the plane of limitations, and thus are able to enter into and complete a greater purpose in life.

Who expands consciousness becomes enlightened in the climb of life's mountain.

Each frame of human consciousness has its own momentum and its own speed. It lengthens or shortens the distance between man and God, reaching finally a state of suspension and then becoming the whole, immersed as one.

True consciousness is but the opening to a unique and divine principle, God.

Thoughts are the bringers of physical life, for their activity is an activity of imperfect expression towards a state of perfection through the medium of experience.

The first elementals of the soul to be conquered by the gift of free will are desires; each individual has desires in some shape or other, but must eventually leave them one by one by the wayside, for they block God from the heart and confuse the individual.

In vanquishing desires and giving more space to God, true communion is born and by such daily conquests emerges the warrior of unequalled might.

Having mastered desires we master life itself in physical form and are then free to wander through the perfect realms.

To have no desire for earthly wealth leaves a man free. To have no desires at all makes a man truly great. Unburdening himself makes a man swift and in his speed he pierces the heart of God and is absorbed in true consciousness.

Each incomprehensible will one day be comprehended fully in true consciousness and that day will be the time of the great awakening outside the limitations of physical form and consciousness.

Love

THE way towards overcoming the personalised EGO is through love for the divine Principle.

To love selflessly is to know true harmony and to grasp its essence.

The greatest gift bestowed upon all is love, for love is the Eternal Flame of God dispersed throughout all creation. If then love be pure in that purity of giving and accepting, the heart receives the highest honour bestowed upon it and is elevated above all earthly wisdom, for of wisdom love is the crown and of all virtues love stands supreme.

Of all the laws that have ever been made and given from the higher realms, love is the embodiment of each and their sum total, for the greatest of all commandments is to love thy neighbour as thyself and upon this law all others are hung. If this law be obeyed, there is no other law to observe for it is the supreme law in all things.

Love is the archer seeking a target for his arrow, weighing carefully the amount of skill given to each by its aim; in stretching the bow it lifts, pushing forward towards the target; in drawing the string it pulls back to anchor and swiftens the arrow of its choice, thus giving a different penetration to each, knowing which is more deserving of its depth.

Love cannot be conquered, but conquers; reflecting its beauty it gives to those who wish to share its illumination; by illumination it heightens; drawing inward each towards its centre it makes each passive to an understanding within.

. . .

As we are born of love so must we become the vessel of love in all that we do, for that is the way, and through love we mould all and bring together purity and simplicity in effortless unfoldment.

True love knows no hoarding, but is given and received with an open heart and mind; these being open align themselves, widening the channel inward to encompass much more, one-pointed towards communion.

Love overcomes hate and is no more conscious of desperate

expression and no longer conscious of expressing a will of its own but a will of truth and divinity.

They who seek to understand all through the works of love see themselves as they truly are and in doing so they see the God within.

A loving heart is the heart that seeks the God within and reflects this principle in its highest form.

The heart that brings forth the sweetest fruit of love and sweeps all before it through that love is indeed a precious one.

The corridors of the heart can only be illumined by the lamp of love, for love is the flame lit by the one eternal Spirit.

In giving lies richness and in accepting the gift there is love; such are the ways of a pure heart and mind; these are held in high regard and valued by what they give and accept from God the Infinite.

. . .

Only those who are new in the ways of love need refilling, but love itself is not new in its own ways of giving and thus is the eternal flow of life.

If our epitaph to physical life were the great love that we had for all things, and if in that life we managed in some way to help the evolvement of others, surely this would have been enough to leave behind for a while, and return to later, to begin anew.

Who truly loves does so from the centre, for there is where true love is born within each individual.

Where there is love there is life, for God is love and God is life; as God unfolds each wonder, so unfolds the beauty of wisdom and each sees itself in the mirror.

A wealth of wisdom is known only from the wisest aspect of impartiality; and impartiality is the silence of God's radiant love for all.

When the season turns upon itself giving the flower of beauty to sight, and the sweetness of its scent fills the air that you breathe, then can you say that all is but an expression of the love that the Spirit radiates through earthly garments.

Life must be the lesson of obtaining and passing on great love to others; if the lesson be learned well God draws each one closer to its own immortality.

Giving and Sharing

How many things can be given freely?

Consider those things and add to your own freedom by giving them as such.

As you received those gifts let others also be their recipient; you will have given much, gained much more and be a great deal wealthier in the eyes of God.

As numberless gifts are given from above so they should be shared in the communion between man and man to be blessed.

Whosoever gives unselfishly has absorbed the principle of life and turned it into great purpose.

If one man is given a gift from heaven for his labour and another is given the wealth of his evil deeds who will be the richer?

As one labour is paid so is another, and as one tree is known for its sweet fruit so is the other for its bitterness, and the harvest will single out each and set them accordingly in a like manner.

For the woodman's axe will mark well that which is unfruitful and the hands of the sower will plant another in its place for a greater profit in time to come.

It is giving that makes all things worthwhile and all things great.

Thus shall your gifts be returned in the way of your giving and by your own ways shall you reap that which you have planted and that which awaits your scythe to be eaten at your own table when the time comes and you find hunger at your very door.

Every selfless gift given from the heart is counterbalanced with its own riches for the future. And every thoughtless and selfish action holds unto itself a repercussion of equal force, yet to be made manifest within the life or lives of the individual.

Beauty survives in the love of sharing. If each gives its heart in the form of the infinite spirit, what greater gift and more unparalleled beauty could be offered?

. . .

The significance of all endeavours lies within the space that is given to the spirit, for within that inner space lies the true and untapped source of life.

Space is that which gives room to live and expand, to reach forth and extend one's own boundaries and to become part of the whole.

Thus is sharing the reaching out for the space within One's Self, and since there is no mathematical point that does not contain its essence there can be no point devoid of life or inspiration within its realms.

To be as space itself is to know all that it contains.

Thus it is possible to sit within the silence of oneself and know what occurrences are about to take place, to know this world and the bounds beyond it, and the true meaning of oneness.

Faith

FAITH is that which aligns experience and soul understanding as a unity of harmony.

Yet it is so much more than this: without it a physical and spiritual universe would not be possible, for faith is the essence that moulds each thing, bringing it to life, vibrancy, beauty.

It is the unseen hand that guides each towards its own infinite point and towards the bosom of God.

Since faith creates and gives to each its design by way of inherent vibrations or oscillations, it must be that which also changes in some way the inner self of man. Thus with faith we change not only our own oscillations internally but also our geometric pattern, our environment, our life; through faith we change the internal design or pattern and recreate another; bringing ourselves to a closer understanding of a higher law of ourselves and God.

Each thing brought into existence cannot know its own lifespan and as such remains, lives and functions on the seed of faith and hope, surviving by learning perpetually.

None survives without hope or faith for these are the hinges upon which life hangs. Without these nothing would be possible.

A flower comes into being from a seed and the seed knows its purpose. It sends forth a shoot and drives itself towards the light against any opposition.

Those who have seen and witnessed the strength of a shoot when it grows through concrete, know of the force it creates and are aware of the flimsiness of its structure. Here is faith and here is hope in operation creating an unexplained force that will move any mountain.

And so in all things faith and hope are a combination of strength and flexibility. Both are the combination and the pattern of each visible and invisible manifestation, therefore both are vital for all things.

For man faith is the test of endurance against all opposition and the rope to which he is anchored, overcoming the storm of his own life in the stage of its proving and maintaining the balance of hope throughout towards attainment and mastery of a true and everlasting state of awareness.

Belief is the foundation of faith and faith its proving, therefore man should know his own direction and consider his course by inner action and sight.

Wisdom

Of priceless possessions surely wisdom is the most precious. Lend yourself to its ways of wonder and then will you see. Count not external gains but the store you hold within, for there lies true wealth.

Wisdom is a jewel made manifest to those who seek understanding and are moulded by its ways. It motivates unseen wonders and gives perception to the human heart and definition to the human eye, but above all makes kings from beggars, elevating them towards God's bosom.

Rarely seen in all its beauty is the gem of wisdom, and precious are they who hold one grain of it to light life's path from within, reflecting its quality. Rarer than the emerald found in the depths of the ocean is wisdom, yet where is he that seeks it out within himself and knows of its true value?

The approach to wisdom has many paths but wisdom has but one source and one reflective quality; it is woven of many threads but is one garment; has many operations but one function of unity.

Wisdom cannot be found except through endless search within and cannot be used unless it be shared collectively towards a unification of understanding.

It resides not within the unprincipled nor the unwilling, but seeks the just, truthful and righteous, and guides them for the sake of humanity.

Nothing is more guarded than wisdom and none more careful than the wise in thought and action.

The still tongue knows it only through careful thought but does not speak it for fools to digest lest they find it unpalatable and degrade it with foul words.

Only those of stout heart seek and find it amongst the perils that lie about its crown.

Wisdom is the pattern of life in the making, cancelling each mortal frame and integrating higher forms towards unity; creating the vessel perpetually to hold its essence, it moulds a new form of each from the fire that is spirit.

Wisdom is the flower of the eternal, ever seeking to nourish and sustain, ever bursting forth towards full bloom, enriching those knowledgeable of their real selves, knowing the quality of a kind heart and still tongue; creating a knowing mind, full of silence, is the apex of wisdom.

Endeavour therefore to know that true light of wisdom and understand existence anew in unity of the spirit that your wisdom may outshine the purest of earthly gems and reflect its innermost quality back to its Creator.

. . .

Though a man be wise he has not found the ultimate in wisdom. Since there is room for more he lacks an understanding of its true application and therefore follows its source; in following its source he creates the way, unfolding himself within to expand; expanding within he contracts and focusses; in focussing he sees more clearly the purpose; opening within one door, he closes the other along a never-ending corridor; therefore he defines, and in defining gives himself clarity, singling out true reality; singling out reality he has more room for selfless love, appreciating its unity; appreciating unity he becomes one, moulding deed and thought; aligning thought he creates the pattern, and in creating the pattern he knows his own silence and God, taking counsel from within.

. . .

In wisdom there is serenity for the wise know the way to God's heart and carefully choose their path.

To be neutral in all things is to be accomplished in the ways of wisdom.

The light that shines in the heart of the wise is of God for God has measured them and knows of their ways.

The wise man is a builder, his foundation is strong in the Principle of God, therein is he renewed and his house remains forever, whilst other houses rise and fall about that which he has fashioned in his silence.

A wise man is like the sun on a summer's day giving warmth and comfort to creation.

He is like the rain bringing forth the seed towards full maturity and the time of harvest. In his fruitfulness he nourishes all and in nourishing all he is renewed.

A wiseman is active in the sphere of overcoming his own shortcomings: he is bound to higher values, and reflects those values in all that he does.

The wiseman knows all things to be expressive of God and God to be the ultimate expression in each. He knows all things that pass away on this plane to be aspects of eternity itself.

A wiseman does not take that which will burden him or confuse him, therefore he battles against desires and in that battle keeps only that which speeds his progress to his own innermost point; his heavenly Father's mansion.

A wise man's attention is turned within for that is the way he learns. From within he projects his own understanding and thereby makes himself complete.

The wise take councel with the foolish, being themselves not fully equipped to their own advantage. They carry on the perpetual search and in doing so find a greater field of nourishment and greater heights of awakening.

It is unwise to mock those who have found peace of the highest order for they are kept wise in the ways of the Infinite; and can teach great wisdom by just being themselves.

. . .

In seeking out the Self there is truth; in finding yourself within the eyes and hearts of others there is wisdom.

The ultimate in wisdom is to expand towards the Infinite One.

Wisdom brings forth creation; the man brings forth himself; the wise understands the law of God and adheres to it in all things.

Wisdom is the light that gives countenance to each, when used unselfishly and shared for the benefit of all to bring about a great understanding.

It makes each confident of the way, expanding knowledge from within.

It is wise to remember that no man outgrows his own expressive qualities, therefore express fully your wisdom and be revitalised by its renewal.

Of earthly wealth are there many rich men, but of wisdom very few who become wealthy in its ways or learned of the inner potential that lies hidden in the depths of each heart.

One word of wisdom can enlighten a kingdom, for the wise are kings who prefer rags to earthly riches, but have great wealth within.

Wisdom is the anchor that holds the ship of the heart through the most violent storms.

Folly

GREED is the ultimate in all follies for what is stolen by way of deceit and greed from others is taken back in equal quantity from the soul.

A greedy man is unable to comprehend himself; therefore he has not seen within; seeing not within he expands in the wrong direction; thus he remains unwise; in remaining unwise he becomes selfish; in becoming selfish he starves his soul; in starving his soul he slows down the cycle; therefore he takes longer to evolve; in taking longer to evolve he punishes himself.

To crave for and obtain by false methods power and dominion over one's fellow beings is to obtain that which belongs to the realms of illusion and ignorance and not to the realm of God.

Riches themselves are not bad, but what is the height of ignorance is to recognise those riches as one's own God and to obtain them through the misery of others; since all that we can take after our bodily death is that which belongs to the spirit, we have cheated ourselves and others for nothing and obstructed our own understanding and our own evolution in the sphere of creation.

To kill, to steal, to covet that which does not belong to one can only lead to the filling up of the vessel with poison and through that poison the self is destroyed.

The fool learns not his unwise ways by experience; he jumps into the waters of life without learning to stay afloat, and in his unreadiness sinks without preparing for his eventual death.

Since many do not strive to understand themselves or the God within their hearts, they live a life of ignorance perpetually creating trouble and disturbance for themselves and others, remaining divided from their better qualities and trying to make up for this by living too active a life in their illusionary being.

Such is the product of an unwise and ignorant individual that he will go to any lengths to be wholly oblivious of the truth about himself, but in the end he must learn and come to know himself fully.

That which judges others in ignorance knows not itself to be unwise, understanding nothing.

A man that considers all things to be as his physical senses dictate is steeped in foolishness for the physical senses deceive him and hide many truths.

To consider oneself too wise for fools is the pinnacle of stupidity, for each is wise in his own way.

It is better that a man keep his own counsel and train himself in silence, than for him to speak that which is foolish and false unto others and tear away from himself that which is true.

He who is wise possesses not great earthly wealth, but wealth of the spirit on his way through life. He who is foolish gathers unto himself that which he cannot take with him to lay at the feet of the infinite.

Goodness

Goodness is the alpha and omega of all for therein it rests in unadorned beauty.

Goodness is found where life is found, under the stone or at the centre of the universal heart.

Goodness is the perpetual seed of life upon which each depends.

Goodness knows its own quality and compares not with itself; it has but one expression and one aim towards unity.

Goodness moulds wisdom, experience and harmony, making them into a bell that rings in its own parish and sowing the seeds of all creation to bring forth the strong oak of immortality.

From goodness nothing can be extracted that is not of its ways or of its store of renewal, for each thing is the interwoven garment of its web and thus being so, lives on from age to age as eternity.

. . .

The Good is the cup that a man fills from the heart; thus the good man is never empty but always seeking to renew himself that he may derive greater nourishment.

The essence of the good is always flowing; always giving its store of wealth in quantity and quality; is never empty and thus never renews itself.

The good are patient in their gift of love towards all things; they turn the face of anger set against them into serenity and the heart of fierce storms into murmuring brooks of contentment and peace.

The good is as bread cast upon the waters for it shall be found, and like the truthful word it feeds many.

Who is good is never fierce of face but truly compassionate and just unto the whole of creation.

. . .

He who is like the sun, touching all things with the warmth of his radiance and setting creation aflame with his incandescence;

He who sets his heights amongst the stars in the heavens but conquers so much more within the precincts of his own heart;

He who masters himself with the greatest of truths and arms himself with the mightiest of virtues
Is the true warrior
He alone is the height of goodness and he alone serves truly God, the undisputed and sole Master.

To give rein to what is good and feel inadequate in service is to be accomplished in life, and known alike by man and God; for he who is forever empty is forever renewed and God sustains him in the highest of his accomplished tasks.

Good reflects its own quality against ill-will as a mirror reflects and scatters light from beyond its surface. Thus to reflect upon good tempers the spirit towards greater harmony and opens the path towards God.

Evil seeks good to destroy its seeds through discontentment and disunity; therefore seek out that which is evil unto your sight and pluck it from your midst as a gardener uproots all that which would destroy the crops; so must you take that from yourself which would destroy your immortality.

PART III

The Way

SEEK the universal in all matter and spirit, in places where there is fear and darkness, turmoil and strife, sickness and death, see all its aspects and become wise of the path towards unity.

Within that unity lies the peace and understanding which lead to the true insight of the Godhead, of that which exists without separation, timeless under one order, that of tranquillity, of harmony, of oneness.

Seek the truth with anger in your heart and you will only see the anger of yourself and others.

Seek God by being in league with opposition and you will see your own opposition and that of others.

Be uncharitable unto others and ask for God's guidance, then will you be severed from God and unable to reach your own peace.

Wage war on another and ask for God's help in winning the battle, then will you reap the storm that you cause and destroy yourself by your own conflict.

God can only be there to help you if you desire truth and justice in your own being and wish these to be the guiding light reflected throughout your life unto others.

. . .

The struggle has been for man to change through the animal from the depths of ignorance to a point in which the light is discovered.

When man realises that the struggle for him has long since ceased, then he has found himself and can begin to learn and find his own peace.

The struggle is through the futile, the meaningless; the acceptance is of the worthwhile, the beneficial and meaningful.

Separation leading back to integration is the way of experiencing. Thus the man in his physical form expresses his inherent attributes in order to see his path more clearly, for there lies his potential in wait and there is the point to which he must aspire before returning as an immortal one into his final home and final rest.

. . .

Seek that within you which is silence, free yourself from the illusion of judgement; be charitable to others for they are an extension of your essence, and all is but an extension of the Godhead.

Thus has the way towards finding God been opened up to you, for when you seek God in wisdom and earnest, with but one thought in your heart and with but one aim, then will you know that you have found the way by the peace reflected within your own being and the stillness of your own mind.

The path that a man treads towards himself and the spirit is indeed difficult, for he faces the storm of opposition within a physical world that seeks to dislodge his foothold from the ledge upon which he stands, casting him into the void far below.

The nearer to an inner understanding man gets, the fiercer the storm becomes, until at last he merges with the true harmony and in that harmony sees only oneness from the centre of opposition.

When man is at peace with himself and undisturbed by the fury of opposition from others, then he has gone beyond the milestone of self expression, and in being selfless sees only love in all things, knowing this to be the eternal.

See then opposition only as a function towards unity and be at harmony with your world.

Those who would give up all for the sake of a greater knowledge see God face to face and in that infinite grace and joy find that they have lost nothing of value, but have gained much more than life itself.

Without inner vision man has not learned his path and without the path each is lost to the truth. Consider then inner silence; consider your time to be well spent in meditation and meditation a reflection upon all that which gives nourishment.

Reflection

To learn is to reflect upon the folly of each one and by reflection extract wisdom.

A voice reflected in the pool of eternity is as the sparkling dewdrops in the eye of morning awaiting the rising sun, golden washed, arisen for yet another eternity giving birth to itself.

Each song sung so sweetly on the morning air is the song for you to awaken and join in its chorus with but one heart and one mind and reflect your thoughts on the singularity that is of God.

The wings upon which you are born rest in stillness upon all that beauty and grace encompass and hold in singularity all, pointing to but one harmony, reflecting but one love.

Each thing is but your reflection and you are the reflection of your Source; to give up the light that shines within for the sake of your own desires is foolish and to gratify yourself with selfishness fulfills no purpose.

An extended insight into the spirit is merely the turning inside out of the garment of physicality; for all is but a mirror image reflected in space and eternity, being extended indefinitely from within, the centre of one's own being.

A heart is known to others by action, and the mind is but a mediator between thought and motivation. Thus the mind turns intention into purpose, and the heart meditates upon that which is reflected through good or bad.

The heart aligns the body as the universe is aligned from within itself to purposeful ends, and reflects the aspirations of the soul. The mind governs in conjunction with soul and spirit the human frame and reflects the needs of both physicality and spirituality.

Thus are mind, soul and spirit governed by their own medium and extended indefinitely towards a point of the Absolute.

Give space to the mind and it will act as the universe itself. Constrict it and it will not understand intent or purpose but reflect darkness, confusion and ignorance.

Supply it with the finest trappings of a spiritual nature and only then will it begin to comprehend fractionally what God is and reflect the harmony of the inner heavens.

Each mind is like the mirror that cannot reflect the light when heavy dirt lies upon its surface, but when the surface is cleaned it becomes a great medium for reflecting. The work that each one does upon its own source within is the polishing process. The harder the work done internally, the greater the light that shines through its surface unto creation.

• • •

That which is reflected from within is that which shall be known to others, and that which is not reflected cannot be acted upon. For reflection is guidance towards the light and lack of reflection a step towards the darkness.

The soul is as a star reflecting its position in the sky to guide the voyager through the abyss of darkness and safely plot his course in a particular direction towards an ultimate goal.

The soul is illuminated from within and followed without by the incandescence of its own making, its reflection in the human heart, and by its position amongst the stars of the inner heavens.

Thus is it likened to the illumination of a house and the warmth of the sun, to the daylight and the joy of new birth, to the cry and laughter of that wishing to be heard and known in understanding. Amidst the source of light lies your own illumination and that of its making.

Many do not recognise their own eternity because they do not recognise God and the true self that exists within each individual as being the extension of that God's love for each thing and that God's reflection.

Why is it that man reflects upon his innermost thoughts? Only in the depths of stillness, in the pool of inner silence, can that intangible principle he calls God be reflected, free from the chains of complex structures and organisations; only beyond these, away from all mental and physical trappings, can he meet his true Maker and his true self within the precincts of his own deeper being.

The Central Point

To be central in action and reaction is to know the finer point of wisdom and operate that wisdom wisely; therefore become not ensnared and entangled in the rights and wrongs of others, and weigh not heavily in judgement on one side or the other; then will you not become unwise.

Judgement, by a man, of others is not the way towards finding himself, but the way towards being caught up in the marshes of life and lured into the trap laid by the hunter for the unwary, to die chained by the lack of insight into what is truly wise.

That which is central considers not force or reaction and is truly placed at the core of all, since it is greater than opposites and perfected beyond these.

Might opposed to might is lack of progression; being held still at one point it cannot advance or retreat or learn by the opposition it creates and therefore is destroyed by its inability to yield.

Learn of opposition and through that opposition seek unity within that house of matter that you inhabit and by the experience of that outer casing create a unity and a bond which can never be broken.

Know unity within your very being and sit upon the true throne of harmony, merging all as one and one as all; thus knowing your true self, impart that knowledge and radiate it amongst all who seek it for self-betterment.

. . .

Consider the grass blown by strong winds and reflect upon its ability to be wise. Never does it try to oppose force but bends and remains intact and by doing so lives to experience a new day, greeting the sun after the storm has passed and spent itself.

And so does all creation yield to a greater force in order to survive and experience what its survival has taught. Becoming resilient it overcomes and outlives that which otherwise would cause its destruction by learning to become meek in the face of opposition and sure in its anchor upon life, it own central point, it achieves its purpose.

Therefore be as the reed in a storm; do not oppose the storm for it will break your structure and cast you before it; then will you have been wasted to no just end by your own opposition and have learned nothing of your own yielding nature.

Opposition is but a spiral directed towards a fuller state of being. Through the opposition created externally and internally one learns to maintain the central axis which is stillness and exists at the point where life begins.

. . .

Were each to see its own central point within itself, then no more would it wage war upon itself by what it does to others, but give a life full of joy and thus renew itself perpetually through the channels of a greater love.

The law that keeps all apart is polarity. Polarity is opposition, and counter movement; the positive and the negative for ever seeking a state of equilibrium.

Since there is movement there is opposition to that action of

movement and therefore those aspects of opposing forces are set up as an inherent law of the universe.

The existence of all is but oscillation about a point of balance and neutrality.

The point at which all meets all is but the interface of interaction where two spirals rotate in opposing directions and their neutral centre reconstitutes both.

Meditation

EACH person has the power to look within himself, for each is an idea of perfection in the vast unfolding mind of the universe, living as a unit to change not only himself or herself, but their surroundings, and thereby embrace all in wisdom and knowledge as one.

Those who know not what silence is must first seek it through meditation; for while there is no silence within their hearts there is opposition, and while there is opposition they cannot find stillness; God is found in the depths of stillness.

The light of man comes in the silence when he meditates upon his Source, and God touches his heart.

The silent way is the greatest of ways for man to be renewed, for in meditation he leaves the world of physical being, of human consciousness, and for that short moment he is free.

In true meditation the activity of the mind ceases. Thus the imperfect is transcended and a greater awareness of the perfect opened up and extended.

The focal point of all efforts is to clarify an inner reality, thus obtaining a working knowledge of what truth consists of. In themselves all efforts are not wasted when served for the little truths that they contain and put to the test within life's daily toil.

In meditation, if the highest order is attained, time is frozen and the individual wanders amongst the sphere of the great, for God will have touched the heart and brought true consciousness and true communion, making him one in perfect knowledge.

As our whole being is merged into a perfect harmony of oneness, thoughts fade and die and in their turn give way to great illumination, making communion possible between the inner self and its Source.

In our meditation we leave the world and its ways, and thus

cannot oppose God's will, for in our silence we are deep in communion with the Eternal.

When our thoughts are turned inward towards God, then are we conscious of all things as they truly are; in such illumination how can we harm anything at all?

The true self captured in stillness is the timeless experience in operation beyond thought and knowledge of the physical, a realm in which all ties and shackles are broken and a new world discovered without limitations.

In the silence of the heart's meditation the divine Principle flashes upon the inner mirror; one polishes it again and again through meditation until it becomes the diamond of life and sheds the radiance of its majesty upon all, giving life and hope anew.

God's kingdom comes not with physical fanfares nor with loud drums but with observation and silent meditation upon the Source.

The silence in which he meditates upon the Source of his own being and the being of his own soul leads man towards the Godhead. In a mood of contemplation, he learns to withdraw from the conditions imposed upon him, to transcend the limitations of the body and thus experience a new life beyond such restriction; on planes beyond physicality there exist realms in which space, time and matter have no meaning.

That is man's goal and one of innermost expression towards that infinite being of unknown Essence that he wishes to express.

As the flame attracts the moth, so the wisdom that emerges from the depth of silent contemplation attracts all spheres of life and motivates that life towards a higher perfection.

Silence

SILENCE is the voice of reflection in the mirror of understanding and wisdom.

Who keeps the silence within holds the key to the eternal and with that key is able to pass beyond all manifested life.

Reflection is the silent existence within; in deep silence the mind ceases to wander away from the path of the creative.

Silence has many levels; even in silence is heard sound, the soundless sound of distinguishable notes, each an illumination; but when true silence is attained full communion with God is gained, and true insight into the eternal wisdom.

In quiescence all things are brought to life and understood and in the silences of perfect music they return to their home, clothed in light, in their hour of awakening.

In silence we are raised up into the sphere of light, beyond which lies true consciousness and from that shore of immortal being we are renewed in the Principle of God.

In the silence we are illuminated and made whole; we are free of physical shackles and in the freedom that we maintain within, we give rise to a greater awareness and expression of the true self.

Man must seek silence, for it is therein that he begins to understand the purpose for which he was created and it is therein that he is renewed with might and fortitude.

If a man has not found his inner silence, then he has not found his own peace, or his greatest expressive potential and therefore cannot see himself within all other aspects of creation as a body of complete oneness.

Silence reveals the essence of perfect harmony. Who dares to argue against silence is not knowledgeable of the self or the wonders of creation and thus will lose his peace.

. . .

If man then is silence itself he is eternally expressing his own creativity in perfect sound.

Who is knowledgeable of silence is knowledgeable of creation. From the silence the worlds came into being and into the silence all will return and know their Maker.

To be silent is to be like the river flowing onward to the sea; to be silent is to be waiting to meet a greater expression and a new creativity.

In silence each is brought forth into life and in silence each returns to meet the dawn of his renewal.

The man of silence listens to the voice within and learns much to his own advantage. He does not judge through separation, and by remaining neutral becomes the child of innocence, knowing the measure of himself.

In silence each heart is seen in its nakedness; its full value is known by that which is the Eternal in us. In silence there is no need for justification.

Man is never silent until he finds the truth and in that second he is all that silence could bring and eternity itself could murmur.

Who masters the silence masters the meaning of oneness, and in that oneness finds the domains of God.

The reality that silence brings is the true path towards that point in which God resides; in knowing the reality of the spirit that in us is God, we extend our awareness wholeheartedly towards the Infinite, thereby constantly renewing ourselves.

To enter into the domain of silence is to forget time and motion and to realise that the material garment or outer shell with which we are clothed is but a containment of impure substance to be transcended by effort towards the pure, the infinite, the eternal.

From the nucleus of silence flowing as a crystal clear pool, does God manifest and bring about all that is great in the eyes of spiritual man.

If a man should see himself as he truly is in unadorned beauty, he would become silence itself, in awe at the wonder of his own nature as well as the beauteous works of God.

Silence comprehends all; it is a jewel within the casket of many secrets, opened in a flash of eternity wherein resides the void of wonder.

Peace

A MIND contented is a mind at peace; its application is in enhancing all things peaceful.

The peaceful man is great in the love of his God and in that love that he has bestowed upon all things lie his great radiance and his potential of wisdom.

Whosoever is peaceful has gained much and become the conqueror of his own self.

If we have inner peace then we understand ourselves and in doing so make life more pleasant for others and evolve ourselves in the process.

So much is given unto us to understand and from that inner understanding derive peace, harmony, joy.

The central sphere, the core of things, the aim of life, can only be obtained in peaceful and harmonious existence, for that central point is the creative hearth from which come all good tidings and spring forth all purposeful actions.

For where can a feather remain stationary whilst there is a strong wind and where can man find peace whilst the storm in his heart still rages and he knows not why?

The justice of man is filled with action and reaction in a physical world, but the justice of God is stillness and silence and without expression but still is and remains true justice.

Know this that the peace within man's heart leads to an understanding of silence and a course of action away from all that seeks to disrupt and destroy. For it is in knowing the silence that a man becomes rich and finds wisdom.

Whosoever can hold a great peace within remains undisturbed in the middle of turmoil, for in peace truth is reflected and in truth serenity is supreme.

Truth

TRUTH is like the seed of a flower; when it falls the birds swoop down upon it to fill their hunger.

It the seed proves to be indigestible the birds cannot use it; thus it is carried far afield and planted anew to begin a creative life some way from its parent.

Great truths fill the hunger of longing; they provide the stuff of life to give life cause and substance.

If truth proves to be too great an argument for the unwise, it becomes unpalatable and is discarded.

Where truth is thrown to the four winds, there will the wise also be to bring it back to life, so that it may once again bear fruit and feed many.

Great truths are like the branches of a tree; they grow outwards from a trunk of strength.

The unwise are like the wind and blow from many directions, seeking to topple the whole structure; but the tree endures because of its resilience and the roots hold because of their firm anchorage upon the soil.

The truthful know the secret that lies within their heart and in knowing that secret can unlock God's very heart in their ways of wisdom; therefore those who are great in truth are able to pass where none have trodden before.

In the renewal of truth we make fast the anchor upon the infinite; we become resilient and thus mighty in strength.

. . .

What is truth?

Unity is the greatest of all truths and those who divide it for self-satisfaction cheat themselves.

Many seek truth but do not hold it above all else. Kingdoms supposedly hold it dear but are nevertheless brought into desolation by lack of its application. They being separated internally against themselves, destroy by division many kingdoms within their souls.

The infinite is the truth at the heart of all and the passage towards the infinite the reality to which all must come to terms finally.

Only that which is the truth will last eternally and that which passes away with the wind of time notices not the eternal in passing, and is in its turn not noticed.

Man weaves a web of truth within the depths of his own soul, and upon reflection of that purity finds a pearl of wisdom therein to share with all who seek it.

Each one has the light of truth within himself to be brought forth and shared amongst all. For each one inherently is given the light of truth by God, therefore it is up to each of us to search ourselves for ourselves and God.

If a person carries the light of truth in its purest essence; is he not wise and knowledgeable of God?

Who can stand up against the light of truth?

Carried in every dark cavern it glorifies its Creator, shields and guides the way of the feet and overcomes all through its wisdom.

Whosoever kindles the truth within his heart lights also his eye and illuminates each dark cavern of the body to his own advantage and the advantage of others.

But he who locks away the truth, guarding jealously its store and illumination, darkens his own soul, eye and body, and by his action locks God away from his heart.

The one who knows the truth, hides not his lantern of truth in dark places and away from others, for there his truth shines not and cannot be seen by those who seek the light.

They who are truthful and cling to the principle of truth are not vain for with vanity comes self-importance and self-importance hinders the master within.

. . .

To mirror inner reality is to reflect the truth; inner reality is the unification of spirit centred about the law of God; being centred about God each resides under the roof of one mansion; therefore God is the focal point towards which all manifestations must tread and in treading turn inward towards their own silence.

Never is the light that is truth taken from the window that is life even for one second, for the light inherently shines from each window but is illuminated by one for all to follow.

Should man be even for a second without that light then would he be in darkness and robbed of all eternity.

For those who see truth, beauty forever shines perpetually expressing itself, for they have found the true reflection of God.

The flower of truth is born amongst weeds that would strangle it; therefore must each be on his guard and wary, and trust in that alone which would bring about full bloom and beauty.

The higher Self reflects the truth that throbs within; the light of truth when attained is the ending of our journey; only then can we be fully free and fully alive.

The sword of truth is strong, being tempered in the furnace of God. The word of the Spirit is subtle but commanding; hence those who wield both the sword and the spirit are gentle unto all things, yet know of their power and are true warriors.

Light

ILLUMINATION comes from within but the light shines without and is scattered beyond your bounds and collected elsewhere to give birth to a new day.

Thus does each scatter the light and thus does each create or die by his own hand.

The candle burns not from its distance of illumination but from its source.

Thus does all creation burn from within and illuminate the darkness without.

Thus does true creation illuminate its source.

Thus does light follow light and darkness darkness, each going its own way.

The more one's light of understanding is shed and shared by creation, the more one illuminates one's own source of understanding and spiritual attainment.

The brilliance of your light is the choice of your making, for you are as the air and its purity, being the guardians of that light and feeding it, tending to its every need.

In light lies all physically manifested forms, for light gives clarity to form in its various aspects and light is perceived by the eye as a picture with its various forms and colours; yet an inner sight probes the sphere behind the colours themselves and thereby learns the secret of the manifest and the unmanifest.

To share your light as it radiates from within each selfless deed is to mirror your own deeper self; for to be central in all things of importance is the only way towards the true spirit.

Each creature exists as but a fractional light from the true Source within the life of all creation; each individual creates a greater light of understanding within itself and therefore remains at its conscious stage of understanding. Each time it goes back to its spiritual world it maintains the light of its own attainment to give it greater illumination to reach an ultimate understanding within its own life span.

What can you say of your fraction of light? Can you state that you, a ray of that light, illuminated a dark corner of the universe and gave it joy by your presence.

Then speak not of darkness where there is the light of truth; or the darkness of your sorrows yet to be overcome; but merge your light with all that you survey and illuminate your surroundings and your fellow beings with that light of truth.

Go as a traveller along all the dim and darkened highways and seek out those who exist in darkness and, carrying your lantern, give them light.

In knowledge, the true self is brought to light and in that light the oneness of God flashes out and God's illumination shines.

Self

Of what use is it to feed the outer self and starve the inner Self?

That which is purified externally is of little value if its interior is neglected.

Within the self all things are waiting to be brought into the light and known; for there, in that oneness of the universal Source, lies all and there all that is to be is seen and known.

Do not look abroad for the signs of true life; there you will find but the external world and be no wiser; instead look within; there you will see a light laid before your eyes and a guidance that will take you upon hallowed grounds.

To be inward turned is to know the self; to know the self is to know all; thus truth brings inner awareness; this is the key towards accomplishing many miracles within the self.

The long walk and the climbing of the mountain bring about physical endurance by test. Even so, the man eternally testing himself within brings out the diamond of God into the radiance of a new dawning and the age of a new day of eternity.

If a man conquers himself, his thoughts and his actions, he in turn is conquered by the Principle of God; it is therefore that man conquers not God but himself and in his turn is conquered.

To conquer the self is man's goal; to be taken over by the Principle of the spiritual Self, the complete accomplishment of man's purpose; for both are brought about by acceptance of being made 'one'.

In knowing the way towards the inner self there is assurance; with that knowledge there is humility; therefore the assured claim no self importance and as such remain apart from judgement; they hold no position in life and thereby remain separated from worldly action.

Were each person to become aware of the Godly consciousness dormant within, all could be changed instantly. It is in accepting true knowledge that one recognises what lies behind the form and draws nearer to the perfect expression of the Source.

Who knows the Self completely in its ultimate manifestation also knows the key to God's heart and there finds immortality.

Soul

THE sun's light holds dominion over the earth.
The moon's light holds dominion over the night and its stars.
Whosoever holds dominion over the fortress of his own soul illuminates his own countenance by the sun of awareness and his light is the light of all.

To search the soul in silence is to find that illumination beyond all dreams.

The soul is the consciousness of life, it is the illumination of the heart, the lamp that warms and lights the depths from within.

The heart and soul remain the same in quality, only conscious awareness is extended and remoulded in the furnace of life to form a different vessel and accept a purer substance sent from the source.

The unconscious desire to live is the force that drives on each thing towards its own progression and maturity; the soul is that perpetual force forever seeking its own perfection and eventual state of rest.

Memories are but of the soul's past and present experience gained through the vessels of bodies past and present, and hope and aspiration towards perfection are but the soul's memories relived within a new body.

Man is the sum total of his understanding and beliefs, weaving each pattern about his own soul.

It is wise for a man to reflect upon his actions since these actions are impressed upon his soul and he carries them with him throughout his travels.

They are not broken after he leaves his material body but remain intact, tied up, until they are released by a better expression of himself and one closer to the laws of God.

In this way the soul finds its own level in the spiritual world and orientates itself towards its own state of conscious awareness and being, and by its own efforts it is rewarded.

The attainment of the soul is the ability to outreach and outgrow its limited physical vesture and to produce a greater awareness within the stream of spiritual progression.

Through the vehicle of the soul we are born again and again until finally that soul has reached its highest pinnacle of human understanding and in its turn is dissolved by the true Spiritual Self.

The highest point of earthly life is the attainment of the ultimate in soul development, and therefore the first battle through the medium of experience is the battle to be at one with the soul and know that soul completely.

It is only when the soul has been mastered that the perfect or expressionless inner Self is released fully and, at this stage, the soul, no longer needed, is dissolved in the true spiritual awareness.

Upon reaching the realisation of oneness the spirit conquers and destroys the soul, becoming that which expresses a divine will beyond the shackles of containment and outside the momentum of life and death.

The final process of the soul's dissolution by the true Spiritual Self is the opening out to immortality, since beyond the bounds of the soul and mind there lies no death. Death is for those who live a life of physical illusion and therefore belongs only to that realm.

The Spirit

WONDERFUL is it to behold the sun in the sky and the moon in the cool night air; more wonderful than this is the light of the spirit captured in the eyes of the truthful and reflected in each thing as the only and supreme light.

The spirit fills all, is the motivating force and thus motion and emotion, the inward expressing itself in the outward; being the great engineer in all it takes the seat to guide the mechanism and thus increases, slackens, changes or suspends motion and function.

The pure spirit is ever present in magnitude and creative force; it moulds the universe and gives to each creative individuality.

The true spirit is indeed the centre of creation: for ever weaving a web of intricate wonder; within which lie the perfect geometry and symmetry, towards one aim and one ultimate purpose in its finality.

Being indivisible it cannot be separated from itself.
Being eternal it has no limits within time.
Being limitless it is omnipresent in all spheres, yet falls outside the reference of what is termed time and space.

It does not travel since it knows no distance but is in all and fills all with its great light of illumination. For the spirit is the hearth, the blazing focus wherein abides the Godhead.

The spirit within holds the reins of eternity, guiding its course within the NOW, from the eternal to the eternal, remaining for ever youthful and vibrant, for ever expressing itself.

Is not the body a filter for the spirit and the spirit that which the body filters?

Even as dark is not devoid of light and as light is not without darkness, so the flame of spirit is hidden within the evil-doer; it is there and can be brought forth in its time to true brilliance, for nothing lacks the spirit or its light.

The house in which your spirit resides is the house of creation and the centre of the universe that links you to the infinite.

Thus should you weave your web inwards through the soul to the spirit, knowing inwardly the truth of your eternity within the system of natural creativity.

All born of the spirit must return to the spirit through the same door and be reborn by the same method. With each step each makes straight the way, gathering experience through foolhardiness, joy from within the realms of sorrow, hope from the seed of its own helplessness at the time of sowing.

The spirit in bliss, suspended in another dimension, pursues its lawful course amongst the spaces of infinity to link itself with the Source of all that gave it expression on this plane, and vision on another.

PART IV

Progression

PROGRESSION is the way towards achievement of perfection as all moves onwards in creation towards perfection and immortality.

All things start life from a point in darkness; thus it is that finally darkness gives way to light and true illumination.

It is through the lower forms and by evolvement through the stages above those lower forms that each one learns to aspire towards true knowledge and see itself unadorned.

Upon the ladder of progression each thing stands, being not a unit unto itself but unto the whole, thus making that whole creative when combined under one universal principle and under that One Order unified, each becomes a great strength.

By way of external experience each creates internal equilibrium; with internal equilibrium each realises its own peace, knowing contentment; knowing both brings richness; in that richness each moulds the vessel of its own life; in moulding that vessel each treads the path; in treading the path each accepts a purer substance; in accepting a purer substance each outgrows itself; outgrowing itself each learns the truth.

Through the passage of learning is the progression of all; and by the experience gained from futility a greater purpose is sought.

It is in seeking that progression is made and through a progressive evolvement that consciousness becomes expanded. Each step of the conscious being is towards the unseen spheres, from the darkness of an unknowing mind to the true light of consciousness.

. . .

To rid oneself of that which restricts one's progress is to climb the ladder towards the spirit and God; therefore the path through life is the experience of learning and letting go of that which is useless to the individual in order to grasp something of use that is less restricting.

It takes time to progress, but each is given many life times in which to express its own evolution through different forms and from different states of consciousness towards the ultimate.

Man lives many lives and reaches a state of progression evolving towards the Godhead; exchanging his own understanding all the time through physical experience, that physical experience being the medium towards understanding and changing his geometrical or oscillatory pattern; he thereby creates a greater awareness of himself spiritually and thus tunes his higher faculties and aligns them to the one universal Law.

We as human beings must work together towards perfection of our species and thus maintain all things under our domain and serve them well with a willing heart as much as we serve one another. Only by sharing can we be complete.

Since the cycle of evolvement can never be stopped at will one can never remain stationary at one point, unless the apex has been attained; therefore all things must expand and reach out for a greater conscious being continually; in hiding behind the cloak of ignorance there is no shelter and no peace of mind, only foolishness in which fools are trapped with the unwise as their guides.

Therefore each is great when measured as the whole and each is definable in terms of the eternal, for all is one – immeasurable, unfathomable, inseparable, known only in true consciousness, distinctive only in true silence.

Destiny

LIKE a stone thrown into the pool, so are the ripples sent out from the one Source and in time return to that Source.

None sings his own song unless first sung by the gods of destiny impressed upon the other and brought into being by a hidden hand.

Nothing is ever created, brought about or made manifest on any plane by chance alone, for all has a planned creation, purpose and destiny to fulfil within its allotted time of evolution.

Destiny chooses its own road through life, unchanged by personal will, for the will of the individual in physical form is no substitute for the oneness that is and remains universal law.

We are all, whether we like it or not, whether we know it or not, the product of an immortal Fountainsource and are thereby eternal; for life is eternal, however ephemeral and myriad forms it assumes.

We indeed change our internal design by what we do; being the sum total of what we believe ourselves to be, with that belief we illuminate or darken our own existence, unifying a God-given-law or dividing the truth we see or do not see, understand or do not understand, act upon or do not, and thus receive or do not.

What we do is what we are; the pattern of actions to follow is in our hands for we weave our destiny and make each design with the passage of physical time and effort.

Each individual, through thought and action, operates the machinery of his own destiny and sets its course.

The seed yet to be harvested is planted with each passing second and the pattern of events yet to emerge is woven by each individual's hands.

It is by thought and deed that the future of all is determined, for we are the mirror and each life is a reflection of our quality.

No man can argue against that which has been laid down for him, nor against that which will be, for his own innermost self has laid down the law and the path and is concentric with the universal Source.

If he were offered the choice between one human lifetime and an eternity, which would he choose? How great then would become his argument against his own immortality?

It is because a man cannot see what is in store for him that he prefers to remain blind and continue to bring forth arguments. But in the final analysis God has the last word in all things of importance, and not man.

Ultimately no individual can escape the destiny laid down by universal Law, since its truth remains the truth forever and the very essence of man's being, and is never changed from age to age. Therefore it is wise to reflect upon the truth and find one's true path to the Source.

Chance or quirks of fate were not your making, nor you their products, for you exist about the precincts of the infinite and are a product of but one Maker.

The divine will within its creative sphere does not and cannot rely upon the happenings of pure chance any more than it can act upon pure speculation.

Consider the future, for one cannot change what has gone by, but one can change what will be in distant times.

The Universe

THE heart of the universe beats within each thing; its rhythm is one rhythm, its order is but one order under one Law supreme.

In the universe all is alive and breathes in unison.

Truth is not ours to change at will, nor the universe ours to set limits upon, for he who limits the universe, limits his own expressive existence and his own understanding.

The universe is as the sea gaining ground upon the shores, ebbing and flowing; as liquid poured from its container spreading and expanding its area upon the ground to reach an equilibrium with that space it shares; a tide, a fluid, an expanse of equilibrium under but one law.

Think not of the bounds of the universe as a fixed and rigid container; for the universe has no mathematical point of origin or of ending; and like to the sea it expands to no single shore and graces no one place with its bounties in preference to another, but as the sun shines on all within its realms, recognising no species great or small in its order, so is the universe.

The universe is unknown because on the conscious human plane there are limitations that one has imposed upon one's self; and one has also imposed these upon the universe, and therefore created a gap between one's self and the universe, blocking an understanding of what that universe is.

The creative power that is at the heart of the universe is the fountain of wisdom, knowing not separation nor recognising individuals for their traits of indifference towards it, yet giving individuality, quality of state, consciousness and above all eternity in which to discover all realms.

Intelligence works through the universe from which none is separated, therefore all is intelligence on a progressive scale of manifestations.

. . .

What we look at each passing day is indeed a symmetrical universe whose pattern is in the depths of our being, and without beginning or ending.

Each is placed within the sphere of its own consciousness and spiritual progression within the being of the universe. Each life-form exists as the centre of that great creation, performing its own limited task within a structure purposely made for all manifestations of form and spirit.

No universal structure is one of rigidity but exists, changing from construction to expansion, rest to unrest, equality to inequality all the time; it is in this way that each evolves.

Within the realms of divine will and inherent energy from that divine will all is equal within a creative structure, and all is given the same life-force without prejudice or favour.

There exists within that creative structure highly evolved life, and on its opposing scale life of little evolvement, one serving the other and, in its turn, being served.

Thus the servant knows the master and the master knows the servant, there being no difference between them, except that of quality and state.

No separation exists within the universe of matter from matter, life from life, or energy from energy.

All there is from the oneness of initial truth is creative individuality, evolvement and quality within the sphere of manifestations.

This and other worlds were designed as an unpainful and inspired calculation by a hand that caused all to appear; from nothingness all came into being as a candle lit by a match, and into that realm will sink when all have passed the trial of life and hold dominion over death.

That candle, my friend, to which the Creator put a match, which He ignited, burns not haphazardly unto its close, but was calculated to burn within a definite time and to give a definite luminosity; thus you and I, being a fraction of that light, must help all burn to its close within this creation.

Life, my friend, in this universe is as abundant as the drops of water in the ocean and as countless on both planes of conscious existence, here and beyond.

Therefore think not that you are alone in the universe and that there are none like you in form or measure within that infinite structure, for beings upon beings there are that dwell within the bounds of their own separate spheres and conscious existence.

The keynote of each thing in the universe is held within its silent sphere; from that sphere springs into being the seed that matures into full growth and expands towards the Infinite.

Deity

WHO gave the word its wings and thus created motion with a myriad of vibrations, each a silent blessing?
Without movement there would be no creation, for movement is natural to all creation.
Who set the spark to the creative? and the universe aflame? dispersed and diffused each spark to become a thing of wonder?
The initial force or word of God brought into being movement, the ebb and flow that creates, moulds and nurtures all.
Who created purpose within that motion towards its own fulfilment?
Who lives eternally and knows each thing by name from the void within the immeasurable?
The dance of God goes on under God and thus all becomes the One.

The essence that is God is an essence of oneness, a oneness that can never be divided from the initial WILL-FORCE, for God cannot compare with Itself, and has no comparison with or separation from what It creates, but remains active, passive and neutral within all.

God is the point of no action in all, existing at the nucleus wherein opposites merge but to re-emerge at the centre of all, at the very heart of silence, of harmony. Be it a spiritual essence or a physical manifestation, each central point belongs to God and God is omnipresent.

God exists at no direction of up or down; and so in order to express the domains of God, one has to remain at the point of no action or reaction, and in finding that point one will find in existence a whole new world, free from movement, extended beyond the bounds of the illusion of physical existence, and new laws in operation.

The Godhead being the innermost nucleus of evolution, its alpha and omega, its impulse and its resolution, has neither beginning nor end, neither highest nor lowest, seeking neither. It is.

Each thing seen and unseen is God in its very essence; therefore be careful in thought and action, for you observe and are observed within the sphere of both dimensions, the inner and the outer, the material and the spiritual.

Everything in creation evolves, everything moves towards that purest essence that the Fountainsource radiates, the Godhead. The Godhead Itself does not evolve by that movement, but is the Pinnacle of all expression, of all movement.

Being at all points, God's essence does not travel as rockets and cars travel, since it is an omnipresent force of divine will, existing at the centre of all points, in all time-streams and on all planes of consciousness; it does not move, it does not grow old, it does not evolve, involute, evolute, change, alter directions or otherwise. Being timeless, it exists in the void and womb of eternity and knows not the restrictions or limitations of time.

Being expressionless it does not feel emotion as we feel emotion, since it contains the purest of all expressions, and merges them as a unit of harmony.

Not knowing movement within Itself, God is motionless in relation to the movement of God's creation; being like an axle God remains stationary, whilst the wheel of all creation spins, alters course, decays and begins to emerge on other planes of consciousness about God's nucleus.

God does not grow old as the tree grows old; God does not evolve as a human being evolves; for God is an Essence of perfection and therefore does not and cannot evolve; everything revolves around God, but God remains stationary in relation to the evolution and to the cycles of evolution of everything.

. . .

The domains of God lie at the central point of all creation, within all that is neutral and beyond the realms of opposition.

Here, one finds God through the operation of God's law and through separation of action and interaction involving opposition within one's self.

The more one is at peace with one's self and one's surroundings, the nearer one is to finding God.

Search your very being without awareness of opposition at the very heart of interaction; at that point will you meet God and have knowledge of the purpose awaiting you; at that point will you see that God has no direction and is the expressionless essence about which all else revolves.

To know the principle that is God one must understand the principle of harmony within one's self; and live in that harmony and shed its radiance amongst one's fellow beings and all creation.

Only in this way will each individual reach an understanding of what God is and what God can do for each.

And so it is that those who seek God's domain must act within themselves to bring about peace and understanding, first by reflecting upon their own actions and thoughts to create good within themselves, i.e. find their centre, and secondly, to create harmony and a true balance within all things, these being but a true extension of themselves.

The miracle that is God can only be found by transcending our own will and by searching deep in the cavern of our own hearts to bring by unification our outer self with our inner self and both as one in touch with our essence.

God is not like a vessel that is used for one purpose only and then discarded or shelves until the next time comes when we need its essence again. God cannot be left upon some isolated shelf like a cup to collect dust and apprehend the light until we wish to fill that cup with our own fluid.

If the highest form reaches the lowest depths of self-expression, degrading the inner light, it neither sees nor understands the Godhead; it has forfeited its right to express that inner light. For God exists within the higher realms of selflessness; God cannot be expressed through disharmony and strife.

Where there is oneness – unity of purpose, harmony of relationship, peace of heart – there also can God's presence be sensed, and where birth and death occur there also is God's hand.

Where the presence of God is sensed there is beauty and grace beyond the comparison of all that is beautiful and graceful and there is purity beyond all visions of that which is pure.

Only by loving everything in life can we show our gratitude to God, for God is reflected in each thing; if that reflection be mirrored through our conscious state of being, then we become the radiant light of the now darkened world and bring in our footsteps a great beauty that will outlast our faulty and seemingly useless past.

The world is never devoid of its masters or of the voice of awakening; so it is that, within, none is cut off from God; for there, in that central point of existence, God waits to be heard in the silence of the heart.

Oneness

MANY roads converge onto one and many efforts end at one attainment.

Apprehension of oneness is spiritual insight; that is born from within; knowing its own direction it sets the course and it is never lost or separated from the Principle that is God; being the Infinite it is immortal.

The point which is the beginning of all is also its ending, the infinitely small and the infinitely large are not separate, but the same. All things in truth start from a point undefined and return to an infinite expanse also undefined. Since the two can never be known fully, who are we to judge by setting limits upon what is or is not. Only God has ultimate power and God alone judges all things in their hour of true awakening.

Worlds revolve about worlds in opposition, each with a task to perform and perfect within their cycles heading towards a state of equilibrium in which oneness is found. Thus will all return into the void whence all issued and a new world emerge, triumphant and unrestricted.

All things are one in essence; therefore true knowledge lies in acknowledging all things as such. Even though the mind pulls everything apart to inspect components and constituents so it must put all things back together and acknowledge the one Source.

Seeing all things from within, each becomes knowledgeable of the oneness from which none are separated, nor any distinct, since all is one and in that Oneness is God in its ultimate.

Matter and Spirit are inversions of one another that co-exist under one mansion and therefore within the realms of all manifestations that one mansion is the Cosmic Order.

Each form, visible and invisible, is part of but one body, differing only in quality and state, in degree and rarity of consciousness.

Since the essence of all is the Godhead without restriction or division from the oneness that manifests as the universe, nothing is a unit unto itself, and therefore each form of creation is the interweaving of knowledgeable and unknowledgeable, known and unknown, complexity and simplicity, of but one extended dimension and unification to which there is no end.

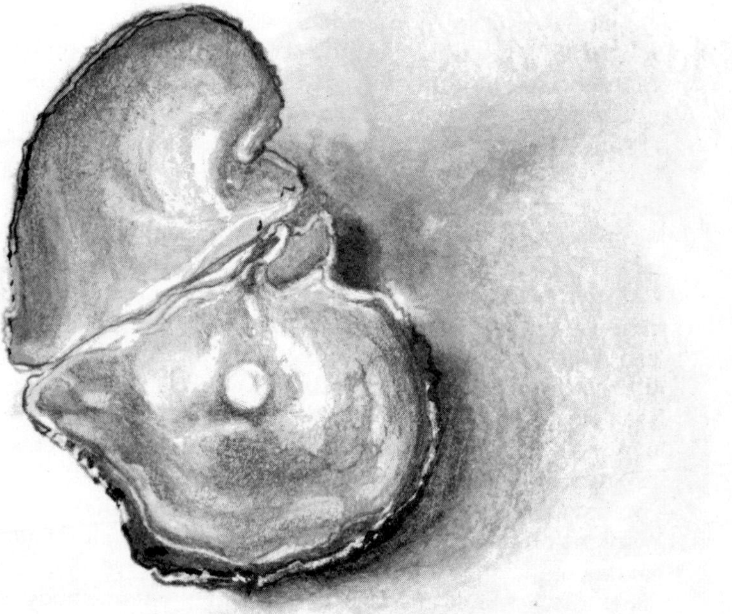

Nothing is a unity unto itself, nor is it self perpetuating, unless it be composed of the whole working in harmony towards a greater awareness of itself; thus is each the extension of just one essence.

That which compares with itself has not found the way towards true unity; that which cannot exist in harmony cannot become at one with the universe for it knows not unity within itself.

Each project of creation is different from the other and is individual in its own actions, thoughts, aptitudes, making it unique; though unique, it falls inherently under one family, the family of God.

There are many images but one reflection and many states of consciousness but one Source, thus each is that which it collects internally and projects from the source of its own soul and from that point it is known unto others.

The perception of the oneness to come is the greater illumination, the understanding of God, and the progressive tuning in of each and everything towards its own God-centre. When the Godhead is reached the world will go back into the Hearth from whence it came and man will become once again one with God. When that day comes will each and every individual being march back to but one illumination, sing with but one voice, see with but one sight and express harmony with but one heart.

A day will dawn when all creation will see and recognise its Maker, and when that day arises, as a butterfly from its cocoon breaks into a new sphere of life, so will all creation sing one song with one voice of unity and see with but one set of eyes.

A day will dawn when all men will become at one with the Godhead, and all animals will become at one with men, for the evolutionary cycle of universal events is geared to this eventual change, and is timed as the sand through the hour glass has its own time.

Consummation

THE glorious beginning and the glorious ending are but one day apart.

As each thing is hastened through the doors of life so it is sped like an arrow through life unto the Source.

The beginning and the ending are one for each manifestation in the manifestation of Oneness; it is like the endless snake whose tail is swallowed by its mouth, and thus is continuous.

As the circle has no ending, life itself has no ending and as the circle is engulfed by itself, so is all life engulfed and brought back back into being by God.

Brief is the pleasure in this physical life for it passes quicker than the wish for more time. It is wise therefore to extract from life the nectar beyond life itself, for it passes not and gives more pleasure in the end.

Then sing your praises to that which gave you your existence and be glad that you were made, for sorrow is but a fleeting shadow towards joy, and darkness but a span of illusion towards the light of reality and true existence.

Is not the joy of life the way we live it and what we do with it? Life, my friend, is a precious jewel to be shared amongst all for the experience gained and passed on to the spirit.

The constant battle to become as one is not in vain for in the end the essence of all emerges supreme and the victors of life share the blissful shore beyond.

The Canticle of Creatures Symbols of Union

The Canticle of Creatures Symbols of Union

An Analysis of St. Francis of Assisi

by
Eloi Leclerc O.F.M.

Translated
by
Matthew J. O'Connell

FRANCISCAN HERALD PRESS
1434 WEST 51st STREET • CHICAGO, 60609

The Canticle of Creatures: Symbols of Union by Eloi Leclerc O.F.M., translated by Matthew O'Connell from the French *Le Cantique des Creatures ou les Symboles de l'Union,* Librairie Artheme Fayard, 1970.

Library of Congress Cataloging in Publication Data

Leclerc, Eloi
The Canticle of creatures.

Translation of Le "Canticle des creatures."
"Canticum Solis" in English: p.
Bibliography: p.
1. Francesco d'Assisi, Saint, 1182-1226. Cantico de lo frate sole. I. Francesco d'Assisi, Saint, 1182-1226. Cantico de lo frate sole. English, 1976. II. Title.
BV489.F74C37413 242'.1 76-44545
ISBN O-8199-0624-7

IMPRIMI POTEST
Rev. Gabriel-Porte O.F.M.

NIHIL OBSTAT
Rev. Martin Steiner O.F.M.

IMPRIMATUR
E. Berrar V.E.

June 13, 1970

"The Nihil Obstat and Imprimatur are official declarations that a book or pamphlet is free of doctrinal error. No indication is contained therein that those who have granted the Nihil Obstst and Imprimatur agree with the contents, opinions, or statements expressed."

MADE IN THE UNITED STATES OF AMERICA

Contents

Introduction

Finally they understood and knew that it
was the soul of their holy father that
was shining with such great brilliance.[1]

Our purpose in this book is to offer a new reading of Francis of Assisi's *Canticle of Brother Sun.* The *Canticle* can, of course, be understood in its direct and obvious sense as a hymn of praise to the Most High for (and by) the various parts of his creation: sun, moon and stars, wind and water, fire and earth. That is how it has most often been interpreted. Such a reading is content with the primary, obvious meaning, that is, with what is expressly stated; it is content, if you will, with the cosmic or cosmic-religious dimension of the poem.

When the poem is thus understood, its inspiration seems very much like that of the Psalms and biblical canticles which praise God for his creation. The image of the universe which the *Canticle* supposes has been seen as a reflection of the cosmology current in St. Francis' time: a cosmology characterized by the geocentrism of the ancients and their theory of the four basic elements.

Such a reading of the *Canticle* is certainly valid. But is it the sole possible one? We think the poem can also be read at another level. In such a further reading we will be sensitive not only to the objects being praised but also to the unique and original way in which they are imagined, appreciated, and ordered among themselves. We then become aware that the cosmic elements are subtly differentiated and grouped in fraternal pairs according to an order that reflects neither objective reality nor cosmological system. More unsettling still is the fact that some of the elements are given epithets that evidently correspond to nothing in the objective order. In other words, the elements are assigned values according to a norm that is established not by the object as such nor by the cultural context of the times but by the subject who sings the *Canticle.* The cosmic elements manifest depths that are correlative to interior values of man's unconscious.

The *Canticle* thus shows Francis fraternally communing not only with the material elements of creation but also with what these elements are made to symbolize, namely, with the unconscious values which are assigned to the elements and for which the latter act as a kind of language. What are the interior values thus given a material shape and form? What profound experience is it that here, unconsciously, finds symbolic expression? In short, what is signified by each of the elements and by their ordered sequence? Such questions compel us to a reading of the *Canticle* in which we endeavor to find and decipher in the primary, cosmic meaning another meaning that is of the interior order.

We are led to such a reading in terms of interiority not only by a greater attentiveness to the text itself but also by an examination of the circumstances of its composition. It has been said that the poem accompanies Francis throughout his life like a refrain and that bits of it are constantly surfacing in his everyday life and activity. It is a fact nonetheless that in its finished form the poem springs into existence at the end of a lengthy spiritual journey.

Almost twenty years had passed since Francis' conversion to the evangelical life. They were years during which he constantly meditated on the "advent of gentleness" and the passion of the Most High Son of God, and strove daily to walk in the footsteps of the Lord. Now, on Mt. Alverna, he had just received in his flesh the stigmata that completed his likeness to the crucified Christ. Bleeding from every wound, exhausted by fasting and illness, blind and almost brought to his final agony, Francis was simply "identified with Christ in redemptive suffering," to use the language of Claudel. Suffering filled his body; his suffering of soul was perhaps even more intense. The evangelical values of pure simplicity, poverty, and peace that were, in his eyes, so essential to the revelation of divine Love, had been shunted aside in a Christendom engrossed by power and ruled by the idea of the crusades. They were even questioned at times by his own followers. It was eventide in Francis' life, but he still had not experienced the full peace that evening should bring.

It was then that the decisive event took place. Francis descended from Mt. Alverna, almost at the end of his strength, and stopped at the monastery of San Damiano where Clare and her sisters were living. It was there that he had first heard Christ speaking to him, inviting him to restore the house that was falling into ruins. Clare settled Francis in a house adjacent to the convent, where he remained in constant pain. "For forty days or more, blessed Francis could not bear the light of the sun during the day or the light of the fire at night. . . .His eyes caused him so much pain that he could neither lie down nor sleep, so to speak."[2]

Then, "one night, as he was thinking of all the tribulations he was enduring, he felt sorry for himself and said interiorly: 'Lord, help me in my infirmities so that I may have the strength to bear them patiently.'"[3] Celano gives us to understand that a conflict was raging in Francis' soul and that he was praying that he might overcome the temptation of discouragement: "as he prayed thus in agony. . . ."[4]

> And suddenly he heard a voice in spirit: "Tell me, Brother: if, in compensation for your sufferings and tribulations you were given an immense and precious treasure: the whole mass of earth changed into pure gold, pebbles into precious stones, and the water of the rivers into perfume, would you not regard the pebbles and the waters as nothing compared to such a treasure? Would you not rejoice?" Blessed Francis answered: "Lord, it would

> be a very great, very precious, and inestimable treasure beyond all else that one can love and desire!" "Well, Brother," the voice said, "be glad and joyful in the midst of your infirmities and tribulations: as of now, live in peace as if you were already sharing my kingdom."[5]

A supernatural joy immediately filled Francis' soul, the joy that comes from the certainty of possessing the kingdom. Now he knew for sure that the road he had been following —the road of suffering with Christ—was indeed the road that "leads to the land of the living."[6] At this moment it was as if a glorious sun had risen in his soul. In the morning he called his companions together and, unable to contain his joy, sang to them the *Canticle of Brother Sun* which he had just composed.

In the light of this account it seems impossible to understand the Canticle *properly* unless we directly relate it to Francis' innermost experience, his bitter suffering, his heroic patience, his daily struggle for evangelical values, and his supernatural joy, or, in a word, to his life of intimacy with Christ. The *Canticle* springs from existential depths. It is the end result and surely the supreme expression of a whole life.

At first sight, there is something rather surprising in all this. Here is a man whose diseased eyes cannot bear the light nor any longer enjoy the sight of cratures, a man who is interested only in the splendors of the kingdom. Yet, in order to express his joy, this man sings of matter: matter that burns and emits a brilliant light—the sun and the fire; matter that nourishes—the air, the water, and the earth, "our mother." And he does so in terms strangely reminiscent of ancient pagan hymns in which men gave thanks for the sun's mastery and for the earth's maternal fruitfulness. His language is the ancient language typical of the sacred, the language of the cosmic hierophanies, and he uses it with the spontaneity, directness, and warmth that mark a man's words when he speaks his mother tongue. Moreover, in the entire *Canticle* there is not a single reference or slightest allusion to the supernatural mystery of Christ and his kingdom! It is only material things that are used to celebrate the glory of the Most High.

We would indeed have every reason to be surprised, were it not that these cosmic realities, given the manner in which they are celebrated and the rich affective and oneiric freight they unconsciously carry, constitute a kind of language expressive of an inner experience of the sacred. "To manifest the 'sacred' *on* the 'cosmos' and to manifest it *in* the 'psyche' are the same thing. . . .Cosmos and Psyche and the two poles of the same 'expressivity;' I express myself in expressing the world;' I explore my own sacrality in deciphering that of the world."[7] On reading this statement, we saw in it the key to a reading of Francis' *Canticle* in terms of the interiority it reflects.

In this book we try to use the key, inquiring into each of the cosmic elements being celebrated as well as into the order and structure of the whole hymn of praise. At each step we seek to profit by the many possibilities made available to us in contemporary hermeneutical theory and practice. As our investigation proceeded, we found the *Canticle* being illumined from within. No longer were we dealing simply with a poetical religious discourse on created things. On the contrary, these created things proved to be, as it were, the outward garment of a deeper kind of discourse. Praise of the cosmos was revealed as the symbolic, unconsciously spoken language that gave expression to an interior journey in which the very depths of the soul were being explored. In more precise terms, the *Canticle* turned out to be as it were a "poetics" for man's reconciliation with his own "archeology" and for his opening of himself to plenary existence in the light of Being. Like the first disciples of Francis when they inquired into the meaning of the solar chariot that had visited them in the night while the master was absent, we too came to understand that "it was the soul of their holy father that was shining with such great brilliance"[8] in this *Canticle of Brother Sun.*

Although we interpret the *Canticle* as the symbolic expression of an experience that unfolds in the night of the soul, we are not by any means giving an allegorical interpretation of the poem. On the contrary, we deliberately reject such an interpretation. For, if Francis' praise of creatures can be regarded as significant of interior values, it is because Francis' communion with created things was so real and deep that it involved his soul and all its powers.

There can be no question, therefore, of playing down the properly cosmic, realistic aspect of the text. To do so would be to go counter to everything we know about Francis' attitude to creatures. His love for them was real, deep, and religious. In his eyes, each of them in its own way and by its very being was a manifestation of the power or the beauty or the goodness of the Most High, and the manifestation sometimes caused him to fall into an ecstasy. There can be no doubt that Francis experienced the sacred in the cosmos and entered into communion with God through the medium of created things and indeed in the very depths of created things. It is this aspect of his religious experience that the *Canticle of Brother Sun* expresses.

Real though it is, however, this aspect of his experience cannot be separated from another: his union with God along the lowly ways established by the incarnation of the Most High Son of God. In fact, all that is original in Francis' religious experience derives from the synthesis he effected between an interior and very personal evangelical mysticism and an ardent cosmic mysticism.

Francis unites, in a wonderful way, a life of union with the person of Christ and the profound religious feeling with pantheistic religions entertain toward the cosmos. He unites the Sun and the Cross. Max Scheler, the German philosopher, speaks as follows in his book on the nature and forms of sympathy:

> It was left to one of the great artificers of the spirit in European history to make the memorable attempt of uniting and harnessing this [a non-cosmic personal love-mysticism of universal compassion],

> within a single life-stream, to the animistic sense of union with the being and life of Nature. This was the very remarkable achievement of the saint of Assisi.[9]

The synthesis resulted in one of the most profound and fascinating spiritual experiences any human being has ever had.

The *Canticle of Brother Sun* is both praise of the cosmos and a hymn to the inner depths. When read according to its full meaning it proves to be the expression of the spiritual experience just described. What this brotherly praise of creatures, to the honor of the Most High, ultimately reveals to us is an approach to God that involves the saint simultaneously in a humble, fervent communion with all creatures and in the soul's opening of itself to its own innermost depths. Somewhat more precisely, it is an approach to God in which the soul, while communing in a humble brotherly way with creatures, is reconciled both to its entire self and to the entirety of reality.

Abbreviations

Adm	*Admonitions* of St. Francis
1C	Celano's *First Life of St. Francis*
2C	Celano's *Second Life of St. Francis*
Fior	*Fioretti* or *Little Flowers of St. Francis*
Lds	The *Lauds* or Praises written by St. Francis, added to his paraphrase of the Our Father
1Let to 13Let	The thirteen *Letters* of St. Francis
LM	*Major Life of St. Francis* by St. Bonaventure
LP	*Legend of the Perugian* (*Anonymus Perusinus*)
PLeo	*Praises of God for Brother Leo,* by St. Francis
1Reg	*First Rule* of St. Francis
2Reg	*Second Rule* of St. Francis
Sp	*Speculum Perfectionis, Mirror of Perfection.*
SV	*Salutation of the Virtues,* by St. Francis
Test	*Testament* of St. Francis
1Vesp	Vespers of the first schema in St. Francis' *Office of the Passion*

The Canticle of Brother Sun[1]

Most high, all-powerful, all good, Lord!
All praise is yours, all glory, all honour
And all blessing.

To you alone, Most High, do they belong.
No mortal lips are worthy
To pronounce your name.[2]

All praise be yours, my Lord, through all that you have made,
And first my lord Brother Sun,
Who brings the day; and light you give to us through him.

How beautiful is he, how radiant in all his splendour!
Of you, Most High, he bears the likeness.[3]

All praise be yours, my Lord, through Sister Moon and Stars;[4]
In the heavens you have made them, bright
And precious and fair.

All praise be yours, my Lord, through Brothers Wind and Air,
And fair and stormy, all the weather's moods,
By which you cherish all that you have made.

All praise be yours, my Lord, through Sister Water,
So useful, lowly, precious and pure.

All praise be yours, my Lord, through Brother Fire,
Through whom you brighten up the night.
How beautiful he is, how gay! Full of power and strength.

All praise be yours, my Lord, through Sister Earth, our mother,
Who feeds us in her sovereignty and produces
Various fruits and colored flowers and herbs.

All praise be yours, my Lord, through those who grant pardon
For love of you; through those who endure
Sickness and trial.

Happy those who endure in peace,
By you, Most High, they will be crowned.

All praise be yours, my Lord, through Sister Death,
From whose embrace no mortal can escape.

Woe to those who die in mortal sin!
Happy those She finds doing your will!
The second death can do no harm to them.

Praise and bless my Lord, and give him thanks,
And serve him with great humility.

Chapter 1

When Creatures Speak

"Supposing truth is a woman—what then?"[1] Nietzsche's practice of hypothesizing has not lacked for followers. In fact, since his time "the whole of philosophy has become interpretation," says Jean Lacroix.[2] The philosopher now knows that language, whatever its form, is never exhausted by what it shows on the surface and that its obvious meaning hides another. Is this disguise, mask, symbol? No matter! All language requires interpretation. Philosophers have therefore learned to "read slowly, with penetration, respect, and caution, with a sense of what lies behind the scenes, with open-mindedness, with a delicate touch and a subtle eye." The effort to interpret means a tension between a "willingness to listen" and a "willingness to suspect."[3]

Anyone who nowadays would offer a new reading of a text such as Francis of Assisi's *Canticle of Brother Sun* finds himself in a somewhat embarassing situation. On the one hand, he cannot evade the demands laid upon him by the nature of interpretation with its "double motivation: willingness to suspect, willingness to listen." On the other, he finds it hard to cultivate a willingness to suspect when the text he is dealing with seems so transparent. After all, is not the thing we find most striking about this poem its amazing simplicity?

Everything about it is simple. It has simplicity of form, being so bare as to be disconcerting. There is no effort at style, nothing lavish, nothing to stir the imagination.

The ideas are simple; the author seems almost to withdraw from the scene, leaving only the objects of which he speaks. Can we even speak of "images"? Do the words not simply make us *see* the objects they designate? After all, what is the poem really about? Only about the sun that brings the day, the moon and stars that shine in the heavens at night, the wind and the air which creatures breathe, and so on. It all adds up to a very unsubjective picture of the world.

Finally, the emotions are simple. The text suggests no dramatization, no conflict. From beginning to end, it is a serene assertion of universal brotherhood. Everything in it is direct, clear, and full of light.

What can justify a willingness to suspect? Is not the simplest interpretation the truest one in this case? Does not Francis himself advise this kind of interpretation when he says in his *Testament:* "God inspired me to write. . . these words plainly and simply, and so you too must understand them plainly and simply"?[4]

And yet—Francis has put his whole self into this poem. Chesterton writes: "It is a supremely characteristic work, and much of St. Francis could be reconstructed from that work alone."[5] The manner in which Francis here looks at the created world is a key to his inner self, for the *Canticle* undoubtedly has elements that reveal in a special way the personality of its author. There are the choice of and the values associated with the cosmic elements; the designation of things as "brother" or "sister"; the archetypal character of the images; the structure of the poem; the addition of the last four stanzas.

These are points that must be examined if we are to grasp the "interior" meaning of the poem.

1. Choice and Appreciation of the Cosmic Elements

In this *Canticle of Brother Sun,* which is a poem of praise to God for and through all his creatures, some of the latter are mentioned and celebrated by name: the sun, the moon and stars, the wind, the water, the fire, and the earth. Others have pointed out the resemblance of this celebration of the cosmic elements to some of the biblical canticles like the canticle of three young men in the furnace, or even to certain liturgical hymns. Brown, for example, cites a liturgical hymn of the eleventh century, *Jubilemus omnes,* which urged men during the Advent season to rejoice on account of all God's creatures: sun, moon, stars, air, winds, etc.[6] But despite their similar inspiration, there is an important difference between Francis' poem and the biblical or liturgical hymns: in the canticle of the three young men and in the liturgical hymn mentioned the various cosmic elements are simply named and listed, whereas in the *Canticle of Brother Sun* they are also described, and described abundantly. Not only is each of them given the title of "Brother" or "Sister," a point we shall discuss further on, but it is accompanied by a series of epithets that assign a certain value to it.

We must pay close attention to these extended descriptions, for they represent an appreciation of matter, a setting of value upon it. The adjective "precious," which occurs in two contexts, is significant in this respect. The universe of which Francis sings is made of a "precious" matter: the stars in heaven are "precious" and the water on earth is "precious."

Each cosmic element possesses a profound splendor. Brother Sun, regally beautiful, is haloed with a divine radiance, and regarded as the symbol of the Most High. The earth, which sustains us and produces every kind of fruit, is greeted as "mother," for she is filled with a mystery of life. Brother Fire, with his power, radiates an invincible joy: the joy of the light that triumphs over darkness. An in Sister Water, "so useful, lowly, precious, and pure," we glimpse the image of an inward, sacred presence; the whole mystery of the soul's inviolable depths is present at the heart of matter!

Evidently, these material images of sun, moon and stars, wind and water, fire and earth are not simply reflections or descriptions of external realities. It is not even possible to give an objective meaning to some of the adjectives Francis applies to the cosmic elements, such as "lowly and pure," used for the water, or "precious," used for both stars and water. The least that can be said of such adjectives is that they imply a choice. Water is not always "lowly"; there are waters that overflow and rage unhindered. Fire is not always satisfied to give light and a sense of joy; it also burns and destroys, and it causes fearful destruction. The wind is not always a life-giving breath; sometimes it rises and becomes a storm or whirlwind, and then it seizes upon and devastates everything in its path. As a matter of fact, therefore, the *Canticle* contains a selection of material images whose "imaginary" character, though not thrust upon us, is nonetheless definitely asserted.

A literary education that concentrates too exclusively on the formal imagination and its creative role has not accustomed us to pay sufficient attention to material images (images of substance) and to understand the creative power they exercise. We too often think of them simply as material we passively absorb from outside in the process of perception. Gaston Bachelard, the philosopher, however, in books on literary esthetics which are also essays on the imagination as it deals with substances, has set out to show that there is a basically creative imagination of material things. Contrary to what is usually assumed, an image of something material is not always a simple reproduction nor even a combination of elements derived from the object perceived. In addition to the image of a material thing as simply perceived, there is an image that is created by the imagination. The former derives from perception and memory and is connected with our capacity to grasp the real. The latter, on the other hand, is connected with our capacity to grasp what is unreal; its domain is the realm of the imaginary; its subject matter is oneiric.

Imagined or oneiric images of material things have their roots in the soul. We did not have to wait for Bachelard to learn that "every landscape we love is a state of soul." The philosopher's contribution was

> to understand that all aspects of nature are not equally revelatory. Lines, forms, and colors correspond to zones of the psychism that have been permeated by reason. The substratum of the self, on the other hand, is homologous with the substratum of things, with substances, with the four elements which an ancient physics, deeply rooted in the collective imagination, regards as constitutive of matter. The imagination that deals with air, water, earth, and fire therefore makes accessible to us the hidden pathways of the soul and enables us to decipher the secrets of men's psychic constitutions.[7]

It is from man's own depths, then, that images of matter

derive their substance. In fact, they have "a twofold reality: a psychic reality and a physical reality."[8] But here the psychic reality dominates the physical reality. The activity of the imagination goes on, in a way, even before perception; it anticipates perception and thus makes us "see" the physical reality in a certain way by imposing on it an existence created by the imagination itself.

When we are confronted by such images of material things, we must ask what they mean, and we must learn to decipher them. It is here that attention to the way in which values are attributed to substances or elements becomes extremely important. Matter to which a value has been given is matter that as it were expands under the action of unconscious interior values. Nor need the attribution of values be accomplished in a cumbersome fashion. It can be quiet unobtrusive; for that reason it is often more profound and meaningful.

Consider, for example, how Francis praises the Lord for "Sister Moon and Stars": "In the heavens you have made them, bright and precious and fair." But is that not a straightforward observation of fact? It seems natural and artless to say of the stars that they are "bright and precious and fair." If we search here for a hidden meaning, are we not just looking for figs from thistles?

And yet the adjective "precious" should indeed jostle our attention, for it is not as "natural" as it might appear. In fact, as we noted earlier, it is enough by itself to show that an attribution of values has occurred. The word immediately evokes the image of a treasure of great wealth in some form. Such an image is all the more striking when it comes from the mouth of the Poor Man of Assisi, since it was not Francis' habit to look at material things from this point of view. In his other writings he hardly ever uses the adjective "precious" except in the letters when speaking of the respect due to the Body of the Lord in the Eucharist. In this latter context he seems spontaneously to use the word "precious" to describe the kind of place in which the

Body of the Lord is to be kept, as well as the objects used in connection with the sacrament of the altar.

> In this world there is nothing of the Most High himself that we can possess and contemplate with our eyes, except his Body and Blood, his name and his words, by which we were created and by which we have been brought back from death to life . . . . If the Body of our Lord Jesus Christ has been left abandoned somewhere contrary to all the laws, It should be removed and put in a place that is properly prepared for It [*in loco pretioso*], where It can be kept safe.[9]

> With everything I am capable of and more, I beg you to ask the clergy with all humility, when it is called for and you think it a good idea, to have the greatest possible reverence for the Body and Blood of our Lord Jesus Christ . . . . They should set the greatest value [*pretiosa habere debeant*], too, on chalices, corporals, and all the ornaments of the altar that are related to the holy Sacrifice. If the Body of our Lord has been left in a poverty-stricken place [*pauperrime collocaturm*], they should put it somewhere that is properly prepared for It [*in loco pretioso*], according to Church law, so that It will be kept safe.[10]

> Above everything else, I want this most holy Sacrament to be honored and venerated and reserved in places which are richly ornamented [*in locis pretiosis*].[11]

Thus, whenever Francis uses the adjective "precious" in his writings, he applies it to things closely connected with the sacred reality of the Lord's Body and Blood. Of course, what was really precious in his eyes was the sacred reality itself. Here the word "precious" acquires a new meaning. It still signifies something of great value, a treasure, but the treasure is no longer one on which society can set a price or which men can lust after. It is a mysterious, sacred treasure, not to be "possessed."

Given the lofty connotations of the adjective "precious" as used by Francis, we are surprised to see him apply it to the moon and the stars. We are justified in asking what can be meant by such an attribution of sacral value to the stars.

The image is, of course, a poetic image: the "precious" star is a star of imagination and dreams, for the quality of "preciousness" cannot be an object of simple observation. We see the stars sparkling in the heavens. The poet's imagination passes from "sparkling" to "precious," and the sparkling star becomes a precious thing. But to see the stars as precious, one must do more than simply look at them, one must dream of them, and dream of them until one no longer sees the stars themselves but in their place an enchanted world of precious stones. Bachelard cites an apt line of Mallarme: "What a precious gem, the changing sky!"[12]

Only dreams can thus combine star and precious stone and transform the one into the other, so that the stars become "the diamonds of heaven." As a poetic and oneiric image, the "precious" star originates in dreams and stimulates dreams. It is always to some extent the mysterious star, fascinating and enchanting, and linked with the depths of the soul. One who loves to watch the "precious" stars in the heights of heaven carries a hidden treasure in the depths of his own soul. The "precious" brilliance in the heavens reflects a great interior brilliance. And thus we are led to ask: "What does this language mean?"

This question arises not only with regard to the "precious" stars but with regard to all the cosmic elements in Francis' canticle of praise. The sun, beautiful and radiant as a god; the wind that sustains life; the water, "so useful, lowly, precious and pure"; the fire, beautiful and gay, "full of power and strength"; and the maternal, fruitful earth: all these elements become bearers of value and creations of the imagination. To what inner forces, what archetypes in the unconscious do these cosmic images give expression? In a word, who or what is speaking here?

In order to answer this question, we must examine each of the images and its position in the poem as a whole.

We must try to discern the direction taken in the attribution of values to the elements, since there are various ways of experiencing a substance and, consequently, of dreaming about it. It is important to determine the orientations underlying the assignment of values. We must also ask whether the text shows a marked preference on the poet's part for one or other cosmic element. Such a preference can be highly significant, for it reveals a "basic illusive temperament." For example, "a fondness for fire is evidence of a particular temperament, different from that which leads an individual to prefer earth, or air, or water."[13]

It will be evident by now that we are dealing here with a text whose meaning is not exhausted by its immediate material sense. The cosmic realities named and praised are symbols as well as material things. They continue to be material things, of course, and we must not lose sight of the realism of the *Canticle.* When Francis praises the sun, moon and stars, the wind and the water, the fire and the earth, he is speaking of the realities everyone can see. But the poem is not simply naming the material elements. Once values are associated with the cosmic realities, they become expressive of something further; they form an unconscious language. The cosmic universe here symbolizes an interior universe. Therefore the full meaning of the poem is to be sought in the relation between these two universes.

Before embarking on our quest we will profit by enlarging the scope of our investigation and collecting all the data pertinent to the problem.

2. THE DESIGNATION "BROTHER" OR "SISTER"

Even a superficial reading of the poem cannot fail to pick up one very striking point: the familiar, brotherly fashion in which Francis speaks of the various cosmic realities. He addressed each of them as "Brother" or "Sister." He is acquainted, not with sun, moon, wind, water, and so on, but with Brother Sun, Sister Moon, Brother Wind, Sister Water, etc. We are far removed indeed from the Cartesian universe and the

> practical [philosophy], by means of which, knowing the force and action of fire, water, air, the stars, the heavens, and all the other bodies that surround us, as distinctly as we know the various crafts of our artisans, we might also apply them in the same way to all the uses to which they are adapted, and thus render ourselves the lords and possessors of nature.[14]

The very names "Brother" and "Sister" given to subhuman things show a quite different manner of presence to the world than that which is characterized by the will to dominate and possess things. In Francis' poem things do not cease to be useful, but they become the object of a respectful, brotherly sympathy.

Francis' language may nevertheless surprise us, especially when we reflect that for him "brother" and "sister" are not mere stylistic formulas nor a purely allegorical mode of expression. Even in his everyday life Francis addressed all creatures as "brother" or "sister." He considered himself to be thereby expressing the true reality of these creatures.

But what is this reality? The reader will probably hasten to observe that this manner of addressing creatures springs, in Francis' case, from an essentially religious intuition: that of the universal fatherhood of God. Admittedly, if there is a single basic intuition governing his thinking, it is this one. We can cite in this regard the testimony of St. Bonaventure: "By the power of his extraordinary faith he tested the Goodness which is the source of all in each and every created thing as in so many rivulets."[15]

Such considerations as these are fully justified. At the same time, we must bear in mind that this theological intuition was, in Francis' case, never a purely intellectual matter. It was rooted in, and inseparable from, a profound affective and esthetic experience. When he spoke of material creatures as "brother" and "sister," he was expressing not only a dogmatic truth but a psychological truth as well; the names expressed a genuine love and a "sense of union with the being and life of Nature" (to use Scheler's words). In short, the declaration of brotherhood is also the affirmation of an intimacy and a kind of consanguinity that is experienced in a vital way.

But an intimacy with what or with whom? The reader may find the question surprising. Is not the meaning of Francis' canticle sufficiently clear? In its direct and immediate sense, the assertion of brotherhood certainly looks to the material elements themselves: sun, moon, stars, wind, and so forth. Therefore it expresses an intimacy, a familiarity, with the realities themselves. Francis speaks the language of a man who lives close to material things; who feels things co-existing at his side, mysteriously connected with his own destiny; and in whom these things elicit a genuine feeling of brotherhood.

Yet, if a man of mature age is to think of various material realities as his brothers and sisters, and to do so in a fully authentic and spontaneous way, he must have established links with them that are deepiy rooted in his past. He must be finding in them, quite unconsciously, something of what filled his earliest dreams. Chesterton is quite right when he says that this poem of Francis is "full of the mirth of youth and the memories of childhood."[16] A person who has not had this early experience of familiarity with the elements, this child's delight in dreams that center on things and are stimulated by them, someday reaches the metaphysical idea of the common origin of all created realities and of the universal brotherhood that consequently binds them together. But he will never experience the innocent job of existing in the midst of these realities and of a fraternal community with all existing things. In any event, he would never feel in his heart the need of calling material things "brother" and "sister." And if he decided to use these names, he would do it in an artificial, pseudo-naive, and calculating way. He would write bad poetry. "You must take things to your heart for a long time if you are to give them life," Debussy used to say.

You cannot improvise the poetic imagination of matter. That imagination has lowly origins; the ground for it must be prepared long before it becomes active. Bachelard writes: "There are times when the creative poet's dreams delve so deeply into his nature that he rediscovers in them, beyond all doubting, the images he cherished as a child."[17] The dream experience of the child is the earth into which the poetic imagination of matter sinks its most life-giving roots. There, among the organic impressions and material images that lent enchantment to the dawning life of the child, the imagination finds the substances it regards as most precious and fraternal.

If this be so, then the terms "brother" and "sister," which Francis uses with regard to the natural elements, look in fact beyond these elements to an imaginary matter; the names are addressed to certain primordial images of matter. Francis' sense of brotherhood relates to this imaginary matter and these material images. The names "brother" and "sister" relate, by way of the material elements, to that which these elements, once values have been attributed to them and the imagination has worked on them, now represent and signify.

Evidently the meaning of these names is not as simple as it seemed initially. The first and explicit meaning, which is that Francis feels a brotherly familiarity with the material elements themselves, leads to a second, hidden meaning that concerns a brotherly familiarity of a deeper kind with the unconscious interior values signified by the material elements. In short, the assertion of brotherhood with the cosmos cannot be separated from that attribution of values to the elements. Brotherhood and attribution of value go together; each reinforces the other. The ultimate meaning of the one is closely linked to the ultimate meaning of the other.

There is a further point to be noted. Although Francis in his poem considers himself "brother" to every creature, the relationship is slightly different in each case, depending precisely on the value attributed to each element. The differentiation is especially clear in the choice of sex. The superficial reader of the text might think the choice of sex depends solely on the grammatical gender of the element in question, but in fact the matter is not that simple. The significance of the choice of sex is not determined by the rather arbitrary grammatical gender, but is connected with the way in which the substance itself is dreamed, imagined, and assigned a value. The choice of sex depends on the play of the imagination as it focuses on material substances; it is called for by the values attributed to the element and is given accordingly.

As a matter of fact, the choice of sex is made in the very process of attributing values to the elements. For example, it is not by accident that Francis uses "Brother" in addressing the fire, which he says is beautiful and gay, "full of power and strength," for the illusive image is characterized by a dynamic vigor. "Sister Water," on the other hand, is praised as "useful, lowly, precious, and pure." Obviously, in these two instances we have the attribution of two different types of value. In the case of fire, the values are those of action, vigor, and the dynamic; in the case of water, the values are those of depth and intimacy. The first attribution yields an essentially masculine image; the second, a wholly feminine image.

The names "brother" and "sister" which Francis gives to the various cosmic elements are addressed to the imaginary image: to it and all it may signify. The names are part of the "imagined" image; they help form and complete it by stripping the material element of the anonymity proper to things and giving it a human shape. The names introduce the images into the universe of human and domestic relationships. The meaning of the names is thus inseparable from the meaning of the material images. Like the latter, the titles "brother" and "sister" certainly have a cosmic significance, for they express an openness and a fraternal presence to the world, as well as an affective communion with all creatures. But the cosmic meaning contains a further meaning, an interior one relating to the depths of affectivity and imagination.

It is still too soon to attack directly the problem of this interior meaning. We must continue for a while to explore the text itself.

3. THE ARCHTYPAL CHARACTER OF THE IMAGES.

Attention to the values attributed to the cosmic elements in the *Canticle* has shown that we are dealing with material elements that have been "imagined" and are freighted with meaning. One aspect of the symbolism is directly shown by the text itself, since "my lord Brother Sun" is expressly acknowledged as being a symbol of God: "Of you, Most High, he bears the likeness." For Francis, the radiant image of the sun is rich in transcendent significance; its "expressivity" is sacral.

The same can be said of all other cosmic images in the poem. The values attributed to them are essentially religious, so that they lead us to see beyond the thing itself, a sacred reality, a reality which is supremely powerful, good, and beautiful. Each image of a material substance is a stimulus of praise to the Most High. The "preciousness" of matter in each instance is closely related to the being's sacral "expressivity." The stars in heaven and the water on earth are "precious" to anyone who knows how to read the sacred language they speak.

We must, nonetheless, raise an important question: How profound, from a psychological point of view, is the religious symbolism in the poem? Does it derive from an original and radical mystical experience? Or is simply the outcome of biblical and liturgical reminiscences or references? Does Francis' symbolism sink its roots into our interior "archeology," that is, into our primal, unconscious powers of affectivity and imagination? Or does it spring rather from a fervid pious imagination that is relaxing its ascetic rigor for a moment? In short: Is the symbolism here nothing but the allegorizing proper to the literature of edification, or is it really a language spoken by the depths of the soul, the language of the great archetypes?

If we turn to the testimony of Francis' early biographers, we will see that the symbolism he used in speaking of nature operates at several levels. In a straightfoward reading of the obvious meaning, the symbolism belongs to the scriptural and liturgical tradition in which Francis was thoroughly at home. Celano, for example, writes: "He [Francis] spared lights, lamps, and candles, not wishing to extinguish their brightness with his hand, for he regarded them as a symbol of the Eternal Light. He walked reverently upon stones, because of him who was called the Rock."[18]

The author of the *Mirror of Perfection* is even more explicit:

> Since in Holy Scripture the Lord Himself is called *The Sun of Justice,* and because blessed Francis thought the sun the loveliest of God's creatures and most worthy of comparison with Him, he gave its name to the *Praises of God in His Creatures*. . .and called them *The Song of Brother Sun*.

"Next to fire he had an especial love for water, because it symbolizes holy penitence. . . , and at Baptism the soul is cleansed from its stains and receives it first purification."[20] Speaking of Francis' compassionate love of creatures, St. Bonaventure tells us: "He reserved his most tender compassion for those creatures which are a natural reflection of Christ's gentleness and are used in Sacred Scripture as figures of him."[21]

There can be no doubt about the scriptural and liturgical

inspiration of Francis' symbolism. At the level of explicit consciousness, this inspiration is certainly the most important. The images and symbols of which Francis makes use must be related to the Lord's revelation in history. In this respect, Francis shares the attitudes of his time with regard to symbolism. We must also recognize that behind and beneath the scriptural and liturgical inspiration there operates another which is altogether original and wells up from the psychic depths. The *Canticle* shows an attribution of values to the cosmic elements that cannot be explained simply by reference to Scripture and the liturgy but must derive from a basic oneiric expeience.

In this regard, the testimony of the early biographers is important. "We who were with him have seen him take inward and outward delight in almost every creature, and when he handled or looked at them his spirit seemed to be in heaven rather than on earth."[22] Francis experienced a profound sense of wonder as he looked out at the world; it stirred the deepest forces in his soul and brought him into contact with the sacred. By "contact" here we mean a direct communion with sacred, mediated by the reality of the world's elements as grasped in dreams.

Celano, for example writes:

> Who would be able to narrate the sweetness he enjoyed while contemplating in creatures the wisdom of their Creator, his power and his goodness? Indeed, he was very often filled with a wonderful and ineffable joy from this consideration while he looked upon the sun, while he beheld the moon, and while he gazed upon the stars and the firmament.[23]

The images of the material elements in the *Canticle* are precisely the expression of this sacral experience of wonder in the face of the world. They are therefore images that also symbolize the deepest powers of affectivity and imagination at work in the soul; they are images that are "imagined" under the influence of the great archetypes.

The images of "my lord Brother Sun," who is a symbol

of the Most High, and of "Sister Earth, our mother," are especially revealing in this respect, and we must pay them close attention. They have a marked archaic flavor, and their archtypal origin comes through quite clearly. They mark an unconscious return to the most primal kind of symbolism. The symbolism certainly has a new dimension, but the new meaning should not make us fail to grasp the original meaning. For, as Louis Beirnaert observes with regard to Christian sacramentalism,

> Christianity has assumed into itself the great images and symbols of natural religion, and along with them all the power and virtue they exercise over the depths of the psyche. The dimension of myth and archetype, though it has become subordinate to another, does not therefore cease to be real.[24]

Does it not follow that this cosmic symbolism, which is a kind of explication of the sacred in the world, is also an explication of the sacred within the soul itself? What, in the last analysis, is the dream-mediated depth of the cosmic elements in which the Most High may be glimpsed, but the living soul of the poet who is endowed with such powers of establishing communion? Authentic poets find their symbols only where these symbols really are, and that means in the oneiric depths of the psyche where the archetypes exist. It is there that life, with its radiant god-like suns, is to be found. It is there that the nightly heavens shine with their infinite plenitude of precious stars, and the wind sings its song over the headwaters of creation. It is there too that death gnaws at being—but at the same time the invincible light of eternal childhood blazes out with its crystal-clear mornings, those marvelous mornings when it is good "to be a child forever."

The mystical, archetypal aspect of the *Canticle* only renders our investigation more complex. For what does this language mean? What deep realities and experiences do the cosmic images symbolize?

4. THE STRUCTURE OF THE POEM

The *Canticle* is intriguing not only for its images of material reality but for its structure as well. The poem is not a mere series of images. Rather, the images are interconnected and form a structured whole. If we leave aside for the moment the last four stanzas, which deal with forgiveness and with "Sister Death" and which were composed only afterwards, what shape does the poem have?

The remainder of the *Canticle* has nine stanzas. The first two are an introduction and a kind of dedication, indicating the one to whom the praise is addressed:

Most high, all-powerful, all good, Lords!
All praise is yours, all glory, all honour
And all blessing.

To you alone, Most High, do they belong.
No mortal lips are worthy
To pronounce your name.

Then the *Canticle* proper begins. It is divided into seven stanzas on six subjects (Brother Sun is given two stanzas). The series is as follows:

1. My lord Brother Sun (stanzas 3-4)
2. Sister Moon and Stars (stanza 5)
3. Brothers Wind and Air (stanza 6)
4. Sister Water (stanza 7)
5. Brother Fire (stanza 8)
6. Sister Earth, our mother (stanza 9)

We need only reflect carefully on this ordering of the elements in order to be persuaded that the poem is following a definite principle of construction of which the author was most probably unaware but which is nonetheless strictly applied and very meaningful. Two points are notable about the order.

First, there is the regular alternation of the titles

"Brother" and "Sister." The names are not applied at random, but go in pairs. The result is three sets of brothers and sisters: "My lord Brother Sun" and "Sister Moon and Stars"; Brother Wind and Sister Water; Brother Fire and "Sister Earth, our mother."

The cosmic elements are not paired off at whim. They form imaginary couples in accordance with the laws of the imagination as it works on matter. Bachelard has some pertinent remarks on the association of images dealing with matter:

> One characteristic strikes us immediately: the imaginary combination always contains only two elements, never three. . . . If a union of three appears, we may be sure that the image is merely factitious, an image elaborated by the reasoning mind. Authentic images of an oneiric kind are always single or dyadic. . . . If such images seek to enter into associations, the combination will contain two elements. There is a definite reason for the dualist character of the associations effected by the material imagination: the association is always a marriage. As soon as two elemental substances unite with one another, as soon as they fuse with one another, they acquire each a sexual character . . . . In the realm of the material imagination, every union is a marital union, and there is no marital union involving three.[25]

The second point that strikes us about the structure of Francis' poem is the fact that all the other elements are bounded as it were by the two great cosmic images of "my lord Brother Sun" and "Sister Earth, our mother." The praise of creatures begins with the lofty, virile, celestial image of the Lord Sun whose dominion and splendor symbolize the Most High, the Father. And the sequence ends with the solid image of the feminine and maternal, that of the earth, our mother, who supports and feeds every living thing. All the other elements are set between these two great images of fatherhood and motherhood.

Such a structure certainly does not mirror any objective structure to be found in the world. Nor is it to be explained in terms of any particular cosmological system. It is possible to appeal to medieval cosmology with its geocentrism and its theory of the four elements, which had been inherited from antiquity. This cosmology certainly could have provided the external framework for the *Canticle,* but it cannot explain the various associations or pairing of the elements and the values attributed to each.

In fact, as has been pointed out,[26] the order among the elements that Francis adopts is contrary to that followed by the ancient physicists. In their view, the basic elements could be ordered according to their heaviness; the order then would be earth, water, air, and fire. Or they could be ordered according to lightness, and then the sequence would be reversed: fire, air, water, and earth. The *Canticle* pays no attention to this theory and puts wind and air first among the basic elements. Why this priority given to wind and air? We must recognize that we are confronted here with an order and with pairings that do not embody rational meanings but are the work solely of the imagination.

The imaginary pairings are not, however, to be taken as arbitrary. Imagination has always paired certain cosmic realities: for example, sun and moon, wind (spirit) and water, fire and earth. Archaic myths and religions provide numerous examples of such pairings. The cosmic pair, heaven and earth, of which Hesiod speaks, is a theme of all mythologies, and is truly the primordial couple. Sometimes the couple is specified as sun and earth. Mircea Eliade, in his *Patterns in Comparative Religion,* gives examples of solar cults in which the "Lord Sun" is regarded as the husband of "Lady Earth," with the world being the fruit of their union.[27]

In the biblical tradition the water-spirit (breath) pair plays a very important role, from the first image in Genesis, that of the creative Spirit sweeping over the waters, down to the prophetic image of rebirth through water and Spirit. Such imaginary pairs are to be found in all religious traditions as well as in the literature and art of all periods and civilizations.

This is to say that the associations of the elements in the *Canticle* belong to a universally operative symbolism, to the basic imaginative structures, or archetypes, of the collective unconscious. With the help of these comprehensive structures men have always spontanously represented to themselves their own deepest experiences, the ones most important for their destiny. Consideration of the *Canticle's* construction thus confirms the conclusion we reached earlier with regard to the various images of material realities: that we are confronted here with a symbolic language that is strictly archetypal in character. What is unconsciously expressed in the text in the garb of cosmic praise has to do with man's own depths.

5. The Addition of the Final Stanzas

One last point requires our attention: the addition of the final stanzas. It is common knowledge that these were not originally part of the *Canticle.* While the praises of creatures were written in the fall of 1225, the two stanzas on pardon and peace were composed only in July, 1226,[28] at the bishop's palace in Assisi, in order to end the conflict between the bishop and the mayor of the town. The final two stanzas are a welcome to "Sister Death" and were composed shortly before Francis' death in early October, 1226.

These final stanzas are in sharp contrast to the rest of the poem. This is true, to begin with, from a literary point of view. They are indeed introduced with the same formula: "All praise be yours, my Lord," but they also contain quite new phrases such as "Happy those" and "Woe to those." The style too is more abrupt and heavy; relative clauses abound.

It is by reason of their object that these final stanzas differ from the rest of the *Canticle,* for they focus directly and exclusively on man, his relations with his fellows, and his attitude to illness and death. Only the specifically human dimension of man and his life are kept in view; the aspect of cosmic praise has disappeared.

Finally, these last stanzas have an element of the dramatic that plays no part in the stanzas devoted to praise of the great cosmic brotherhood. They take note of our human conflicts and also of the unhappiness brought by bitter death. They are, of course, a hymn to peace and serenity, but to a peace and serenity that are preserved amid suffering and by virtue of a love that rises triumphant over hatred and even over the anguish of death itself.

Despite all these differences Francis chose to add these stanzas to his *Canticle of Brother Sun* and to have them sung along with his praise of creatures as if they really were a continuation and climax of the latter. In his mind the addition was not an accidental one, due to external circumstances. Rather, the added stanzas were likewise part of his praises of creatures. They sprang from the same basic inspiration. In both parts of the poem it is the same fraternal presence to the world that is being asserted: a total presence that is at once cosmic and human.

If this be so, then the final stanzas with their essentially human focus, oblige us to inquire into the ultimate significance of earlier stanzas with their properly cosmic hymn of praise. Since the latter finally leads over to the world of man with his conflicts and his total destiny and is transformed into praise of the man who has achieved peace, does it not by this very fact suggest its own deeper orientation and meaning? Does not the praise of the cosmos, by the fact that it is prolonged and completed by the celebration of man as fully reconciled to his fellows and his destiny in its entirety, hide a strictly anthropological meaning under the great cosmic images? Are we not to "read," behind and under the fraternal presence to material things, the approach of something further: the quest for the reconciliation, at the deepest level, of man with man?

Chapter 2

A Hypothesis for Interpretation

Our analysis has shown that the *Canticle* contains a set of images of material things, the meaning of which is not exhausted by reference to the objective realities reflected in the images. The direct and obvious meaning does refer to cosmic realities: sun, moon and stars, wind, water, and so on. But the images also contain and say something further. Their matter is a matter that has been imagined and profoundly dreamt and is now filled with interior values relating to the unconscious; in short, it is a "precious" matter.

Careful examination has also brought out the mythical and archetypal character of both of the cosmic images and their pairings. Finally, the addition of the last four stanzas, which are so thoroughly human in their reference, has proved to be invitation to us to inquire into the links between the properly cosmic part of the poem and its conclusion that refers to man. Is the former, at a deeper, hidden level, not already oriented to the latter?

Our initial examination, therefore, leads us to believe that the *Canticle* constitutes a language of symbol, in the proper sense of this last word. We give the word here its full meaning. "A symbol exists when language produces complex signs in which the meaning, not satisfied to point to a reality, points to another reality which is accessible only in and through the first."[1] "I define 'symbol' as any structure of signification in which a direct, primary, literal meaning designates, in addition, another meaning which is indirect, secondary, and figurative and which can be apprehended only through the first."[2]

At this point in our inquiry we cannot say what this "other meaning" is. It must still be deciphered. Two points are already fairly clear. First, the *Canticle* must be the work of an especially rich oneiric temperament, one endowed with great imaginative and affective powers, open to the world of the archetypes and thereby to man's great dreams. Peter Lippert writes: "There must have been something in Francis that was universal, that touched and attracted everyone. Both the splendor and the tragedy of man must have found in him a privileged interpreter."[3]

Second, we observe that these great powers of imagination and affectivity, with their archaic structures, issue here in light and serenity. In none of the cosmic images in which these powers find expression is there any trace of anxiety or conflict. Everything is filled with light, so much so that we might readily mistake the character of the poem and see in it simply the expression of an idyllic vision of the world and life. We must guard against such a mistake, for it would mean we had forgotten the circumstances in which the hymn of praise came to be written, and failed to take into account that Francis' life was a daily struggle, filled with keen suffering.

The *Canticle,* we must remember, came at the climax of a long pilgrimage marked by trials and struggles. The fact that the poem radiates light and serenity is proof, that the poet has achieved a profound and complete reconciliation with the primal vital powers of his own psyche. The great illusive and affective forces have been purified of disturbance and ambiguity, and can now deploy themselves in the light of day; they have become fraternal powers leading man to the Most High and to communion with all reality.

At this point, and in the light of all this, a hypothesis suggests itself quite naturally: Perhaps the *Canticle* expresses in symbolic language this profound reconciliation of the man with the totality of his psyche? Perhaps it is the imaged expression of

> a unique confluence of Eros and Agape. . ., occurring in a soul of native saintliness and genius; an interfusion of both, in short, which has become so complete as to present the greatest and most sublime example of a simultaneous "inspiriting of life" and "enlivening of the spirit."[4]

Or perhaps the *Canticle* is to be regarded as the poetic expression of the reconciliation in man between the highest purpose (the quest of the Most High) and the lower, obscure links with "mother earth"; a poetic expression of the reconciliation between our "archeology" and our "teleology"? The reconciliation would take place on the occasion of an extraordinary experience of God, namely, the encounter with the Most High in the depths of the psyche and in the course of communion with what is simplest and lowest in the scale of being.

With this hypothesis before us, let us read the text once again and try to enter into its inner movement. The *Canticle* begins by addressing the Lord as "Most High." It is noteworthy that of the three adjectives in the initial invocation only this is used in the remainder of the poem as a designation for God. The name "Most High" thus occurs four times in the poem, three times in the first four stanzas. There can be no doubt but that it expresses a deep-rooted attitude of Francis' soul, his highest desire, his thrust toward the divine. This upward movement is strongly affirmed in the first two stanzas:

Most high, all-powerful, all good, Lords!
All praise is yours, all glory, all honour
And all blessing.
To you alone, Most High, do they belong. . . .

At this point, the movement toward the Most High is jarred by self-awareness: "No mortal lips are worthy to pronounce your name." This is not a phrase intended merely for edification or tossed out in passing. It expresses a basic attitude of innermost poverty before the transcendent God. No praise, however sublime, can manifest the mystery of God. Francis is aware of this; he recognizes and accepts it.

Francis now turns to creatures: "All praise be yours, my Lord, through all that you have made." Since he cannot name the Transcendent One, he will name things and sing the praises of this world. "On" things and "on" the world (recall Paul Ricoeur quoted in chapter 1) he will speak and sing of the Ineffable One. The visible universe will be his path of praise, his path toward the Sacred. "Of you, Most High, he bears the likeness," says Francis of the sun, after voicing his enthusiasm for this fountainhead of pure light. He will proceed to manifest the Sacred "on" all the other cosmic elements, which are gathered up and made the subject of praise in accordance with the basic flavor that is peculiar to each of them. Each of them in its own way is something "precious" to Francis, a hierophany, a language that gives expression to the Most High.

We see that the opening movement of the *Canticle,* which had been entirely upward and completely oriented to the transcendent, is now matched by a horizontal movement of openness to the brotherly communion with all creatures. The man who had recognized that he was unworthy to name the Most High now acknowledges himself the "brother" of all creatures. Let us look more closely at this second movement. It is a descending movement. The name "Most High" is used for the last time in the second of the stanzas on Brother Sun and will be absent from the remainder of the cosmic praise.

The abandonment of the name is significant. It does not mean that Francis has ceased to be alert and open to the call of the Most High. It means that henceforth his way toward the Most High will, paradoxically, be a way that leads from heaven to earth. From the heights of heaven where "my lord Brother Sun" radiates his light, Francis in his praise gradually descends to things ever closer to us, ever more accessible, and ever more humble as well. His way now is not only that of the dazzling sun and the "precious" stars but also that of wind and water and finally of earth: a humble journey of return to mother earth. Francis' itinerary in his song of praise brings us back among things and sets us in their very midst; he calls us back to our lowly origins. "Praise and bless my Lord . . . with great humility," says Francis at the end of his *Canticle.*

But this journey through the cosmos is also a journey to the interior. As we pointed out above, all the cosmic elements with which Francis enters into brotherly communion manifest a dimension of depth. Once they have been submitted to the imagination and have had unconscious values attached to them, they present the soul with a way of entering into its own inner depths. Under the guise of these sensible realities, which are so beautiful and desirable and to which it finds itself closely related in a mysterious way, the psyche is unconsciously dealing with itself. And when the psyche opens itself thus to material things it is also opening itself to all that these things symbolize for it. As it praises elements that are increasingly lowly and obscure and as it sings finally of "Sister Earth, our mother, who feeds us," the psyche is descending into its own depths.

There can be no doubt that Francis praises God "on" the cosmos. But would such praise be possible if the various cosmic realities had not awoken profound echoes in his soul and symbolized his soul's primordial powers? A purely positivist outlook will never read the sacred "on" the world. If the world is to manifest the sacred, the psyche must, on contact with the world, resonate with the world in its own depths and must thereby be set in motion toward itself, its own mystery, and its own native sacrality.

In and under the cosmic dimension of Francis' praises the psychic dimension makes its appearance. The two dimensions cannot be separated, being but two sides of the same thing. As Paul Ricoeur rightly observes, "To manifest the 'sacred' *on* the 'cosmos' and to manifest it *in* the 'psyche' are the same thing. . . .Cosmos and Psyche are the two poles of the same 'expressivity'; I express myself in expressing the world; I explore my own sacrality in deciphering that of the world."[5] The world will be for me a manifestation and cipher of the sacred only if I scrutinize it at a certain psychic depth, and if the image I form of it puts me in contact with the deeper levels of my being. The man who reads the sacred "on" the world is always a bit like those shepherds at Bethlehem, of whom Pierre Emmanuel says:

They plumb
The heights of heaven in their souls
And their souls
Beneath.[6]

The exploration of the sacred in the world is therefore accompanied by a more hidden exploration of the sacred in the soul itself, and the one unconsciously symbolizes the other. When the soul imagines things and has dreams of them that evoke their depth or inner dynamism, it is at the same time exploring its own hidden powers. It is as though man were incapable of finding a way into himself and his own depths except by detouring through the lowly things of creation and by living "in union with the totality of the world that carries him along, cosmically."[7]

Can't we see in Francis' celebration of the various cosmic realties not only the expression of a profound communion with the material world but also the symbolic evocation of a spiritual adventure that is taking place in the night of the soul, and the description of the soul's journey in search of its own sacrality? "The soul," writes Jung, "is a sequence of images, in the broadest sense of this last word. It is not a chance juxtaposition or succession of images, but a highly meaningful and purposeful structure, a kind of vision, through images, of the vital activities."[8]

May we not say that the ordered sequence of cosmic images in the *Canticle* contains a kind of (retrospective) vision in imaged form, of an interior process? In this view, the hymn in which Francis praises God "on" the various elements of his creation and in which he speaks of himself as brother successively of the sun, moon, and stars, of wind, water, and fire, and of Mother Earth, would be in its own way the expression of what Jung calls "a process of transformation of the soul and its symbols." In this process the soul opens itself to its own totality, including its own depths. It starts with the highest and most ambitious kind of contemplation, that of the "Most High." Then, recognizing that it is not "worthy to pronounce your name," it returns, under cover of the images of the great cosmic realities that are welcomed as brothers, into itself and its unconscious depths, back to its lowly origins and to the obscure forces of desire, to Eros. While remaining fully open "to the summons of highest heaven," it accepts its own fraternal communion with "Sister Earth, our mother, who feeds us." In this manner it succeeds in in descending into its own archaic depths where irrational forces dwell.

This path of "great humility" and fraternal communion with creatures becomes a path to the soul's complete reconciliation with itself. The obsure forces of desire come under the control of the spirit's lofty aspirations, while the spirit in turn humbly consents to draw vital energy from the forces of desire.

It will not surprise us that the *Canticle* should also be a hymn to great mercy and peace: "All praise be yours, my Lord, through those who grant pardon for love of you." The final four stanzas no longer appear to be a mere fortuitous addition to the praise of the cosmos. Instead, they show where the praise was leading. They celebrate man as fully reconciled: the man in whom Eros and Agape have met and fused in a vast desire for pardon and peace. The *Canticle of Brother Sun* turns into the song of solar man, who is filled with good will and mercy toward all things, thereby resembling the Most High who makes his sun shine on the bad and the good.

The reconciliation leads to an authentic encounter of man with God. He who begins by recognizing that he is unworthy even to pronounce the name of the Most High and settles for praising him in union with rest of creation, as he humbly takes his place among his fellow-creatures and enters into a brotherly communion with them and all that they signifiy, finally encounters the Most High himself.

And he encounters him precisely via the path of profound reconciliation: "Happy those who endure in peace, by you, Most High, they will be crowned." Here the expression "Most High," which had been dropped after the fourth stanza of the *Canticle,* reappears now that the soul has reached the end of its journey. But it no longer expresses a distant and inaccessible Transcendent One. Rather, the Transcendent One is immediately present to the man whose will set upon mercy and peace. The Most High sets a crown upon such a will, and his transcendence proves to be identical with that plenitude of all-embracing, merciful love to which man has opened himself.

If our reading of the *Canticle* is valid—and the rest of this book will be devoted to showing that it is—it sheds a great deal of light on the secret of the Franciscan wisdom that so wonderfully joins the highly detached mysticism of the Gospel to a highly enthusiastic cosmic mysticsm; spiritual detachment to a radical communion with the earth. In fact, it is in Christ that Francis sees fully embodied the movement by which the soul renounces equality with the Most High and accepts its lowly roots in psyche and cosmos and that fraternal presence to the world that becomes for it the pathway of spiritual ascent. For Francis, Christ is the true archetype, who "though he was in the form of God,. . . did not deem equality with God something to be grasped at. Rather, he emptied himself. . . .Because of this, God highly exalted him."[9]

The humiliation and exaltation of the most high Son of God was the central theme of Francis' meditations, and around it he shaped his whole life. He summed up his religious ideals in these simple words: "to follow in the footsteps of your Son, our Lord Jesus Christ, and so make our way to you, Most High, by your grace alone."[10] It in unthinkable, then, that his ideal which inspired the entire life of Francis should not also have influenced at the deepest level his *Canticle of Brother Sun.* There must be a hidden but immensely strong link between the object of Francis' constant meditation and his most original literary work. And in fact here is every reason to think that if the *Canticle* contains no special reference to the mystery of Christ, the reason is that it is entirely penetrated by that mystery.

The *Canticle* is the song of a soul which, at the end of its pilgrimage, has united within itself, as Christ did, the finite and the infinite, the depths of earth and the immensity of heaven. The *Canticle* gives expression to that supreme illumination of the soul, of which St. Bonaventure speaks at the end of his *The Journey of the Mind to God:*

> This consideration brings about, the perfect enlightening of the mind, when the mind beholds man made, as on the sixth day, in the image of God. Since, therefore, an image is an expressive likeness, when our mind contemplates, in Christ the Son of God, our own humanity so wonderfully exalted and so ineffably present in Him; and when we thus behold in one and the same Being both the first and the last, the highest and the lowest, the circumference and the center, the Alpha and the Omega, the caused and the cause, the Creator and the creature, that is, *a scroll written and without* [Ap. 5:1; cf. Ez. 2:9]—then our mind at last reaches a perfect object. . . .that peace where the truly peaceful man reposes in the quiet of his mind.[11]

St. Bonaventure adds: "This was shown likewise to blessed Francis."[12]

Chapter 3

The Impossible Praise

Most High, all-powerful, all good, Lord!
All praise is yours, all glory, all honour
And all blessing.

To you alone, Most High, do they belong.
No mortal lips are worthy
To pronounce your name.

These first two stanzas are inspired by a doxology in the Apocalypse of St. John[1] and are a hymn to the divine transcendence. They are entirely dominated by the recurring image of the "Most High."

The "Most High," who is also all-powerful, all good, and Lord, is here the supreme magnetic pole that sets in motion and gives direction to the soul's capacity for adoration and praise. He is acknowledged as alone worthy of praise, glory, honor, and blessing, and therefore as the total and unqualified Good.

This outlook is a familiar one to Francis and finds expression in many passages of his writings. In the *Praises before the Office* which he composed and recited daily at the canonical hours we read: "Worthy are thou, O Lord our God, to receive glory and honour and power. . . . All-powerful, all holy, most high and supreme God, sovereign good, all good, every good, you who alone are good, it is to you we must give all praise, all glory, all thanks, all honour, all blessings; to you we must refer all good always. Amen."[2]

This homage to the transcendent God shows us a basic concern of Francis. In saying that the "Most High" is sole recipient of its praise, the soul already makes it clear that God is for it the sole Good for which it longs, the sole Good that can fulfill its expectations. It thereby expresses its supreme purpose: to attain to the Most High and belong entirely to him. This desire was really at the very core of Francis' being, and is clearly expressed again in the prayer which ends his *Letter to a General Chapter:* "Almighty . . . God, grant us . . . [to] make our way to you, Most High."[3]

These opening stanzas of the *Canticle* give expression to the ascending movement of Francis' soul toward the supreme object of his desire and the sole object he deems worthy of his praise. And—we might be tempted to add—the sole object that could match the soul's capacities. But at this point the soul in its upward thrust becomes aware of what is put into words in the final words of the second stanza: "No mortal lips are worthy to pronounce your name."

We should not dismiss these words lightly as edifying jargon or pious exaggeration. No, they spring from a genuine experience. As Mircea Eliade observes, "The 'most high' is a dimension inaccessible to man as man,"[4] and that is precisely what Francis experienced. Therefore, if the first stanza of the *Canticle* expresses the soul's ultimate goal, the second is the admission of an absolute, radical limitation, and a limitation that has been experienced, tested, and accepted. In his first Rule Francis writes: "We are all poor sinners and unworthy even to mention your name."[5] God has his own mystery, and it eludes our grasp. The Most High is not down on our level, and no human being can put the mystery of God into words.

But must not every voice that would praise fall silent? Is not every desire to reach the Most High doomed to frustration and failure. At the end of these opening stanzas we feel the soul waver in its movement. It has shot upward like an arrow toward the Most High, bent on giving him alone its enthusiastic praise and self-surrender, but now it realizes how inaccessible is the object upon which it has been so totally concentrated. It seems destined, then, to hover between heaven and earth: unable to renounce its loftiest desire, yet unable any longer to think the goal within its grasp.

Are we faced with a contradiction at this point? We might easily think so, and yet nothing in the text suggests the least tension between the soul's aspirations and the awareness that the object of these aspirations is inaccessible. There would certainly be such a tension, of course, if the thrust of the soul toward the Most High masked an unconscious desire for identification with God. Such a desire to possess is not at all impossible. On the contrary, it lurks in the heart of every man and is the special temptation of those who would be "spiritual."

Francis was more aware of this than anyone else. It is to be noted, in fact, that throughout his life he was constantly reacting against the will to possess that is native to man. He came very early to the realization that this will is not satisfied with material and exterior goods but affects even what is most interior, radical, and elusive in man: his drive toward the good, the thrust of his being toward the highest values.

Francis has some far-reaching reflections on the subject. Speaking of original sin, he notes:

> A man eats of the tree that brings knowledge of good when he claims that his good will comes from himself alone and prides himself on the good that God says and does in him. And so, at the devil's prompting and by transgressing God's command, the fruit becomes for him the fruit that brings knowledge of evil, and it is only right that he should pay the penalty.[6]

In other words, man's will to possess himself can become the will to spiritual self-creation. To be like God is man's ancient dream and constant temptation. To be like God: that is, to be his own origin, to depend only on himself, and therefore to escape from his cosmic condition as a creature tied to other creatures. Man's highest aspiration can thus turn into Lucifer's attempt to lay hold of the divine and be identified with the Most High.

When this happens, God becomes simply one element in man's plan for himself; he is simply a name for the stature man seeks to achieve by his own powers. Recall Nietzsche's invocation of the heavens: "O heaven above me, deep and pure! You abyss of light! Seeing you, I tremble with godlike desires. To throw myself into your height, that is *my* depth,"[7] Francis had deeply experienced such desires as that. He was well aware that even the religious man is not sheltered against this temptation and that under cover of the loftiest and purest ideal he can be secretly inspired by the passionate desire to possess, to "have" the infinite God himself.

In his writings Francis constantly warns his brothers against this desire for spiritual possession. He urges them not to regard as their own the good the Lord accomplishes in them and through them, but to refer all honor for it to the Most High who is the source of all good.

> In that love which is God (cf. 1 Jn 4:8), I entreat all my friars, whether they are given to preaching, praying, or manual labour, to do their best to humble themselves at every opportunity; not to boast or be self-satisfied, or take pride in any good which God says or does or accomplishes in them or by them; as our Lord himself put it, *Do not rejoice in this, that the spirits are subject to you* (Lk. 10:20).[8]

Elsewhere: "Blessed the religious who refers all the good he has to his Lord and God. He who attributes anything to himself hides *his master's money* (Mt. 25:18) in himself, and *even what he thinks he has shall be taken away* (Lk. 8:18)."[9] And again: "Keep nothing for yourself, so that he who has given himself wholly to you may receive you wholly."[10]

Francis also knew that men are not even aware, most of the time, of this urge for possession that nonetheless guides them; he understood how easy it is to deceive oneself. The self-deception is all the easier and more profound as the object desired is higher and purer. Consequently he applied himself, as teacher of his brothers, to exposing the delusions. On every page of his writings, and especially in his *Admonitions,* he shows his concern to keep his brothers on the true path. He calls attention to errors in the spiritual life, and points out the signs by which we can unerringly detect the evil of self-will and the will to possession that may be hiding behind the appearance of great virtue and religious commitment. The signs are the disturbance, irritation, impatience, and aggressiveness a man shows when his will is frustrated.[11] To Francis these are sure sysmptoms of a self-will that is for the most part unconscious. Such defensive reactions betray a possessive attitude that may infect even the soul's loftiest aspirations.

In all this we can discern how keen Francis' spiritual vision was. We can also see how attentive he was to the fact that man's highest purpose—his desire to reach God—is in radical need of purification. When a man ventures to pronounce the name of God, he must ask himself who the God is that he is naming. He may discover that this God is really only another name for his own desire, for his will to possession or power: in short, another name for himself.

In his own personal life, Francis subjected himself to an ever deeper purification of his desire for God. It is certainly not impossible, it is even quite probable in view of his evidently fiery temperament, that initially he was swept up toward the Most High with the passionate ardor of one who immediately identifies the divine with the highest aims of his own person and the loftiest expression of his innate spiritual potentialities. As a young man, Francis was immensely ambitious. He wanted to astound the world. He dreamed of winning glory through some noble deed, and even of becoming a great prince.

In the next stage his ambition turned to other types of greatness, and became more spirtiual, but it was still a powerful force in him. "Why do you think I rejoice?," he said on one occasion, "I will yet be venerated as a saint throughout the whole world."[12] Francis may have been joking, but the very joke is revealing. How ambitious a man must be to find joy in the thought of some day becoming an idol for the whole world!

When the young Francis was converted, he did not renounce his lofty aims, but aimed even higher. We may well ask what the "Most High" really meant to him, given the ambition that was so much a part of him. In any event, one thing is certain: throughout his life, he was constantly moving, interiorly, toward a relation with God that was less and less possessive. This was the deeper meaning of his concern with poverty. In the last analysis, his poverty was a refusal to claim for himself what belongs to God, and even to claim God. It was a renunciation not of the call issued to him by the Most High but of the attempt to possess the Most High. At the end of his spiritual journey Francis was completely docile to the call of heaven most high, but he also recognized that he was not worthy to pronounce the name of the Most High.

This is the meaning of the opening stanzas of the *Canticle.* In them the whole ardent desire of Francis to mount up to the Most High is expressed in praise. But the desire is purified of all ambiguity and detached from the will to possess. Francis stands before God in the greatest possible poverty, that of the soul that derives its whole joy from the fact that God alone is God. This is why we find side by side, in complete serentiy and without any tension, the lofty aim of the soul and the full awareness that its object is beyond reach.

All praise is yours, all glory, all honour. . . .
To you alone, Most High, do they belong.
No mortal lips are worthy
To pronounce your name.

This unlimited acceptance of God's transcendence dominates the entire *Canticle.* It is this that opens up the created world as the path of Francis' praise: a path of lowliness and incarnation, in imitation of the most high Son of God: "Almighty, eternal, just and merciful God, grant us to follow in the footsteps of your Son . . . and so make our way to you, Most High, by your grace alone (*et ad te, Altissime, sola tua gratia pervenire.*)."[13]

Chapter 4

The Mediation of Creatures

After the opening doxology comes a transitional verse that introduces the cosmic praise proper:

All praise be yours, my Lord, through all that you have made.

This verse is in fact much more than a simple transition, for it marks a decisive turning point in the movement of the *Canticle.* The opening stanzas ended with an admission that man is unworthy to pronounce the name of the Most High, or to utter the Sacred. But Francis does not on this account simply give up on trying to sing the impossible praise. His eyes turn for the time being to our world here below, the world of creatures. With them he will praise the Most High and speak of the Sacred. His journey of praise will lead him through the things of the world. Acknowledging that he is unworthy to pronounce the name of the Most High, he will instead sing to his Lord the praise of this world. We cannot help thinking here of Rilke's Ninth *Duino Elegy:*

Praise this world to the Angel, not the untellable. . . .
. . . .So show him
some simple thing, refashioned by age after age,
till it lives in our hands and eyes as part of ourselves.
Tell him *things*. . . .
show him how happy a thing can be, how guileless and ours.[1]

The praise of the Most High thus becomes a praise of creatures as well. The upward movement of the soul that is filled with the image of the Most High is now followed by a movement outward to the world of creatures. To understand the full significance of this second movement we must dwell on the words "through all that you have made" and try to grasp their meaning.

"Through all that you have made" means, to begin with, that when confronted with the inaccessible God Most High, the soul humbly takes its place among creatures. Its essential poverty before God has liberated it from resentment at its condition. Francis has no difficulty in accepting himself fully as a creature, one among all the others and linked to the lowliest among them. Many religious men and spiritual thinkers have extolled the divine transcendence but in doing so have set themselves apart somewhat from the rest of creation, especially material creation. At times they have shown haughtiness toward it, or even a contemptuous scorn. They thought that by depreciating the material world and cutting their connections with it they were drawing closer to the Most High.

We find none of this in Francis. Quite the contrary, he intends to praise and to relate himself more closely to the Most High by joining with the rest of creation and cultivating a brotherly closeness to it. Even in his ardent thrust toward the transcendent God he does not seek to escape his condition as part of the cosmos; instead, he humbly determines to appreciate more fully the matter of which he is made and to welcome it as his companion. The expression "through all that you have made" represents a heartfelt consent to our creaturely condition over against the Most High, to communicate and relate himself to God. not worthy to pronounce.

In thus placing himself among creatures Francis expects something from them in return: they are to help him praise the Most High, to communicate and relate himself to God. "Through all that you have made" also expresses, therefore, the fact that Francis is looking for something that will mediate between him and God. He asks creatures to reveal to him something of the Creator and his power, goodness, and beauty.

We must take care to understand this mediation properly. We would considerably lessen the significance of the *Canticle* if we were to think of creatures as simply an occasion for praising God. Francis' relation to creatures is far deeper than that, as the whole of his life makes clear. It is not easy, of course, for a modern man to appreciate the true depth of Francis' relation to subhuman and material realities. We live in a world in which science has taught us to regard things simply as objects for us to take apart so that we may learn their secret, master them, and exploit them. Our attitude to the entities of the cosmos is one of conquest and possession; it is inspired by the will to power and leaves hardly any room for the instincts of sympathy.

Francis' attitude was entirely different. "He embraced all things with a rapture of unheard of devotion," writes Celano.[2] "Who would be able to narrate the sweetness he enjoyed while contemplating in creatures the wisdom of their Creator, his power and his goodness? Indeed, he was very often filled with a wonderful and ineffable joy from this consideration while he looked upon the sun, while he beheld the moon, and while he gazed upon the stars and the firmament."[3] This joy with its sense of fellowship did not stop at the surface of things but went deeper. "He called all creatures *brother,* and in a most extraordinary manner, a manner never experienced by others, he discerned the hidden things of nature with his sensitive heart, as one who had already escaped *into the freedom of the glory of the sons of God.*"[4]

The mediation Francis seeks from creatures is impossible unless he enters into a profound communion with them. The words "through all that you have made" also give expression to a fraternal communion with creation and an affective identification with the cosmos. In his book *The Nature of Sympathy,* the German philosopher Max Scheler has endeavored to analyze Francis' kind of sympathy, which he regards as something profoundly original with Francis. "It does seem to me that in this respect St. Francis really has no predecessor in the entire history of Christendom in the West. Saint Bernard's mysticism of love and betrothal is quite another thing; we look in vain for any sense of cosmic unity there."[5]

In Scheler's estimation, the effective identification Francis experienced with the various elements of the universe cannot be regarded simply as the extension to subhuman nature of an acosmic love, strictly supernatural in inspiration, for God and spiritual persons.[6] It has rather a special emotional source. If we prescind from Francis' own emotional temperament, the source must be the Provencal cult of chivalrous love, "a mode of feeling which Francis certainly cultivated in his youth and early manhood prior to his conversion."[7]

> The self-styled "troubador of God," who kept to the end of his life the habit of humming his beloved French songs to himself, was never to lose hold of this strand of his past life; it can be seen, even in the rigorous and heroic asceticism of his later career, in the almost indescribable tenderness of his relations with St. Clara. And yet, with incomparable *spiritual* artistry, as unselfconscious as it was undesigned, he succeeded, for all his early absorption in the historic emotional attitude of the Provencial cult, in so divesting it of all substance, all worldly or amorous import, that virtually nothing but its serene and ethereal *rhythm* was left behind.
>
> So appropriate was this to the spiritual love of God, of Christ and of persons (which had, of course, a wholly indigenous origin of its own), that the effect was to reanimate this Christian inheritance to an equally unprecedented state of vitality. Just as the Provencial mood acquired, for him, a spiritual and Christian flavour and in so doing became entirely "functional" and dissociated from womanhood, its original object, so now it provided a spiritual key and a new insight into the *whole* of nature, whereby her secrets also were unlocked and stood revealed.[8]

Scheler's analysis sheds a good deal of light on Francis' relation to creatures. It illumines that relation from below. By connecting the affective identification with the cosmos to the roots of the soul itself and to eros (but an eros that has been purified, freed from the oppressiveness proper to the "flesh," and opened to *agapē*), Scheler's analysis not only explains the universality of the identification, but also helps us understand its religious character and the depth at which it operated in the psyche.

We are now in a position to understand better the words "through all that you have made." For Francis, creatures were not simply a book in which all the writing lay on the surface of things. His communion with them reached their innermost reality, and they in turn spoke to him out of the depths of his own being and through the primordial powers of his soul. This is why his communion with them was also an encounter with the Sacred.

When any cosmic reality, however lowly, is welcomed and loved in such depth, it becomes something "precious" and fascinating and acquires a sacral "expressivity." The emotions Francis felt could even reach rapture and ecstasy. "We who were with him have seen him take inward and outward delight in almost every creature, and when he handled or looked at them his spirit seemed to be in heaven rather than on earth."[9] There can be no doubt that Francis communed with God through creatures as such and that he had a cosmic experience of the sacred. Teilhard de Chardin has asked, "Who then, at last, will be the *ideal Christian,* the Christian, at once new and old, who will solve in his soul the problem of this vital balance, by allowing all the life-sap of the world to pass into his effort towards the Divine Trinity?"[10] Francis of Assisi seems to have achieved this vital balance, reconciling within himself the upward supernatural movement of Chrisitanity with a fiery love of the universe. And he does it with typical simplicity: proposing to praise the Most High, and him alone, but "through all that you have made," and entering into an intense communion with the whole of that world of which he is a part.

Have we now exhausted the meaning of the words "through all that you have made"? No, there is a final point. If things enable Francis to relate himself to the Sacred, the reason is (as we noted in connection with Scheler's remarks) that they speak to the depths of his soul. In other words, the cosmic mediation has a specifically psychic dimension. Creatures are a language expressive of the sacred because they put the soul in touch with itself and its primordial powers. Creatures are the outward form of a discourse that goes on deep within man. "All praise be yours, my Lord, through all that you have made"; the words do express a movement to communion with all creatures, but the movement of cosmic sympathy contains something further. It is itself a language: the language of the soul that is in search of its own sacrality through reconciliation with all its own powers, and through the integration of these powers into the soul's highest aspirations.

The manner in which creatures are named, described, and celebrated in the following verses of the *Canticle* will confirm what we have just been saying. As we shall see, the images of material things do not simply point to cosmic realities, but are a language expressing something else. They co-symbolize the primordial powers of the soul and are a mirror reflecting the forces of the unconscious. The words in our transitional verse of the *Canticle* have indeed a specifically cosmic reference, but they also point to a movement in which the highest aspirations of the soul are reconciled with the obscure roots and humble origins of these aspirations. Francis seeks to praise the Most High and deepen his relationship with God, but his language will not be that of a pure spirit. It will be the language of a soul that fully accepts its own ultimate origins and its links with matter, a soul that intends to draw all these things into its praise of God, "with great humility," as Francis says at the end of his *Canticle.*

We have perhaps not paid sufficient heed to these final words of the *Canticle.* They correspond very precisely, though antithetically, to the opening words, "Most high." The two phrases give us the two extremes that are involved in the hymn of praise. "Only humility," says Lavelle, "can bind us to the earth where our roots are; it forces us to draw strength from her."[11] Humility is the opposite of any resentment against our "archeology"; it is the inward ease which enables us to accept ourselves completely, both in our highest purposes and in our deepest and most unconscious links with the cosmos and our own psyche. The journey through creatures upon which Francis is here entering will be a journey of reconciliation.

Chapter 5

The Praise of the Sun

And first my lord Brother Sun,
who brings the day; and light you give to us through him.

How beautiful is he, how radiant in all his splendour[1]
Of you, Most High, he bears the likeness.

Alain says of Plato that his philosophy is a "philosophy of dissatisfaction, that is, dissatisfaction with himself." Plato's aim was to think the pure idea, to lay hold of the purely intelligible, but he knew he could not achieve this. Matter enters into even our loftiest thoughts, and for Plato matter is the dark kingdom.

Idealism such as Plato cultivated is a permanent temptation for the human mind. Many philosophers have sought to escape from matter. Few have suspected that matter, as dreamed and imagined by man, could be a further language of the mind, though a secret language that can be heard only by well attuned ears. Nietzsche writes: "Watch for every hour, my brothers, in which your spirit wants to speak in parables: there lies the origin of your virtue."[1] And Eliade observes: "Today we are well on the way to an understanding of one thing of which the nineteenth century had not even a presentiment—that the symbol, the myth and the image are of the very substance of the spiritual life. . . .The power and the mission of the Images is to *show* all that remains refractory to the concept."[2]

As a matter of fact, the only knowledge we can have of the depth of man and things is a knowledge through symbols. We must bear this in mind as we set about our methodical exploration of the litany of material images that makes up the *Canticle of Brother Sun.*

*
* *

The first of these images is of "my lord Brother Sun." The author of the *Mirror of Perfection* writes in this connection:

And since in Holy Scripture the Lord Himself is called *The Sun of Justice,* and because blessed Francis thought the sun the loveliest of God's creatures and most worthy of comparison with Him, he gave its name to the *Praises of God in His Creatures* which he had written when the Lord assured him of His Kingdom. And he called them *The Song of Brother Sun.*[3]

Before entering upon any study of Francis' image of the sun, a preliminary remark is called for that concerns the method to be followed and applied to the whole of this book. The text celebrates various cosmic realities. If we want to get at the real meaning of these realities as they find place in Francis' text, we must avoid isolating them from one another in his celebration of them and considering them apart from the values attributed to them. In short, we must not separate them from their context in the *Canticle.* To do so would lead to certain misunderstanding.

Each reality celebrated must then be considered along with the total image given of it. Francis will speak, for example, of "Sister Water, so useful, lowly, precious and pure." We must not break the connection between the words, since the true meaning resides in all of them together. The meaning is to be sought in the combination of words that call each for the others, from the first to the last, so that all may together form the complete image. The end result is a material image, but one in which matter that has been dreamed and imagined is associated with invisible, inward values, even while losing nothing of its everyday character. The point is that the images in this text are poetic images, and we cannot explain a poetic image if we reduce it to its material base. Neither, on the other hand, can we explain it if we substitute for it an idea of which the images is regarded as simply the sensuous, allegorical dress.

A genuine poetic image has its own proper, irreducible reality that exists wholly within the imaginary realm the image creates. A poetic image is, at bottom, an energy from the world of dreams, and to understand it means penetrating to its oneiric core. That is where the image truly speaks;

it is at that level that we must be able to hear and understand it. When grasped at that level, the poetic image is bearer of a knowledge that has not been, and cannot be, mediated through concepts. Its mission, as Eliade says, "is to *show* all that remains refractory to the concept."

We must go a step further and add that each image in the *Canticle* yields its full meaning through its relations with the other images and its position within the poem as a whole. The succession and arrangement of the images is thus very important; we will have to pay close attention to the structure and movement of the poem as a whole.

"Francis thought the sun the loveliest of God's creatures."[4] And since to every Lord all honor is due, he begins his cosmic praise with the sun. Francis' praise of the sun expresses his admiration of its "splendour." This man who "with great humility" has renounced the attempt to name the Most High and has turned to the beings of the visible universe as the means of praising God, finds in visible things an inexhaustible source of delight. We will not understand the *Canticle* if we do not read it as the expression of a deep and innocent joy that derives from the heart of reality itself. But this joy was for him, before all else, a joy at light.

Francis loved the light as few men have loved it. It is notable that the adjective *bello* which occurs three times in the *Canticle* is each time applied to a cosmic reality which in one or other fashion is a source of light: the sun ("beautiful"), the moon and stars ("fair"), and the fire ("beautiful"). Francis thus associates beauty with all his images of light. For him, the supremely beautiful matter is matter that is luminous. The cosmos is to Francis chiefly an epiphany of light, and in this epiphany the sun plays the chief role.

The sun that Francis finds so beautiful is for him a wellspring of light:

All praise be yours, my Lord, through all that you have made,
And first my lord Brother Sun,

Who brings the day; and light you give to us through him.
How beautiful is he, how radiant in all his splendour[1]

Such praise of the sun is undoubtedly the expression, first of all, of gratitude for sight. According to the author of the *Mirror of Perfection,* Francis himself "used to say, 'At dawn, when the sun rises, all men should praise God, Who created him for our use, and through him gives light to our eyes by day.' "[5] We could well put on Francis' lips the song which Lynceus the watchman sings atop the castle tower in Goethe's *Faust:*

Born was I to see,
and posted to keep watch;
my oath has bound me to this tower,
and I rejoice to gaze upon the universe. . . .
O happy eyes!
Let come what may,
how beautiful the vision you have seen![6]

Well whatever happens! As we know, during his journey in the East Francis contracted a serious eye problem that caused him a great deal of suffering and rendered him almost blind. Yet he kept his fervent love of the sun's brilliance to the very end of his life, as his *Canticle* proves. When his eyes were an agony and could no longer bear the light of day, the Poverello's inner gaze turned once again to the sun in its splendor, and he felt the same admiration and gratitude as before.

This image which fills and fascinates him is, however, more than a simple remembrance of the material thing he had perceived. "My lord Brother Sun" is no longer merely an object of sight which everyone can see, but an image arising from the depths of the soul and drawing the inner gaze to something beyond itself. But, to what? To find the answer, we must enter into the "inwardness" of the element and make our way, if possible, to the illusive heart of the image.

The sun is greeted first of all as the source of light: it

brings the day. And like all well-springs or origins, it sets men dreaming. The striking thing about it is its magnificence, that is, its splendor and its abundance. "How beautiful is he, how radiant in all his splendour." Brother Sun goes in for expansive gestures. There is nothing niggardly about him; he gives without calculating. He is a great lord, sharing greatly in the nobility proper to the universe.

Here precisely is where the dream begins that gives the image its surrealist cast. The special title Francis gives to the sun is significant in this regard, for it bestows upon the sun a kind of special personality: "My lord Brother Sun" (*Messor lo frate Sole*). We shall return to the title "brother"; for the moment, let us concentrate on "my lord." It is difficult to translate the word *messor* and preserve all the meaning Francis puts into it. The title is more modest and familiar than the *misignore* which Francis directs only to God, but it nonetheless expresses esteem and respect. Perhaps the closest we can come to is the expression "great person," as used with the overtones we give it when voicing our deep admiration for an extraordinary human being. In Francis' view, the sun is, as it were, a "great person."

The image of the sun in the *Canticle* is already more than a simple reflection of material reality. Francis' imagination has unconsciously retrieved the very ancient image of the "Lord Sun." This aspect of it is emphasized by the dominant position the image of the sun has in the structure of the *Canticle.*

As we noted earlier, all the cosmic elements praised in the *Canticle* are assigned a sex, and the end-result is three pairs of brothers and sisters: Brother Sun and Sister Moon, Brother Wind and Sister Water, and Brother Fire and Sister Earth. In addition, to this distribution by pairs we must note that the whole procession begins with a dominant masculine image, that of "my lord Brother Sun," and ends with the female and maternal image, "Sister Earth, our mother." Here then, the cosmic pair, Sun and Earth, embraces the whole of the created world. Such a combining of the elements is, of course, the work solely of the imagination and takes us back to an ancient mythical image. We find it in the solar cults of the archaic religions, where the Lord Sun is regarded as the husband of Lady Earth; from their union the entire world comes into being.[7]

Francis undoubtedly did not share these mythic beliefs; in fact, he was probably completely ignorant of them. He is simply giving expression to an archetype or basic structure of the imagination. If we attend to this mythic infrastructure of the *Canticle* we see that the sun is being imagined and valued not simply as a source of light but also, at a deeper and less explicit level, as the universal source of fruitfulness and the origin of life, that is, as a paternal symbol. The sun is the image of the Father, the image of creative power and generosity. This is confirmed and reinforced by the words that complete the image of "Brother Sun: Of you, Most High, he bears the likeness." Now the image is complete. It has its full dimensions and has become a hierophany.

At his point the image is no longer directed simply to the eye, but also speaks to the soul. The splendor and abundance which it radiates high in the heavens symbolizes a sovereign reality and draws the soul toward it. As it communes through imagination with this lofty image of light, the soul becomes the recipient of a transcendent revelation, for it sees in the sun the imaged manifestation of the Most High, the symbol of the One the soul has judged itself unworthy to name but for whom it ceaselessly yearns and to whom it refers itself in praise.

Some who read these pages may be surprised to see such a role attributed to the sun. For many Christians the sun has completely lost its capacity to express the sacred. The natural sacramentalism that played such a large part in the pagan religions has no role in most Christian groups at least at the level of clear consciousness. What we do see is a supernatural sacramentalism that is focused on the person and historical actions of Christ. After all, is not the humanity of Christ the great manifestation of God that eclipses all the cosmic symbols and hierophanies? Cardinal Daniélou says:

> A Christian is one who is so dazzled by the light of Christ that he no longer stops short at the cosmic symbols; not because these symbols have no value but because they are infinitely surpassed by the brilliance of a new sacrament. . . .We are no longer pagans, just because the sun of Christ is more dazzling to us than the sun of the first creation.[8]

In addition, the natural sciences have considerably blunted our sensitivity to all the cosmic mysteries; they have especially desacralized our image of the sun. It is a simple fact that even for believers the sun is no longer the object of an experience of the sacred. It is no longer "the splendid thing, the everlasting Epiphany in which they have been ushered into life."[9]

For Francis, the situation is quite different, perhaps more than for any other Christian. Christ is the great sacrament of God, the one who reveals to us the Father's love in an incomparable way. But his Christian faith does not destroy or even lessen the impact of the prechristian meanings things have. On the contrary, it strengthens these meanings by adding a new value to them, because it makes its own and fulfills the symbolisms natural religious man had attached to things. For Francis, Christ gives meaning to everything; he makes it possible for us to plumb the depths of the created world and grasp its full meaning. Just as he opens for us the sense of Scripture, so he opens for us the sense of creation—and the meaning revealed is a sacred meaning.

Francis undeniably experienced the sacred in the cosmos. What we must realize, is how deep the experience went, for it is not to be separated from his exploration of the sacred within his own soul. To be convinced of this, we need only return to the text of the *Canticle,* where we shall encounter something surprising and even paradoxical. A moment ago, Francis acknowledged that he was not worthy to pronounce the name of the Most High. Yet now, speaking of himself as brother to the sun, he says that this sun is the symbol of the Most High! What can he mean by calling himself brother to so noble an image? If he can greet "my lord the Sun" as a brother, and do it quite spontaneously, is he not claiming that there is a profound relationship between it and himself? Even a blood relationship? And when he thus fraternizes with this material being that is so drenched in light and that has even been placed in the category of the divine, is he not in the last analysis relating himself to his own self in its totality and thus to what is deepest and most divine in himself?

The interior relation between the soul of the poet and the cosmic element brings us to the heart of the image. When the poet, through his imagination, enters into a loving, religious communion with this wellspring of light, he receives into the depths of his being its illuminating and purifying influence. An image has its own innate dynamism. A poetic image that is intensely experienced creates something new, "expressing us by making us what it expresses."[10] Anyone whose imagination lays hold of the sun with a certain degree of inwardness feels this "splendid" being enter and penetrate him with its brilliance and abundance, expanding his being and exalting it to the region where fire is purity, matter is light, and desire is gift of self.

The image which brings joy to such a person and with which he is in communion expresses what he most deeply desires to be and what he is in the process of becoming: a solar being! Solar in his depths, down to the very root of his desires. Solar like the Most High who makes his sun to shine on all without distinction. According to Jung, the sun is the image of psychic energy in its fullness. "That this comparison is not just a matter of words can be seen from the teaching of the mystics: when they descend into the depths of their own being they find 'in their heart' the image of the sun."[11] St. Teresa of Avila, for example, speaks several times in the course of her interior journey of this "divine sun" which abides "in the midst" or "at the center" of the soul; she is referring both to the deeper self and to God.[12]

Thus the sun which Francis finds so beautiful and to which he discovers himself to be closely related does not shine upon him solely from the heights of the cosmic heaven. It also sheds its rays within him, out of the depths of his soul, like a prophecy of what he is ultimately to become. This sun, too, could say: "I am a star wandering together with you and shining up from the depths."[13] It expresses the inward fullness that the future will bring, and translates the movement of the soul in which obscure primordial affective powers, those of desire and eros, are being transformed into powers of light and self-giving and to that extent have a share in the soul's loftiest aspirations. The man who celebrates the sun as both a brother and a symbol of the Most High is secretly dreaming of his own highest destiny.

In his *Patterns in Comparative Religion,* Mircea Eliade gives numerous examples from ancient or primitive peoples of immediate relation of kinship between the solar god and certain persons or categories of persons. Filial or fraternal relations with the sun god are always regarded by these peoples as the privilege of a few individuals, the prerogative of a small group of chosen ones. The choice is accomplished either by a ritual of initiation or by accession to sovereignty. Thus "in different parts of the world chieftains were supposed to be descendants of the sun."[14] Polynesian chiefs, the heads of the Natchez and Inca tribes, Hittite and Babylonian kings, and the Indian king all had the title and character of "suns," "sons of the sun," or "grandchildren of the sun." In the solar religion of India the sovereign was even directly identified with the sun, and and Sassanid kings called themselves the brothers of the sun and the moon. It was not only initiates and sovereigns who had direct relations of kinship with the sun: heroes and philosophers often enjoyed them too. But whatever the class of human beings, the relations were always the expression of a consciousness of being specially chosen, a consciousness of possessing a higher calling or a higher destiny.[15]

Francis was certainly conscious of having a higher calling, although the awareness had far different effects in him. We should remember the occasion on which Francis described himself as "the herald of the great king."[16] He was a herald of the great King, like the sun that in the heights of heaven proclaims the magnificence of the Most High. A man thus conscious of being chosen and called can without hesitation call this splendid star his brother.

If we wish to grasp the full dimensions of Francis' brotherhood with the sun and the ultimate meaning this image of splendor has in his *Canticle,* we must set his praise of the sun in its psychological and spiritual context. In the light of the facts we recounted in our introduction to this book, it is evident, to begin with, that the cosmic praises followed upon a very profound experience in which the meaning of Francis' whole life was involved. He was overwhelmed with all kinds of suffering and on the verge of discouragement.

> One night, as he was thinking of all the tribulations he was enduring, he felt sorry for himself and said interiorly: "Lord, help me in my infirmities so that I may have the strength to bear them patiently!" And suddenly he heard a voice in spirit: "Tell me, Brother: if, in compensation for your sufferings and tribulations you were given an immense and precious treasure: the whole mass of the earth changed into pure gold, pebbles into precious stones, and the water of the rivers into perfume, would you not regard the pebbles and the waters as nothing compared to such a treasure? Would you not rejoice?" Brother Francis answered: "Lord, it would be a very great, very precious, and inestimable treasure beyond all that one can love and desire!" "Well, Brother," the voice said, "be glad and joyful in the midst of

> your infirmities and tribulations: as of now, live in peace as if you were already sharing my kingdom."[17]

To need such strengthening Francis must have been going through a period of crisis, when the soul has felt the solid ground slip from under it. We can see in the text just quoted how important the images are, especially that of the "immense and precious treasure" resulting from the transformation of the entire earth into pure gold. In this image the heavenly voice tells Francis of the destiny that awaits him as he too is transformed and his entire being is transfigured in the kingdom of light. Jung notes that "the great problems of life are always related to the primordial images. . . .All the great events of life and life's highest tensions evoke these rich images and cause them to manifest themselves in conscious interior processes, once the individual has become sufficiently reflective and acquired the ability to understand his own vital experiences."[18] These great images have the power to draw the consciousness out of its isolation and put it in contact with a transcendent fullness of life.

Let us continue with the account in the *Legend of Perugia:*

> The next morning on rising, he said to his companions: "If the emperor gave a kingdom to one of his servants, how joyful the servant would be! But if he gave him the whole empire, would he not rejoice all the more? I should, therefore, be full of joy in my infirmities and tribulations, seek my consolation in the Lord, and give thanks to God the Father, to his only Son our Lord Jesus Christ, and to the Holy Spirit. In fact, God has given me such a grace and blessing that he has condescended in his mercy to assure me, his poor and unworthy servant, still living on this earth, that I would share in his kingdom. Therefore, for glory, for my consolation, and the edification of my neighbor, I wish to compose a new "Praises of the Lord," for his creatures. . . .He sat down, concentrated a minute, then cried out: "Most high, all-powerful, and good Lord. . . ."[19]

There can be no doubt that after the crisis during the night

Francis was now passing through one of those moments of interior fulfillment and exaltation that are rarely given to men. He was wholly filled and alive with the certainty of the "immense and precious treasure." The light of dawning day had for him the brilliance of the world's first morning. Francis himself was radiant and shared in the being of the morning itself. He wanted to sing of his joy to the Lord and praise the entire universe whose mysterious transformation he had glimpsed. It was at this moment that the first of the great cosmic images came to him: the splendid fraternal image of the sun that is a symbol of the Most High.

During the famous night of November 23, 1654, when Pascal was filled to the depths of his being by certainty about the living God, he too was entranced by one of those great primordial, cryptic images that according to Jung are laid up in the soul and rise into consciousness under the influence of supreme tension. He writes at the beginning of his *Memorial:* "From about half past ten to about half past twelve: FIRE." The image of fire is well known to all religious traditions and especially to the biblical tradition on which Pascal's mind formed.

Francis, for his part, was fascinated by the sun, another primordial, cryptic image. This sun is a symbol of the Most High and yet also Francis' brother; it is both sacred and familiar. He did not contemplete it solely with his afflicted eyes, as it shone above the plain of Assisi. He felt it with his whole being, for this great cosmic image had ascended from the depths of his soul and was the expression of an interior fulfillment.

In this image we must see an unconscious replica of the image of the "immense and precious treasure" of pure gold into which the whole earth had been transformed. The image of the sun expresses the same deeper reality. In it Francis' soul recognized and celebrated in symbol, although unconsciously, its own transformation, its great transfiguration in the kingdom. "As if you were already sharing my kingdom," the voice had said to him. The marvelous substance of the sun, all filled with light,so brotherly and yet bearing the impress of the Most High, is the unconscious but immensely expressive image of a soul that grasps fully its own powers and destiny, opens itself to the entire mystery of itself, and reconciles within itself the lower, dark forces of life and matter with the consciousness of its ultimate destiny and the radiant certainty of its own divine election.

Oddly enough, Francis' image of the sun, for all its mystical character, is neither frightening nor overwhelming. It gives expression to a power that lies beyond the grasp of consciousness, yet it shows no trace of anxiety or tension. On the contrary: the man who contemplates this image is radiant with fraternal joy. This is all the more striking inasmuch as in the various solar myths and cults the cryptic image of the sun is ambivalent. In India, for example, the sun, which is regarded as the real father of man, is sometimes identified with death, because he may devour his children as well as beget them.[20] Among other peoples, the sun is closely related to death and to the darkness from which he emerges and to which he returns, taking men with him either to destroy them or to give them rebirth along with himself.[21]

In itself, the image of the sun is ambiguous; it symbolizes a power of evil as well as of good, a power that can give life or death. The context in which the image appears controls the meaning. In Francis' use of the image, the ambivalence is eliminated. The sun here is nothing but a wellspring of light, and the soul experiences its inward harmony with this radiant plenitude. It is precisely this harmony that finds expression in the title "brother" which Francis bestows upon the sun, the symbol of the Most High. "Brother Sun": in that simple phrase the soul implicitly acknowledges a wealth of being, a totality which for all its transcendence is deeply bound up with the soul. In truth, what the soul is unconsciously celebrating in the form of the cosmic image is its own innermost recesses, that part of it which is divine. The reader may remember here Claudel's verses:

Let me wholly cease to be hidden!
. . . .
Come forth at last,
all the sun that fills me, and the richness
of your light, which now I see
no longer with my eyes alone, but
with my whole body and substance and
the sum of my radiant, speaking quantity.[22]

We are now in a position to identitfy the archetype that speaks through this image of the sun and gives it its full meaning. As a symbol of harmony, union, and wholeness, the sun here proves to be an image of the self. It is not easy, to define the self as an archtype. We must be on guard especially against identifying the self with the conscious, individual ego, our little "personality." With the self we are, on the contrary, back in the primordial depths of the psyche, and at the same time dealing with the ultimate goal of the psyche's development. The self contains both the germ of the soul and the soul in its entirety. It is the center around which the authentic personality is built, and the shaping power that seeks the full development of our being. "The beginnings of our whole psychic life seems to be inextricably rooted in this point, and all our highest and ultimate purposes seem to be striving towards it."[23]

This center embraces the whole of the psyche; the self is the total being that is seeking to come to birth in us and that corresponds to our personality in its full and authentic form. But we must bear in mind that this total being is open to the fullness of being. Jung writes:

The self is our psychic totality, consisting of consciousness and of the limitless ocean of the soul on which consciousness floats.

> My soul and my consciousness—these make up the self, in which the ego forms a part like an island amid the sea or a star in the heavens. The self is thus infinitely more than the ego. Loving oneself should mean loving this totality, through the medium of which one would love all mankind.[24]

The self is an immense inner world in which man feels himself to be in harmony with the whole of being and life.

The self makes itself known to consciousness only by means of certain basic images, a few great unifying and illuminating symbols. The sun is one of these. When such a symbol rises in consciousness and enlightens it with all its rays, then, to the extent that consciousness suddenly finds itself related to a transcendent fullness of life, we are justified in saying that a process of spiritual maturation and fulfillment is going on in the depths of the soul. The psyche is moving toward its full expansion, its divine East, and a new birth is under way. The symbol functions as the heralding and prefiguration of the new being with its radiant beauty and attractiveness. The symbolic manifestation of the self to consciousness always points to an important, decisive moment in a man's life: the moment of illumination. "This is why. . . .most heroes are characterized by solar attributes, and the moment of birth of their greater personality is known as illumination."[25]

Is this not the deeper meaning of the image of the sun that begins and then dominates Francis' *Canticle*? This first great cosmic image corresponds perfectly to the interior event Francis was experiencing at this moment, that is, to the prophetic revelation he has just received concerning his eternal destiny. How, can we fail to see in the radiant image of "Brother Sun" the glorious treasure that has just been promised to him and that is but his soul itself and all its energies, fully saved now and bearing upon it in bodies of fire the mark of the Most High?

Objections will certainly be raised to such an interpretation. The first might take this form: If you give Francis' image of the sun a psychological and anthropological meaning, do you not necessarily commit yourself to a reductionist, "immanentist" interpretation in which both the cosmic and the transcendent dimensions of "Brother Sun" simply vanish? Our few remarks on the nature of the self provide an answer to this first objection, since they indicate that the psychological, cosmic, and religious dimensions are in fact inseparable here. The experience of the self is an experience that comes to a man who is fully open to the total mystery he embodies. In such an experience he submits to a source of power that, though unqualifiedly his own also infinitely transcends him and relates him to the whole of reality: to the whole of man himself and, beyond, to the whole of being and life.

In such an experience a man's center of gravity shifts. It passes from the individual ego with its limited concerns and tends to move to a depth at which the secret of personal being coincides with the secret of the universe. Such an experience is, necessarily cosmic. The man who is open to the self in him does not feel at home except in fraternal communion with "all that you have made." The experience is also religious, and radically so. The symbolic manifestation of the self always turns into a theophany. To be born to the self is to be born to divine life and to the sacred part of oneself. Indeed, "the self never takes the place and position of God, but it can," says Jung, "be a receptacle for divine grace,"[26] and the place where the glory of the Most High is manifested.

This, moreover, explains why "the image of God and the self are so closely linked in psychological 'phenomenology' that they may seem 'identical,' "[27] and why a single symbol (the sun, for example) can signify both at once. Consequently, in making the sun the symbol of the self, we do not strip it of its religious meaning any more than of its cosmic reference. We only think, with Paul Rioceur, that "to manifest the 'sacred' *on* the 'cosmos' and to manifest it *in* the 'psyche' are the same thing."[28] The quest for the sacred in the world symbolizes the quest for the sacred in the soul. "I explore my own sacrality in deciphering that of the world."[29] "God, who said, 'Let light shine out of darkness,' has shone in our hearts, that we in turn might make known the glory of God shining on the face of Christ."[30]

In summary, an archetypal image such as that of the sun in the *Canticle* is a symbolic language for an experience which is inseparably cosmic, interior, and religious, since it puts the soul in communion with the world, the self, and God. To state the matter even more accurately, such an image symbolizes the profound experiential harmony between the inner self, the world, and God. This is why the image possess such incomparable brilliance and exercises such a fascination upon us.

The second objection that might be raised is: Why is this image of the sun, which is regarded as symbolizing the self, that is, the ultimate goal of the soul's development, put first in the poem, since the poem as a whole is a sequence of images expressing the process of transformation of the soul and its symbols? In such a process would not the symbols of "union" and "wholeness" naturally be the last to appear? True enough. But we must take into account that at the moment when Francis composed his *Canticle* he was at the end of his spiritual journey. He had the full experience of wholeness, and in this experience was privileged to grasp the full significance of his earlier advance with its decisive stages. Consequently, there is no justification for surprise that the symbolic image of the sun should be placed first in a sequence that derives its intelligibility from the sun itself.

The *Canticle of Brother Sun* truly deserves that name, for in the other cosmic images in the following verses, we are always confronted with one and the same reality, the very reality already designated by the radiant image of the sun. The reality is the soul of Francis in its resplendent fulfillment and its various transformations. On the other hand, we should not forget that the image of the sun can designate not only the term of the soul's development but also the starting point of a new ascent. The great problems, after all, are never totally resolved once and for all. Francis himself was to say at the end of his life: "Let us begin, brothers, to serve the Lord God, for up to now we have made little or no progress."[31] It is very likely that he thought of the experience of fulfillment expressed in the praise of the sun, as a starting point and the source of a new movement of the soul toward its complete development. The brotherly image of the sun now glowed over his path like a prophecy of the complete being he would become. Francis was now interiorly certain that his development was a journey toward the sun and the light-filled heart of Being.

Chapter 6

The Lamps of Night

All praise be yours, my Lord, through Sister Moon and Stars;
In the heavens you have made them, bright
And precious and fair.

The *Canticle of Brother Sun* is also a canticle of night. Immediately after praising the radiance of day Francis turns to the "flowers that grow in the darkness": "Sister Moon and Stars. . .bright and precious and fair." We must observe straight off that what draws the Poverello to the night is not its darkness but its splendid lights. Francis is thus pursuing his quest for light among creatures.

When we read this stanza on Sister Moon and the Stars, we find it so simple at first that there seems to be no question about its meaning. Yet, we cannot but note that Francis feels a fraternal affection for the moon and stars as for the sun before them. He calls them "sisters," and the name means something to Francis: it is evidence of an intimate link between him and these cosmic realities. On the other hand, the latter are not simply mentioned, but are the object of imagination and dream. The adjective "precious" already tells us a good deal in this respect, for it shows the attribution to cosmic matter values which have little objective basis. "Precious stars" is a combination that changes our usual idea of the stars and turns them into matter that has been subjected to the imagination and made the object of unconscious values. We have the right to ask what the meaning of such matter can be, what further reality it serves to express.

Francis praises God for "Sister Moon and Stars." The first point he makes in his praise of them is the privileged place they occupy in the totality of creation: "In the *heavens* you have made them." The heavens, in the language of poetry and religion, are the place of the Most High. "Sister Moon and Stars" belong to this heavenly region and draw our gaze beyond our world. Nonetheless, it is because of the way Francis sees them and contemplates them that these cosmic elements appear in this context as expressive of a transcendent reality: "You have made them, bright and precious and fair."

Let us dwell on these adjectives. In their simplicity, they express a sense of wonder. The moon and stars are light-filled sisters to Francis, and it is their brightness above all that charms him. We have already pointed how closely the beauty of things is connected with their lightsomeness in the *Canticle.* But of the three adjectives here applied to the moon and stars, "precious" is the one that deserves special attention, for it is the most mysterious of the three and the most laden with hidden values.

The adjective calls to mind realities to which we attach great value; some sort of treasure. As we already pointed out, Francis uses the adjective in his writings only to specify the quality objects must have if they are to serve in the celebration of the Eucharistic sacrifice, or that places must have if the most holy Body of the Lord is to be reserved there. It is the adjective Francis uses each time he touches on this subject that was most important to him. He is explicit on the point:

> In this world I cannot see the most high Son of God with my own eyes, except for his most holy Body and Blood which they (priests) receive and they alone administer to others. Above everything else, I want this most holy Sacrament to be honored and venerated and reserved in places which are richly ornamented (*in locis pretiosis*).[1]

In Francis' writings, the "precious" quality of things emerges in close relation with a sacred reality. The preciousness is required by the latter and must give expression to it. The precious object is not willed for its own sake, but is regarded as a sign of the sacred. In using the adjective "precious" in his *Canticle* and applying it to the moon and the stars, Francis is giving these cosmic elements a religious value and telling us that for him these cosmic elements have power to express the sacred or constitute a language for uttering the sacred.

Is it possible to state more specifically the religious

values attached to moon and stars? In his phenomenological study of the various primordial cosmic mysteries Mircea Eliade has brought to light the special meaning contained in the attribution of religious values to the moon. Unlike solar hierophanies which "give expression to the religious values of autonomy and power, of sovereignty, of intelligence,"[2] lunar celebrations express awareness of the religious value of decline and death as being a passage or stage leading to a new birth. To celebrate the moon in a religious spirit is to open oneself to the mystery of a becoming that reaches fulfillment only through preliminary phases of decline and death. "It might be said that the moon shows man his true human condition; that in a sense a man looks at himself, and finds himself anew in the life of the moon."[3]

> It is through the moon's phases—that is, its birth, death, and resurrection—that men come to know at once their own mode of being in the cosmos and their chances for survival or rebirth. . . .What the moon reveals to religious man is not only that death is indissolubly linked with life but also, and above all, that death is not final, that it is always followed by a new birth. The moon confers religious valorization on cosmic becoming and reconciles man to death.[4]

Christian apologetics has made use of this lunar symbolism as a prophetic illustration of the resurrection. St. Augustine writes: "Every month the moon is born, grows, reaches fullness, decreases, dies, and then is born again. What happens each month to the moon will happen in the resurrection, but only once in the whole course of time."[5]

Does the significance attached to the primitive lunar enigmas reappear in Francis' image of the moon and in the religious meaning he attaches to it? We must acknowledge that it seemingly does not, since Francis' image makes no allusion to the lunar phases of waxing, waning, and death.

We must, nonetheless, situate the image within the

Canticle as a whole and understand it in function of the overall movement of the poem. This movement passes from contemplation of the image of the Most High and its symbol, our royal Brother Sun, to the welcome given to "Sister Earth our mother." It is a descending movement that is reinforced by the addition of the last four stanzas which praise the religious value of negativity, suffering, physical decay, and death as a way of reaching the Most High and the life that never fades. The *Canticle,* even though it is filled with the sunlight and the love of God's creatures, thus accepts and integrates decline and death into the total mystery of life and being. It reconciles man to his destiny attributing a value even to our Sister Death.

It is in the light of this overall structure that we must reread and meditate on the stanza which praises Sister Moon and Stars. When we do so, the values assigned to these beings reveal their meaning. Coming as it does immediately after the praise of the sun, this valuation undoubtedly expresses an initial attitude of acceptance and openness to the mystery of things and the world as seen on their nocturnal side. It tells us that even on this side there is light. Not everyone is able to contemplate in the nightly heavens the "precious" stars. Night is illumined in this manner only for one who accepts the total mystery of existence and entrusts himself to it. The man who clutches the rudder of his own destiny and wills to control his own life as its sovereign and unconditional master by organizing everything in it according to clear and rational concepts, has nothing to do with the mystery of the night. Night has no value for him; it contains no splendors and no precious stars.

As Baudouin observes, the excessive value placed upon the "day" is connected with the will to power, the hatred of dreams, and scorn for meditation. It embodies a rejection of what is strictly unfathomable and sacred in the realm of being. The attribution of religious value to the night, on the contrary, is bound up with an attitude of trusting acceptance when confronted with those depths of life and being which exceed our grasp. We have a striking example of such a valuation with its underlying attitude in Péguy in his poem *The Portico of the Mystery of the Second Virtue.* He puts into God's mouth this eulogy of the night:

> O Night, o my daughter Night, the most religious of my daughters
> The most pious;
> Of all my daughters, of all my creatures, you are the one who is most in my hands, the one who most completely yields;
> You glorify me in Sleep even more than your Brother Day glorifies me in Work.[7]
> You who lay man in the arms of my Providence,
> My maternal Providence,
> O my *dark and gleaming* daughter, I greet you.[8]

When given religious value and taken into profound dreams, night becomes the symbol of the unconscious, fostering depths of being; it is a female, maternal symbol. Péguy again:

> Just as the sea is the water supply, so is night the reserve of being.[9]
> O Night, black-eyed mother, universal mother. . . .[10]
> Night, o my daughter Night, o my silent daughter,
> At Rebecca's well, at the Samaritan woman's well,
> It is you who draw the deepest water
> From the deepest well.[11]

This cosmic and religious significance of night leads us over into the properly psychic dimension of the symbol. It is easy to see that under the symbol of night as a fostering mother the soul is coming to grips with its own nocturnal depths: the depths of its unconscious and of its total mystery. The individual "looks at" himself and rediscovers himself in his image of night and its splendors. Especially in the image of its splendid lamps, for they act as a mirror. "All pain and pleasure must/In darkness hidden be,/But moon and stars make clear to me/What lurks within my heart."[12] Goethe addresses the light of the moon and says: "At last you set/My soul entirely free."[13] And what does he see in the moon's light?

What man knows not
Or disregards,
What walks the night
Within his labyrinthine heart.[14]

What, we may ask, does Francis' praise of moon and stars in the *Canticle* reveal from this psychic point of view? Does the cosmic image of "Sister Moon and Stars," to which a religious value is undoubtedly being attributed, also have an interior and properly psychic meaning? We cannot evade the question. This fascinatingly beautiful image whose "precious" matter God has made, gleams in the depth of night with a mystic splendor. Francis contemplates an immense treasure with which he is obviously familiar. He implicity acknowledges the fact by addressing this material being, so "bright and precious and fair," as his "sister." This surely admits to a close relationship. The soul unconsciously rediscovers in this image of the lamps of night the sacral value of its own innermost substance; it explores its own sacrality in deciphering that of the world. The beings that light the night are language through which which hidden forces within the soul find voice; and their "precious" brilliance symbolizes some great inner burst of light.

Let us try to get at this inward meaning. "To *love* an image is always to *shed light* on a love. To love an image is unwittingly to find a new metaphor for an old love."[15] Bachelard's remark is an invitation to deepen our sympathetic intuition of the image of "Sister Moon and Stars," so that we may identify, if possible, the love on which it sheds light. A first point to be noted is that, unlike "my lord Brother Sun," to which are attributed values concerning action and the dynamic (the sun brings the day and radiates resplendently), "Sister Moon and Stars" are assigned values which have to do solely with their being and substance. No precise function, no special usefulness is mentioned. They are praised simply because they are "bright and precious and fair." These adjectives pass beyond the realm of efficacy and profit; they express an openness to a new dimension, an interior world of values that belong not to the realm of doing but to the realm of being.

Let us look more closely at the values attributed to moon and stars. We should not overlook the association of "bright" with "precious." "Bright" (*clarite*) is the first feminine adjective in the whole *Canticle,* and is immediately followed by "precious," which, as we have already seen, has sacral resonances in the vocabulary of Francis. We may therefore ask what the hidden bond is between these two descriptive adjectives that Francis' imagination should so spontaneously associate them in the first feminine image of his *Canticle.*

The word "bright" *(calarits)* awakens profound reverberations in Francis' soul. "Clara," after all, was the name of the young daughter of an aristocratic house who had been drawn by Francis' evangelical ideal and whom he himself had consecrated to the Lord. It was he, Celano tells us, that "encouraged Clare to scorn the world. . . urging her to keep for the divine Spouse who became man for love of us the *precious* pearl of her virginity."[16] In the spring of 1211, during the night of Palm Sunday, Clare, who was then only eighteen, secretly left her father's house, wearing all her finery. She went to St. Mary of the Portiuncula, where Francis and his brothers welcomed her by torchlight. She cast aside all her jewels and was consecrated to the Lord. "The Lady Clare, a native of the city of Assisi" became "the most *precious*. . .stone*(lapis pretiosissimus*]. . .She was of noble parentage, but she was more noble by grace; she was a virgin in body, most chaste in mind. . .Clare by name, brighter in life."[17]

In both of these texts from Celano the adjective "precious" is applied to Clare and her life of consecration. In juxtaposing these texts with that of the *Canticle* where we find associated the two adjectives "bright" and "precious," we are not at all suggesting that the image of "Sister Moon and Stars" contains the least allusion to Sister Clare or the least trace of allegory. We are at an entirely different level here and looking in different direction. We only ask the following question: may not the values attached to "Sister Moon and Stars" unconsciously symbolize certain interior values with which the name and life of Clare are not unconnected?

The entry of Clare into Francis' world was not merely one episode among many. The event points rather to a profound receptivity in Francis and an openness at the level of being. In order to belong wholly to God, Francis had completely and radically renounced woman. Now he finds her on his path once again, this time as a consecrated virgin. He welcomes her, not as one fulfilling a function, complement to man or as object of desire, but as one with a personal transcendent calling and a being consecrated to God. It is impossible to overstate the psychological and spiritual importance of this event in Francis' life, since it touches the man's very depths. From now on, a woman will always be part of Francis' spiritual life.

It is clear that Clare played a very important part of Francis' interior development. When he is in doubt about the course he ought to follow, it is to her that he turns. Then later on, when the vision of his soul grows dark like that of his eyes, he will turn his gaze toward her in the darkness, looking for light. In every sense of the word, she is Sister "Clare" or "Bright" to him, not only by the advice she gives but, at a deeper level, by the spiritual influence of her being on the innermost forces in Francis' soul.

No man, however devoted to the service of God, can attain spiritual maturity apart from some feminine influence that makes his mind and will more sensitive and provides a kind of spiritual complement. Indeed, it can be said that he will not reach spiritual maturity unless he accepts woman for what she is and acknowledges her true being, her personal vocation, and her spiritual dignity. When woman is thus accepted and loved for her own sake, above and beyond desire, she ceases to be a myth and becomes the symbol of a mystery that transcends her but allows its light, inaccessible by any direct means, to pass through her.

It is at the level of the primordial affective powers that we must locate Clare's action in Francis' life. If the Saint's life manifests "a unique confluence of Eros and Agape. . . an interfusion of both. . .which has become so complete as to present the greatest and most sublime example of a simultaneous 'inspiriting of life' and 'enlivening of the spirit,' "[19] it certainly owes this in large measure to some profoundly feminine source of light. That source was Clare, "brighter than the light of day": *Clara clarior luce.*

Now it was at San Damiano,[20] close to Sister Clare, that Francis received his revelation of the "immense and precious treasure"[21] and that amid the resultant joy he composed the *Canticle of Brother Sun.* There can be no doubt that Clare's presence at this decisive moment in his life helped loose the springs of poetry in him. Nor can there be any doubt that Clare is somehow present in this song into which Francis poured his soul and expressed all his gratitude. The point is not, let us repeat, that we are to look for the least allusion to Clare in the *Canticle.* The point is rather that by the way he imagines and attributes value to certain cosmic substances, especially the moon and the stars, and by the way he relates to them as to "sisters." Francis is unconsciously turning the realities into symbols: feminine symbols in which we may see, not an image of Sister Clare, but the expression of primordial forces in Francis' soul which Clare helped attain an illumination and spiritualization to which she herself was no stranger.

The praise of Sister Moon and Stars thus becomes an unconscious symbolic evocation of the one of the deepest experiences a human being can undergo: the experience of the spiritualization of the hidden forces in him and the transformation of eros into agape. Night, moon, and stars have always been feminine symbols. The symbolism is more than a simple matter of grammatical gender. It has to do with the resonances of the images in the depths of the psyche, with their cryptic power and with the great archetypes they stir to action.

The dark night with its gleams of light, the moon with its phases of growth and decline, the stars sparkling and unreachable—these have always fascinated men and set them dreaming. In the imagination and dreams of mankind, these beings of the night, simultaneously fascinating and inaccessible, spontaneously co-symbolize the nocturnal side, itself both mysterious and fascinating, of man's own being. For the male, the other side finds its essential expression in the fact of woman. Via the face of woman, be she mother or wife, man comes into contact with the most obscure and fearful, yet also the most precious aspects of his own being and of existence: birth, sex, love, God, death, and necessity.

Jean Guitton writes: "It is through the image of woman that the human mind achieves a first, vague awareness of existence, its sudden origin, its movement and transformations; of sexuality and the passions; of love, the sins against it, and its fall; in short, the obscure relation between spirit and body."[22] Woman's face orients man, via his own deepest desires, to the other side of himself and the obscure world of his own origins: the maternal womb, the life of the unconscious, mother earth and the cosmic night. It is not surprising, therefore, that in the imagination and dreams of men of all times, night and woman symbolize one another. Novalis asks:

> Dost thou take pleasure in us also, dark Night? What dost thou hold beneath thy mantle that with unseen power affects my soul?. . . .Dimly, inexpressibly, we feel ourselves moved: a grave countenance I see, startled with gladness, which gently and reverently inclines toward me and amid infinitely tangled locks reveals the mother's lovely youth. . . .More heavenly than those flashing stars

> seem to us the infinite eyes which the Night has opened within us. They see further than the palest of those countless hosts.[23]

What the feminine images of night, moon, or stars symbolize is not this or that human person, this or that individualized form, but the feminine archetype that is all-encompassing—and ambivalent or ambiguous as well. The feminine symbolism of night and its lamps can point both to life and to death, self-giving and desire, soul and animality, salvation and damnation, spiritual progress and spiritual regression. It always expresses a confrontation of man with the "night" of his instinctual origins and of desire and eros. But the confrontation can make him prisoner of that night or, on the contrary, shed the light of the spirit upon it. In the latter case, the image of the lamps or splendors of night translates the metamorphosis going on in a soul that opens itself to its own total mystery by assuming and transforming its nocturnal powers. The immersion in our archaism and that of mankind then becomes the way to "a discovery, a prospection, and a prophecy concerning ourselves."[24]

In the *Canticle,* the ambiguity of the symbol is removed. To be convinced of this we need only replace the image in its context. The image of Sister Moon and Stars follows upon that of "my lord Brother Sun," which in turn follows upon that of the Most High. The whole movement of the poem starts with this initial image of the Most High that gives expression both to the highest aim of the soul—its guest of the Sacred—and to the awarness of its helplessness. The soul judges itself not "worthy to pronounce your name," but does not therefore abandon its longing to unite itself to God through praise. Instead, "with great humility" it turns to creatures, all creatures.

The first of the ensuing cosmic images is that of Brother Sun. Brother Sun symbolizes and gives expression to the entire interior dynamism of the soul: its vital energies, its creative powers, its power to expand, influence, and conquer. Brother Sun represents the power of daylight and of the enterprising, conquering mind. In this image we are still quite close to the Most High, and Francis greets it as a symbol of God. The soul that communes with such an image will be fascinated by the inaccessible heights.

This image of radiant splendor is followed by the image of the bright lamps of night: Sister Moon and Stars. The two images—sun and moon—cannot be separated; they call for and complete one another, and together form a highly meaningful cosmic pair. As Baudouin writes, "a profound acceptance of the solar myth is possible only if that acceptance is complete. They myth of night and the myth of day go together, and the symbol of night. . .is no less essential than the symbol of day."[25] Mircea Eliade approaches the same point from another angle:

> The final result of giving absolute supremacy to solar hierophanies as developed in one sense only, can be seen in the excesses of those ascetic Indian sects whose members go on staring at the sun until they become totally blind. This is a case of the "dryness' and "sterility" of a purely solar order of things which carries its limited logic to extremes. The counterpart of it is a species of "decay from damp," the turning of men into "seeds," which occurs in those sects which give the same sort of total acceptance to the nocturnal, lunar or earthly order of things. It is the almost automatic fate of those who accept only one aspect of the sun hierophanies to be driven to a state of "blindness" and "dryness," while those who fix themselves exclusively upon the "nocturnal sphere of the mind" are led into a state of permanent orgy and dissolution—a return to a sort of larval state.[26]

We think here of that other singer of the sun, Nietzsche, who wanted to "jump over his shadow—and verily, into *his* sun."[27] He too had his eye on the "most high": "O heaven above me, pure and deep! You abyss of light! Seeing you, I tremble with godlike desires. To throw myself into your height, that is *my* depth."[28] But, dazzled by the image of his own sun, he admits that he cannot sing of the stars:

> Light am I; ah, that I were night! But this is my loneliness that I am girt with light. Ah, that I were dark and nocturnal! How I would suck at the breasts of light! And even you would I bless, you little sparkling stars and glowworms up there, and be overjoyed with your gifts of light.
>
> But I live in my own light; I drink back into myself the flames that break out of me.[29]

Francis of Assisi followed an entirely different course. He did not imprison himself in his sun, nor immediately identify himself with the highest and most conscious part of his being. He acknowledged himself brother to all creatures, as one intimately linked to them and rooted in them, as one who had originated in one and the same creative Lord. Consequently, it is in union with them, all of them, that he mounts up to the Most High. He is in communion with the humblest of them, and first and foremost with those of the night: Sister Moon and Stars. The celebration of the lamps of night, coming as it does after the celebration of the radiant splendor of the day, gives expression to a soul that refuses to monopolize the sun, to make it his own and take up dwelling in it as though it were meant to be his home. His is a soul that in its poverty is open to the mystery of being in all its dimensions.

The praise of the moon gives voice to a spirit that is open to the depths, the nocturnal part of our being. But this very openness already represents a transformation of the soul, the kind of transfiguration that can here find expression in a great feminine symbol of the cosmic universe. In the male, spiritual development

> takes place through the vital experience of the Anima, the earthly principle which man sees at work in woman. His object-oriented mind, his world of rational ideas, draw inspiration from her and are liberated from their rigidity and onesidedness. It is only when the male comes into contact with his non-rational eros that his logos becomes a living spirit. For this contact to take place man must descend from the throne of proud intellect and acknowledge the feminine principle in himself.[30]

All praise be yours, my Lord, through Sister Moon and Stars;
In the heavens you have made them, bright
And precious and fair.

Such praise rises from the depths of the soul and is the echo of an interior poverty, but here "poverty is a great inner light."[31]

The poor man's house is like the earth;
the chip of a future crystal,
now light, now dark in its chance flight;
poor as the warm poverty of a stable.
Yet there are evenings when it is everything,
and all the stars emerge from it.[32]

Chapter 7

The Song of Wind and Water

All praise be yours, my Lord, through Brothers Wind and Air,
And fair and stormy, all the weather's moods,
By which you cherish all that you have made.

All praise be yours, my Lord, through Sister Water,
So useful, lowly, precious and pure.

The *Canticle of Brother Sun* is gradually taking on the colors of the earth. It is becoming a song of simple things that are strangely close to us. Wind and air, it is true, are elements that still leave the soul hanging between heaven and earth. But can Brother Wind be really separated from Sister Water? The two are sister and brother; that is how the poets see them. It is not by chance, then, that the two go together and link hands in Francis' hymn of praise. In poetic and religious meditation on the cosmic elements, wind and water are often closely associated. We shall therefore avoid separating them in our reading of the *Canticle.* In fact, the meaning of the image is to be sought in the combination of the elements.

* * * *

The Bible provides us with many examples of the association of wind and water. At the beginning of Genesis we read: "A mighty wind swept over the waters."[1] In Exodus, wind and water unite to help in the deliverance of God's people: "The Lord swept the sea with a strong east wind throughout the night. . . .When the water was thus divided, the Israelities marched into the midst of the sea on dry land, with water like a wall to their right and to their left."[2] The image of the combined elements, now with spiritual meaning, reappears in the prophets foretelling the new exodus after the deportation and exile: "I will sprinkle clean water upon you. . . .I. . .will place a new spirit [breath] within you."[3] And finally we read in St. John: "No one can enter God's kingdom without being begotten of water and Spirit. . . . The wind blows where it will."[4]

The same association can be illustrated from the poets. Thus Goethe, in his *Song of the Spirits over the Waters,* sees the two elements as closely united: "Soul of man,/ how like the water!/Fate of man,/how like the wind!"[5] And in one of his *Five Great Odes,* entitled *The Spirit and the Water,* Claudel writes: "And in turn the wind rises on earth, the Sower, the Reaper./Water is the extension of spirit; it supports it and feeds it."[6]

It would be easy to multiply examples. The important point, however, is that this constant pairing by the imagination has a meaning, and the meaning is with man himself and his condition. When wind and water come together in the poet's soul, his celebration of them points to something deeper which he contemplates.

In attempting to get at this meaning as contained in the *Canticle* we shall adhere to our method. We shall inquire into the values attributed to these elements and into their position in the poem as a whole. The words "Brother Wind" introduce us into a world that is not simply the world of the meteorologist, but a world in which the images of material substances aim at "loosing the moorings of something in us that seeks expression in dreams."[7] "Brother Wind" is no longer merely a physical phenomenon: it now has face and soul. "There is someone/in the wind."[8]

Whenever a man truly greets any material substance in his soul, we get a glimpse of unconscious depths within his being. Not everyone can be a friend of the wind, and there are few who can say and fully mean it: "Brother Wind!" If a soul is to treat a great cosmic force as a brother, that force must set in motion within the soul mysterious and deep-seated energies. "Fate of man,/how like the wind!" Goethe would never have written that line unless he had at times felt himself lifted and carried by inner forces, as a leaf is carried by the wind, and unless he had a stupendous intuition of the profound links between the great forces of nature and human life.

Anyone who says "Brother Wind," is recognizing that

he is interiorly related to, and in harmony with, a cosmic environment. Each cosmic element that is welcomed and becomes the object of profound dreams brings with it a very specific context. The context of the wind is a world open and exposed and swept by a force that will not let you rest and carries you further and further, a force that refuses to be fettered and overturns every dividing wall and every barrier. The wind blows where it will; and one never knows for sure whence the wind is coming and whither it is going.

If a man is to find such an environment congenial and have brotherly feelings for it, or even just to experience it in imagination, he must be greatly detached and open to inner newness, to the great inspirations, and to profound changes. He must be poor "like the flowers along the railway line/So generously poor in the mad wind of journeys."[9] He must be both poor and free. Happy the man who can say, as he approaches his fiftieth year: "All praise be yours, my Lord, through (and for) Brother Wind." Yet that was one of the graces given to Francis of Assisi.

All his life Francis was a man of the "open air," in the fullest sense of the praise. Louis Lavelle writes: "There has perhaps never been a more receptive soul than St. Francis. Of all men he had the most spontaneous and elicate sensitiveness and was deeply moved by all his contacts with nature, his fellow-men or with God."[10] For, while Francis listened to the song of the wind and exposed himself to its fraternal breath, his naked soul yearned to be ever more open to the Spirit of God at work in him and to be caught up by God's inspiration.[11] He could, without pretense, have made his own the words Shelley later spoke to the wind: "Be thou, Spirit fierce,/My spirit! Be thou me, impetuous one!"

We must not think of all this as simple romanticism on Francis' part. No, his brotherly feeling for the wind springs from an interior detachment and openness of soul that a man reaches only after much striving. The *Canticle* in which

Francis gives expression to his presence to God and the world is not primarily a song of Brother Wind. On his interior journey, as in his hymn of praise, Francis undoubtedly began by being drawn to the image of the sun; he was brother to the sun before being brother to the wind.

Let us go on now to the other "qualities" Francis regards the wind as having. But, to our astonishment, we find no adjectives used of the wind! While all the other cosmic elements in the *Canticle* are given detailed description, the wind is left by itself. The image is as bare as it could be. And yet that impression is mistaken, because Brother Wind is praised in all his manifestations: "Air, and fair and stormy, all the weather's moods." All its moods! The good ones and the bad! Paradoxical though it may seem, the *Canticle of Brother Sun* is here transformed into a canticle of all the seasons and all the kinds of weather they bring.

The wind that rages in a storm and brings rain or hail is here blessed just as much as the gentle breeze under a warm sun. Francis has no preference when it comes to weather, but opens his arms in welcome to the four winds of creation. In fact, for him there is no thing as bad weather any longer. It has been said that the poetic evocation of the four basic elements: water, fire, air, and earth, is typical of the psychic quest of its own unity.[12] We can say that the poetic celebration of the wind in all its manifestations shows a soul aspiring to open itself to Being in its entirety and to all its inspirations:

> If I love and admire and sing
> wild songs of the wind. . . .
> it is because it magnifies my being
> and, before it makes its way through lung and pore
> to the very blood by which my body lives,
> has clasped the world in infinite arms
> with stark power or sweetness ineffable.[13]

Francis goes on to tell us why he praises "all the

weather's moods." It is because by them "you cherish all that you have made." The wind, which Francis welcomes in all its manifestations, is here directly associated with God's work as Creator. Brother Wind is seen as the Creator's fellow-worker, the one who "cherishes," that is, supports, strengthens, and invigorates other creatures. This verse of the *Canticle* echoes some of the great biblical images, for example: "If you take away their breath, they perish and return to their dust. When you send forth your spirit, they are created, and you renew the face of the earth."[14]

Because of the cosmic and life-giving role assigned to the wind, the image of Brother Wind here embraces the whole universe. It relates to creation in its entirety and its power becomes as great as that of the Creator himself. "Brother Wind" becomes an image of the Creator's own power, a symbol of the creative Breath that sustains all things in existence. Moreover, the values being attributed to the wind are clear: the wind is imagined not only as energetic and powerful, but as an essentially beneficent and life-giving force. It is only the wind's positive and beneficial effects that are kept in view. Such an unconscious selectivity suggests the illusive depth the image must possess in Francis' soul. For, as we are aware, the wind does not always act for the good of other creatures; it is not always a life-giving, creative breath, but can turn into tornado or hurricane. Then it no longer supports but uproots and smashes, destroying everything before it. Here, however, "Brother Wind" is a dream-image of the wind, an "imaged" image, as Bachelard would say.

In this magnified image to which extraordinary values are attributed, we have left the physical phenomenon behind. More accurately, the image becomes part of the symbolic language a soul uses as it searches its own depths. The image now expresses the soul's relation to the Sacred, and the values attributed to it are essentially religious. In thus imagining the wind, the poet is really asking this image to manifest something of the Most High to him and to enable him to relate himself to that Most High. "Brother Wind" is being praised not simply as an agent in a cosmic work but as an expression of God's attentive, active presence to the whole of his creation.

Such an exploration of the sacred in the world also means an unconscious exploration of the sacred in the depths of the soul itself. Francis' feeling of brotherhood relates to a magnified image of the wind and to the values attributed to it; in the wind thus imagined he sees a substance that is truly brother to him. This airy, energetic, cryptic thing is the imaged, symbolic expression of what is most powerful and divine in the soul's most obscure and deep-rooted energies; it is the expression of that which is constantly being communicated to the soul, the creative Breath of God himself.

Coming as it does after the image of Brother Sun and Sister Moon, the image of Brother Wind undoubtedly gives expression to the same inner reality: that is, to the soul of Francis as he opens himself, in every "pore" and every vital power, to the destiny that has been revealed to him by the heavenly voice in the image of the earth's transformation into "an immense and precious treasure."[15] Only the symbol has changed, but the very change is significant. We should recall Bachelard's words: "Every new choice of cosmic element renews our inner being." In the movement of the *Canticle* as a whole from the lofty image of Brother Sun to the image of our Sister, mother earth, the image of Brother Wind is not simply transitional, that is, just another stage between heaven and earth, but also points to the meaning of the return to the dark origins, to the mother. It tells us that the return is not to be interpreted as a seeking of security in the maternal womb or a relapse into the sleep of the unconscious, but rather as an opening of the soul to the great adventure of creation, the adventure in which God's creative Breath enters into matter and its obscure energies so as to inform them from within and to draw out of them a living soul that is destined for eternal life.

As we mentioned at the beginning of this chapter, we cannot grasp the full meaning of the image of Brother Wind in this *Canticle* of St. Francis unless we closely link it to the image of Sister Water, with which it forms a brother-sister pair. The two images do not merely follow one upon the other; each calls for the other. The reason why we can speak of the two as forming a fraternal pair is not simply the somewhat accidental fact that the two differ in grammatical gender, thus enabling us to address the one as brother and the other as sister. The reason is the complementary values assigned to each of the two elements. The values themselves cannot be fully understood unless we see how the two elements form a pair deep in the poet's imagination. This is a point we must now examine more closely.

Brother Wind, as we have seen, is praised as the one through whom the Lord sustains his creatures; he is associated with the creative work and takes an active part in it. The values attributed to him have to do with energy and action, for he is one who performs a task. It is entirely different with Sister Water. Here the values are attached directly to the substance of water: "All praise be yours, my Lord, through Sister Water, so useful, lowly, precious and pure."

The praise here contains no verb denoting action; no precise task is assigned to Sister Water. Her value resides in her very being. Using the language of Bachelard, we may say that the values attributed to water are determined by a poetics of reveries concerning inwardness. We noted the same thing about the moon and stars as compared with the sun. Now we can see that in the *Canticle* two types of value-attribution alternate: one moves outward to virile action and a delight in vastness (this is true of the sun, the wind, and, as we shall see later on, the fire); the other moves inward to the depths of the poet's being (this is the case with the moon and the stars, the water, and, later, the earth).

Let us try to penetrate more fully into the meaning of

the imaginary pairing of wind and water. We noted at the beginning of the chapter that their association here is not mere chance, since their pairing by the imagination is found everywhere in the symbolism of mankind. It must therefore already have a meaning that relates to the universal human condition. Only by "sympathizing" with the values unconsciously attributed to these elements can we hope to reach the illusive core of the image which the two elements together form. It should be noted that when wind is paired with water, it is usually depicted as mastering the water so as to make the water fruitful. Thus in the biblical image the wind of Yahweh sweeps over the primordial waters to control and fertilize them. In Claudel's image, already quoted, the wind is "the Sower," and the water is a receptacle, a maternal womb. In Goethe's *Song of the Spirits over the Waters* there are the following significant verses: "The wind is tender lover/to the billow;/the wind churns up/the foaming wave."[16]

The examples are enlightening. They show us that, while every imaginary combination of the material elements is a marriage (Bachelard), the special meaning of the union of wind and water in poetic and religious language is to make known a renewal in depth, a new birth, a creation. The biblical image of the wind of Yahweh sweeping over the waters is a prelude to the account of creation. Later on, the prophetic image of pure water and a new spirit (breath) announces the creation of Yahweh's new people. St. John's image of water and wind symbolizes the new birth from on high. The liturgy of the Paschal Vigil, in the blessing of the baptismal water, recalls the image of the Spirit breathing on the waters (Gn 1:2) as prefiguring the new life to be given by Christ. In the older rite the priest breathed on the water and then said this prayer: "Almighty God,. . .bless this pure water with the breath of your mouth. . . .Let the power of the Holy Spirit descend into the water of this font and make it entirely fruitful, giving it the power to bestow new life."

Many poets see the same significance in the pairing of wind and water. In his *Ode to the West Wind,* the wind that has passed over the waters and stirred them up, Shelley prays: "If even/I were as in my boyhood. . . ./O lift me as a wave. . .!" And Paul Valéry, in his poem "The Graveyard by the Sea," suddenly feels new life course through him at the call of the wind as it rises over the sea:

> And, O my heart, drink in the winds reviving!
> A freshness, exhalation of the sea,
> Restores my soul. . .Salt-breathing potency!
> Let's run at the waves and be hurled back to living![17]

To become a child again, to be reborn: such is undoubtedly the profound desire of the soul when in its dreams it embraces wind and water in a single image and with the same love: Brother Wind and Sister Water. In itself, the image of water is highly ambivalent. Water can be the focal point for all the dreams of the ego, and for nothing more. But the image of water, when it is simply a reflection of the ego, is ultimately barren. It contributes nothing to the soul and leaves the latter stranded at the surface of itself; it does not open the soul to its own depths or help it achieve rebirth. It is in vain that Narcissus attempts to recapture his childhood and to render immortal what he used to be. "What Narcissus glimpses in the gloomy waters is only the successive skins he has sloughed off."[18]

But the mirror may break. Then water is dreamed of in depth and becomes a symbol of the unconscious and, more specifically, of the maternal womb and the mother. And yet this symbol is in turn ambiguous. It may symbolize a nostalgia for the womb, a longing for the serene life of unconsciousness in which one is sheltered and without responsibilities. If this be the case, then the illusive image of water once again fails to give life, and rather symbolizes death and the return to nature's sleep.

If the soul is to draw new life from water, it is not

enough to have a brotherly feeling for water. There are various kinds of brotherly feeling. We must pay close attention to the way in which water is dreamed and imagined, to the way in which value is attributed to the water, and the way in which water is combined with other elements. It is clear that association of water with wind is already important. A water that is imagined in conjunction with the wind cannot be barren water; it is always water that is a source of life. The water in the pool of Bethesda cured the sick who immersed themselves in it, but only after the water had been stirred up and thus aerated by the angel of the Lord.

Let us suppose for a moment that in the *Canticle* Sister Water had been paired not with Brother Wind but with "my lord Brother Sun." The image of water would have been quite different and so would its meaning: when associated with and dominated by the image of the radiant sun, Sister Water would have become the mirror in which the god was reflected. Think for example of the marvelous and disturbing line of Jean Clarence Lambert in his *Depaysage:* "The sun lingers on the lake like a peacock." The water on which the image of the sun rests is nothing but a reflection of the heavenly fire; it is a surface that is as it were dazzled. The water over which the wind passes is, on the contrary, receptive of deepest life and being.

"All praise be yours, my Lord, through Sister Water, so useful, lowly, precious and pure." Such praise of Sister Water shows a high decree of poetic and spiritual tact; it may not be handled with insensitive fingers, lest it be spoiled. We may try, however, to sense the poet's feeling of wonder and to share his reverie with regard to water.

As we noted above, the values attributed here to water belong to the very substance of the element rather than to its function or its role in the universe; it is the very being of water that is described. And yet of the four adjectives used, at least three are evidently not susceptible to an objective, material meaning. These are the terms "humble, precious and pure." Only the first glance seems to have an objectively clear and obvious meaning: "Sister Water, so useful. . . ."

At the same time, however, we must avoid isolating the word "useful" from the rest of the descriptive terms and giving it a purely pragmatic meaning without reference to its position within the image as a whole. The first adjective prepares the way for the second; it leads up to "lowly" and acquires overtones which go beyond the simple notion of material usefulness. It implies the idea of service of obligingness or being at the service of another. When all is said and done, this first attribute of Sister Water evidently belongs to the same poetic and oneiric sphere as the others. It plays a part in forming the image that can be glimpsed behind the material element: the image of an obliging, beneficent feminine presence that is also reserved, hidden, and pure.

It is easy, moreover, to see that from the outset the values attributed to water point in a definite direction. When Francis presents water as sisterly, useful, and lowly, he has already made a selection among possible images. In the empirical order water has many faces, from the clear serene surface to the torrential flood that sweeps all before it, with the crystal fountain in between. Each of these kinds of water can, moreover, be imagined and dreamed in many ways. Thus there are waters that lie sleeping; deep waters like abysses that swallow whole cities; the great proud raging waters of destruction. We find in the Bible images of waters that inspire fear:

Save me, O God,
  for the waters threaten my life;
I am sunk in the abysmal swamp
  where there is no foothold;
I have reached the watery depths;
  the flood overwhelms me.[19]

Your furies have swept over me;
your terrors have cut me off.
They encompass me like water all the day;
on all sides they close in upon me.[20]

The water Francis contemplates is quite different. Its face is not threatening, it stirs neither anxiety nor aggressiveness. On the contrary, it is a sisterly face, the face of a "useful, lowly" sister.

But it is the third and fourth of the values attributed to water that we find most striking: "precious and pure," for these take us to the heart of the image as dreamed. With them we evidently leave behind the world of positivist experience, the world to which natural, empirical observation gives access. The poet's imagination forgets about any objective point of reference and creates an imaginary universe that lies beyond material reality; it sees the object in its invisible relation to the soul, as a symbol.

Here we also meet the adjective "precious" for the second time in the *Canticle.* In its earlier use it described the stars. Is the point here that something of the stars' brilliance is also found in water? Our Sister Water can, on occasion, rival the starry heavens and sparkle as through strewn with precious stones. But isn't it odd that Francis, the man of total poverty, should thus dream of precious substances in the heavens and on earth as well? That he should dream of precious stars and precious water? Moreover, the very repetition of this adjective within the space of a few lines and with regard to such different things is enough to attract our attention. It suggests that Francis' inner eye, as it moves from one image of matter to another, continues to gaze, unconsciously, on the same "precious" reality, a sacred "treasure" that rivets his attention because it is extremely valuable.

We have pointed out several times already how infrequently Francis uses the adjective "precious" in his other writings, and how it always refers to something sacred.

Specifically, he applies the word "precious" to everything that serves for the celebration of the sacred mysteries of the Lord's Body and Blood, as well as to the places in which the holy Body is reserved. In Francis' use, the "preciousness" of these things and places seems to be a kind of language that expresses in a sensible way what he regards as most sacred. In short, a "precious" matter, for Francis, is a matter that can symbolize the sacred.

It is not surprising then to see "precious" linked with "pure" in the image of Sister Water; here the two words are of the same order, and complement and illumine one another. "When water becomes precious, it also becomes seminal. Praise of it then has a deeper aura of mystery. . . . Water thus energized is like a seed, a source of inexhaustible vitality."[21] Precious water is living water, and the living water in this instance flows from depths unprofaned, from a hidden, sacred source. In the vision of the prophet Ezekiel, for example, the stream of water that fertilizes everything in its path and even purifies and makes lifegiving the waters of the Dead Sea, flows from under the rebuilt temple, on the right or eastern side.[22] And when Jesus speaks to the Samaritan woman of "living water," he does so while sitting beside a deep well, as the woman reminds him: "Sir, you do not have a bucket and this well is deep. Where do you expect to get this flowing [literally: living] water?"[23] Living water always has a source deeper than the deepest well, a source that is not continuous with the external world but is unsullied, virginal, and sacred.

The image of Sister Water as "so useful, lowly, precious and pure" certainly carries the inward values of the unconscious. This does not mean that we exclude an implicit allusion to the water of sacramental baptism that symbolizes and communicates supernatural life. It means only that such a possible reference to the baptismal rite leaves intact the profound psychological roots of the image. Well, then, what does this image of Sister Water mean? What does the cosmic element praise in these verses imply?

There is a way of looking at things or, more accurately, of communing with them through imagination and dream, that turns them into a language expressive of the soul's depths. In a fragment of verse entitled *German Song* Hölderlin writes: "And he [the poet] sings, when he has drunk/Of the holy, temperate water, and heard the while/The song of the soul."[24] How close the "holy, temperate water" is to the water "so. . .lowly, precious and pure"! In both instances the praise of water echoes a song that rises from the soul's depths. Heidegger situates these verses of Hölderlin in their immediate context, according to which the poet who thus sings has first "sat in deep shadow" but now feels "the fresh breath of the stream."

> The *deep shadow* preserves the poet's words from the excessive brightness of the *heavenly fire,* and *the fresh breath of the stream* preserves them from the excessive heat of the *heavenly fire.* The freshness and the shadow cast by temperance attune the poet to the sacred. Temperance does not negate the spirit but is the radical, ever-poised harmony created by openness to the sacred. Hölderlin's words give expression to the sacred.[25]

The sacred also finds expression in Francis' image of Sister Water, "so useful, lowly, precious and pure," joined with the image of Brother Wind. Francis is here celebrating the sacred "on" an element of the material world. But the celebration of the sacred "on" the world echoes the revelation of the sacred in the soul; it is a symbolic language for a revelation in the inner depths.

Can we specify this inner revelation? We noted above that the values attributed to Sister Water enable us to glimpse within the substance of the element a feminine presence. The image of Sister Water is not, however, an image of a particular woman, but a symbol of the feminine part of the person, the feminine principle which exists in every human being, or, in the language of Jung, the *anima.* In the image of water here the poet is thus unconsciously giving expression to his relation to one of the basic archetypes of the human soul. "The *anima* is the archetype of life. . . .Life takes possession of man through the *anima,* although he thinks it does so through his mind. He masters life by means of his intelligence, but life acts in him through the mediation of the *onima.*"[26]

The archetypes, as we know, are foci of energy. Of themselves they are ambivalent. The great symbols which they inspire and through which they manifest themselves to consciousness (such symbols as sun, water, and fire) are symbols of human desire at its most elemental and archaic level, where it is closest to the basic instincts of the species. At the same time, however, the symbols form a language in which being addresses its call to us from within ourselves, offering itself to us in the form of great creative possibilities that prefigure our destiny as human beings. In consequence, the more than human power that emanates from the archetype can either be a regressive force that draws us back to the archaic, nocturnal forms of desire by making the latter seem limitless and beyond our control, or a progressive force that generates in the personality an upward thrust by opening it to the mystery of being. The ambivalence can be removed only in the course of, and by means of, the experience itself. Depending on how one surrenders to that experience, the power of the archetype will draw one down into the shadowy depths or raise one to the Most High.

It is for this reason that we must pay very close attention to the way in which consciousness expresses its relation to the archetype by means of the image. From this point of view, Francis' image of Sister Water proves highly meaningful. Everything in it is simple and transparent. The feminine part of the being (the *anima*) that finds expression here is not a shadowy realm that is both repelling and fascinating. It is recognized rather to be a "Sister. . .so useful" and "lowly." It has become the dimension of the soul that assures man's soul of a profound communion with life.

In addition, the *anima* is here embraced within the context of praise; it is seen and accepted not only in its relation to man but also in its relation to the sacred. It is the "precious" and "pure" zone of the person that is not focused on the external world, and that can open itself to the breath of the divine Spirit. It is an inward openness to the sacred. Thanks to it, man can receive within himself Him whose name "no mortal lips are worthy to pronounce," that is, the Most High himself.

"All praise be yours, my Lord, through Sister Water, so useful, lowly, precious and pure." If the reader has followed and understood our analysis, he will not be surpraised to find us connecting the praise of Sister Water (which, we must not forget, is linked with praise of Brother Wind) to what Francis says in his *Letter to All the Faithful:*

> It is not for us to be wise and calculating in the world's fashion; we should be guileless, lowly, and pure. . . .We should not want to be in charge of others; we are to be servants, and should *be subject to every human creature for God's sake* (1 Pet. 2:13). On all those who do this and endure to the last the Spirit of God will rest (cf. Is. 11:12); he will make his dwelling in them and there he will stay, and they will be *children of your Father in heaven* (Mt. 5:45) whose work they do. It is they who are the brides, the brothers and the mothers of our Lord Jesus Christ.[27]

Is not a man who thus renounces his own "wisdom" and desire to dominate a man who accepts the *anima* and acknowledges the non-rational part of his being, that is symbolized by "Sister Water, so useful, lowly, precious and pure"? Such a man is mysteriously united to the Spirit of the Lord. The Spirit rests upon him as the creative Breath rested upon the primordial waters and as Brother Wind upon Sister Water. The Spirit of the Lord enters into such a man's inmost self and there establishes his dwelling. From the union comes a new birth: the divine birth of man: "They will be children of your Father in heaven."

Everything suggests that the praise of Sister Water, taken together with the praise of Brother Wind, ultimately expresses the same spiritual experience that is reflected in the *Letter to All the Faithful.* In both writings Francis celebrates the new and heavenly birth of the human being when he opens his inmost self to the Spirit of God. In the *Canticle,* this spiritual experience acquires a cosmic dimension, since it is mediated through a fraternal communion with material substances, the elements of the world. The communion is both the symbol of and the way by which the individual is reconciled to the roots of his being and to his primordial vital powers, in the light of the all-encompassing mystery of being.

Once more we must admit that the *Canticle* yields its complete meaning only in the light of the great spiritual experience in which it originated, namely, the interior enlightenment in which Francis, amid so much suffering, was assured of his election and entry into the kingdom of the Father. Inversely, the *Canticle* also gives the interior event its full dimensions. The man who here sings of his joy at being saved is the man in whom all creatures have been taken up and transfigured by the Lord's Spirit, and have been integrated into man's ultimate destiny. We can see now how deeply meaningful was the image of "an immense and previous treasure" that the heavenly voice used in calling Francis to heavenly joy: "The whole mass of the earth changed into pure gold, pebbles into precious stones, and the water of the river into perfume."[28] The *Canticle* is the son of this mysterious transformation within Francis' soul.

Chapter 8

Brother Fire

All praise be yours, my Lord, through Brother Fire,
Through whom you brighten up the night.
How beautiful he is, how gay! Full of power and strength.

Every poet holds one or other material substance especially dear. He spontaneously embodies his dreams in it, and it characterizes his particular kind of imagination. The *Canticle of Brother Sun,* it has been noted, shows a very clear preference for images of light. These predominate. First comes the radiant image of "Brother Sun"; this is immediately followed by the images of "Sister Moon and Stars," which are also images of light, "bright and precious and fair." Then, in "Sister Water" Francis finds again the "precious" brilliance of the stars. Now comes "Brother Fire": the beautiful gay, unconquerable Brother Fire who lights up the darkness. The adjective "beautiful" (or "fair") occurs three times in the *Canticle,* and in each instance it is applied to a luminous element. It seems clear that for Francis the supremely beautiful matter, the choice matter of his dreams, is matter that radiates a splendor: light and fire.

It is certain that Francis loved fire. He loved it with a special love among all those lower creatures that lack the life of the senses. The author of the *Mirror of Perfection* tells us that "among all lesser created things Francis had an especial love for fire, because of its beauty and usefulness."[1] This statement echoes Francis' own words as recorded by Celano: "My brother fire, that surpasses all other things in beauty, the Most High created you strong, beautiful, and useful. Be kind to me in this hour, be courteous. For I have loved you in the past in the Lord."[2]

These words were uttered just as Francis was about to have his temples cauterized with a red-hot iron (and without any anesthetic), and their tone is unmistakable: they express what must beyond any doubt have been an old and deep friendship between Francis and Brother Fire. Chesterton writes:

> Not to many poets has it been given to remember their own poetry at such a moment, still less to live one of their own poems. Even William Blake would have been disconcerted if, while he was re-reading the noble lines, "Tiger, tiger, burning bright," a real large live Bengal tiger had put his head in at the window of the cottage in Felpham, evidently with every intention of biting his head off. He might have wavered before politely saluting it.[3]

But Francis did not hesitate for a moment to greet his brother the fire. He asks only, in the name of the "great Lord" who made the fire and of the friendship he has always cherished toward the fire, that the latter would temper its heat "so that I may bear it when you burn me gently."[4]

This is a lover's language, and Francis loved the fire. He liked to draw close to it. We see him sitting beside it and meditating in its presence. On one occasion, he even let the fire consume his clothing.

> Once while he was sitting close to the fire, his linen underclothes caught fire near the knee without his notice; and although he felt the heat, he was unwilling to put out the flames. Seeing his clothes alight, his companion ran to put out the flame, but blessed Francis would not allow it, saying, "Dearest brother, do not hurt Brother Fire!" So his companion ran to the friar who was Guardian and brought him to blessed Francis, and against his wishes the Guardian beat out the flame.[5]

Francis' behavior with regard to fire is surprising and reveals an extraordinary love for it, based on the powerful attraction and unqualified respect one experiences in the presence of something sacred. "So dearly did he love fire that, however pressing the need, he would never put out a flame, whether a lamp or a candle."[6] And Celano repeats the same thing: "He spared lights, lamps, and candles."[7]

How are we to explain such a love of fire? The fact, though well known, is mysterious, and we must try to shed some light on it. Many have hastened, of course, to find mystical and theological reasons for the special affection Francis had for fire. Celano was one of the first to do so, telling us that Francis saw in all flames "a symbol of the Eternal Light."[8]

Symbolism such as this, with its Scriptural basis, is certainly not to be excluded. But, in this developed form, symbolism belongs to the sphere of clear and reflex awareness, whereas there is something about Francis' love for fire that eludes clear and reflex awareness. We must therefore try to get inside Francis' vision of things, into his reveries concerning fire and his sense of wonder as he gazed upon the living flame with its shifting colors. Our starting point must be the image he offers us of fire in the *Canticle*. As in our reflections on the preceding images, we must pay close attention to values attributed to the element.

We note immediately that Francis does not offer mystical reasons for his praise of fire. The first thing he says of it, the first adjective he uses, is "beautiful." His admiration has a very simple basis: he finds fire beautiful! As he says elsewhere, fire is for him an incomparably splendid thing; he admires the splendor and abandons himself to the joy it gives him: "Brother Fire, beautiful and gay." But now admiration yields to enchantment and dreams. Fire ceases to be something anonymous; it becomes a living presence that radiates joy, a being that overflows with life and energy, "full of power and strength." Energy, drive, invincible power, along with joy and spirit: these are what Francis contemplates in this companion who brightens up the night. Moreover, in this essentially dynamic image, Francis sees the presence of a brother. He experiences the fire as brotherly, feels himself closely linked to it as though by ties of blood, and so he calls it "Brother Fire."

This image of fire is an image produced by imagination and dreams. Yet we must not stop here. It is an image with the power to move Francis to praise. There is something about it that expands his soul and lifts it to the Most High. "All praise be yours, my Lord, through [and for] Brother Fire." In the radiance of fire and in its unquenchable energy Francis contemplates "the great Lord who made you": "My brother fire, that surpasses all other things in beauty, the Most High made you strong, beautiful, and useful."[9] The fire's splendor and overflowing energy are like a window opening on the splendor and blazing life of God. In this sense it is accurate to say, with Celano, that he saw in every flame "a symbol of the Eternal Light."

We must immediately add, however, that he saw this not by an intellectual analogy or by association with Scripture, but in a direct poetic and affective experience of fire itself. His poetic and affective experience of fire is thus also a religious experience, that is, an opening out to the sacred. We must keep in mind that Francis communed with God through things themselves because of the way in which he saw and experienced and imagined them. In no one else perhaps has the material universe been such an integral part of a human being's spiritual adventure: "We who were with him have seen him take inward and outward delight in almost every creature, and when he handled or looked at them his spirit seemed to be in heaven rather than on earth."[10]

All this amounts to saying that the image of Brother Fire is not only mystical and poetic, but sacral and cryptic as well. The very depth of the emotion linked with it puts Francis in contact with the sacred. Here we have the explanation for Francis' unconditional respect for fire, a respect so great that he would not permit himself to extinguish any fire.

At the heart of Francis' universe stands this great radiant fraternal image of fire, and the image is at once mystical, poetic, and cryptic. It is assuredly a basic image. But what is its meaning? The image, so admired and celebrated, so laden with interior values, certainly relates to more than the natural phenomenon of fire; it speaks of something beyond. If Francis feels such a close and deep friendship with fire, and if he likes to represent it to himself as an invincible brotherly power that expands his soul and lifts it up to the Most High, must the reason not be that the image of fire reflects some profound element in his own life? Must fire not somehow be an image of his own interior destiny? Must it not relate Francis, at the unconscious level, to certain hidden forces and give symbolic form to a discourse being carried on in the psychic depths? In brief, must not the image of Brother Fire—"through whom you brighten up the night. How beautiful he is, how gay? Full of power and strength"—be a symbol for an experience of power and light that unfolds in the night of the soul?

The image of fire has always awakened profound resonances in man. Men have never regarded fire solely as an external reality, but have seen it as something that touches them interiorly. Fire is innate in man's psyche: in the ardor of desire, to become attached, to love and to hate; he feels this force as consoling but also as consuming; in short; he experiences it as a fire. Fire is thus one of the great symbols of the libido. It symbolizes the ardent energies of life in all their forms, from the noblest spiritual action to the wildest and most archaic passion.

The image of fire, then, touches us very deeply. Love of fire, reveries before a fire, fraternal communion with fire: all these bring us, unconsciously, to the center of ourselves, or, more accurately, to the beginning of ourselves, to the original source of our life. "In the beginning there were not coldness and darkness: there was the *Fire*."[11] The poetry of fire and the dreams about fire are always an attempt to re-experience "primitiveness," our own "primitiveness."[12] They immerse us in our own archaism—that of our infancy. To commune with fire by the power of imagination is to return to the first "hearth," to the warmth of the maternal womb and the primal affectivity; it is to relive, in the unconscious, the primal impressions of intimacy, union, and well-being.

But the dream of fire can also reach even greater depths; it can enter into a past that lies beyond the experience of the infant and the individual unconscious. The image of fire draws us into a far more distant past, into mankind's archaism, that of the collective unconscious. In such moments, "the dreamer lives in a past which is no longer solely his own, a past when the primal fires of the world were lit."[13] The image of fire now takes on a superhuman, mythical dimension, makes us dream the destiny of the world itself. This primordial fire "illumines all the transcendences."[14]

The appearance of so profound an image as this is always a great moment in a soul's life; at such moments, life itself becomes incandescent. "Fire": that simple word stands at the beginning of Pascal's *Memorial,* for during the night when he wrote it he had a personal experience of the biblical image of fire, the fire of the great theophanies. "The voice of the Lord strikes fiery flames."[15] "Fire goes before him."[16] "Is not my word like fire?"[17] God speaks to Moses from out of a burning bush. At Elijah's prayer a fire from heaven descends and consumes the victims on the altar. In prophetic visions, fire surrounds God's throne; Ezekiel's cherubim and Daniel's angels are fiery beings.

In the Gospel, Jesus himself says: "I have come to light a fire on the earth. How I wish the blaze were ignited!"[18] And John thus describes the Son of Man as seen in apocalyptic vision: "His eyes blazed like fire. His feet gleamed like polished brass refined in a furnace. . . .and his face shone like the sun at its brightest."[19]

The image of the cryptic fire is not restricted to the biblical tradition, but is found in most religions, often in association with the hierophanic image of the sun. Jung writes: "The visible father of the world is the sun, the heavenly fire, for which reason father, God, sun, and fire are mythologically synonymous."[20] And in one of his poems Jean-Claude Renard has these lines: "Father pure through tree and fire, / O source of the sun, mysterious Father."[21]

How does the image of fire become thus magnified? What gives it superhuman mythical dimension, it power to fascinate and move so deeply? "Whence does matter receive its power to rise into the category of the divine?" Paul Claudel asks as he gazes at a flame.[22] Mere observation of the empirical phenomenon is not enough to explain all this. When an image acquires this kind of cosmic value, we can unhesitatingly assert that it rises from an interior center of energy, a center that belongs to the universal psyche. But how can one describe this psychic center?

If we would know the answer, we need only listen to the voice of the god who speaks in the fire. This god is essentially a living god; he is life itself, life as a creative force. "Since the time of Heraclitus," Jung notes, "life has been conceived as a *pûr aei zôn*—a living, everlasting fire."[23] More accurately, the god who speaks in the fire is a life-giving force that seeks union, communication, and self-propagation, as does a flame. "The arrow of fire, never flagging, crosses the vast universe and leaves nothing at rest" (Heraclitus). This living fire, "this power that seeks to fuse all things into oneness," was named Eros by the ancient Greeks; it is the power to love, that great active energy of the soul.

The man who by imagination communes in an intense and cosmic way with fire is dealing with eros, the primordial affective power of the soul. The depths of his own being are crossed by the "arrow of fire that pierces every inch of the vast universe and leaves nothing at rest." Within him dwells the life-giving force that he cannot consciously grasp or dispose of as he wishes, and yet is embodied in his deepest desire: the desire to live in a total communion with all reality.

The force that speaks in the illusive image of an elemental, living fire is both fascinating and terrifying. The reason for its dual nature is that what it promises and foretells is a plenitude of life that can lift a man out of his narrow individuality and limited ego by eliciting from him a creative assent to the immensity of reality, but this possibility is initially clothed in the elemental, archaic forms of passionate desire. The life-giving force which eros contains is threatened by the blind power of chaotic passion. This is why life-giving fire is also imagined as a devouring fire, for it can destroy as well as give life. The archetypal image of fire is thus ambivalent.

After all, what does man really know about "this force that lays hold of the entire universe in its winding coils"?[24] It is "fire, flame, and serpent" all at once. The voice of the living God is not the only thing that makes fiery flames leap up. Leviathan[25] and the dragon and horses of the Apocalypse[26] spit fire. And the monstrous, destructive fire into which anyone is thrown whose name is not written in the book of the living[27] is also an interior fire: "Their worm shall not die, nor their fire be extinguished."[28]

This great mythical, ambivalent image of fire is thus connected with man's inner destiny; it is an image of that destiny. Man does not have the power to extinguish the elemental, living fire, but it is up to him whether the fire is to burn him or enlighten him, destroy him or give him life. He decides whether it is to be a conflagration or a light, hell or heaven. This does not mean he can claim to master this fire and dispose of it at his whim; the creative fire from heaven always consumes those who wish to steal it and make it their own. But man can give his consent to the mysterious inner force that speaks to him in the mythic image of fire. He can do this in a humble, fraternal way, in a spirit of poverty.

The man who consents to this force, while practicing a profound detachment from self and renouncing any attempt to dispose of the fire as he himself decides, accepts within him the creative energies of eros. Eros here does not serve egoistic pleasure and self-satisfaction; it is the mystery with which the earth is filled, a religious mystery that draws all life out of its own narrow confines toward other beings. A man can then surrender with wonderment to his dream of fire and celebrate in the fire's power and splendor both the presence of a brother and the image of the Transcendent One.

This kind of fraternal, religious celebration of fire undoubtedly brings man back to his most remote and hidden origins, indeed to the prehistory of mankind, putting him in contact with the primal energies of life. Yet this re-immersion of man in his archaism, when accomplished in a spirit of humility and self-detachment, enables him to relate himself to these great vital psychic energies, especially eros, in their purity, and not in their infantile forms, in the blind forms of chaotic passionate desire. When these energies are thus freed from their limitations, they can operate in the light of the spirit, and man can receive them as forces that create communion, forces that enable him to give a creative assent to the whole of reality. Then, the fire of which a man sings no longer burns and destroys, for it has been wholly changed into an irresistible energy of light and joy. The fire that has thus become man's brother symbolizes the reconciliation of life and spirit, the meeting of *eros* and *agape.*

In the light of these very broad considerations on the symbolism of fire, we can grasp a bit more clearly the meaning of the image of Brother Fire that stands like a beacon at the center of Francis' universe. Must we not say that Francis' praise of fire is symbolic language for "a unique confluence of Eros and Agape"?[29]

All the early writings on Francis of Assisi leave us with the clear and inescapable impression of overflowing vitality. Here was a man endowed with an extraordinary capacity for love. As Peter Lippert writes:

> If we wish to offer even a superficial assessment of Francis' life, we must say that it strikes us from the very beginning as a life devoted to loving. Here, of course, "love" must be given its highest and most sacred, its purest and most primal, in short its most divine meaning. His life is one long loving, or rather a prodigious capacity for loving, a charistmatic, even miraculous capacity. It is fervent, heartfelt, spontaneous communion with every creature and with him who brought every creature into being. . . .In this utterly immense soul, in this man who advanced to meet every creature with outstretched arms, we find a truly maternal devotion to all things, a genius for loving. . . .For him, to love meant to give himself overflowingly, to give without calculating, to liberate, fecundate, and conquer.[30]

We must not think of this "charismatic, even miraculous capacity" for loving as emanating from a purely supernatural source that is simply external to Francis' own deeper nature. This life of simple, strong love is too straightforward and too rich not to have sprung from the deeply hidden psychic regions of Francis' being. His love is not something he puts on like a garment; the very freedom and energy that mark it show it to be the expression of great primordial affective powers. His is a love that must be rooted in the vital psychic regions that lie deeper than thinking and willing; it must spring from an inner dynamism and make its way out by an inner necessity.

St. Bonaventure was not mistaken when he wrote that "his [Francis'] tender love made him the brother of all creatures."[31] Even in his madcap younger days, Francis showed an exceptional capacity for communion with other beings.

> His good life, his gentleness and patience, his almost superhuman readiness to oblige, together with his generosity which exceeded his means, and his pleasant manner were so many indications which marked him out as a young man. They seemed to be almost a foretaste of things to come, indicating that the abundance of God's blessings would be heaped upon him more plentifully than ever in the future.[32]

In those days Francis responded with his whole being to songs of love; he listened with enthusiasm to the adventures of the knights and the heroes of the courtly love stories. And he dreamed of similar adventures with himself as the hero. So rich a nature as his could not long remain locked into a narrow individual life or the confines of petty middle-class passion; it was made for adventures on a world scale. The great dreams Francis used to have as he slept are highly significant in this regard.

One night, he saw his father's house transformed into a splendid palace and filled with weapons and a beautiful bride; a voice called him by name and enticed him with the promise of all these things.[33] Imagine, his father's shop where he sold cloth, transformed into a noble court that was a meeting-place of military glory, beauty, and love! And all for Francis! What an omen! He accepted the dream as a call, but what the dream really meant was still hidden in the forms of primordial desire and passion. Young Francis thirsted for knightly glory and therefore at first he saw in the dream only a reflection of his desire and the prediction of a brilliant future. He therefore set out on a military adventure, which, in the chivalric view of the time, was also a search for love and a conquest of woman.

Celano comments: "A carnal spirit prompted him to make a carnal interpretation of the dream he had had, while a far more glorious interpretation lay hidden in the treasurer of God's wisdom."[34] And St. Bonaventure: "He had no experience of interpreting God's secret revelations and he could not penetrate beyond the appearance of what he saw to the truth which he could not see."[35] But soon the voice that had drawn him the first time spoke to him in another dream: "Go back to the place of your birth for through me your vision will have a spiritual fulfillment."[36] So Francis returned to Assisi and "began to be changed into a perfect man and to become other than his former self."[37]

"Go back to the place of your birth." It is significant that Francis' spiritual conversion begins with this mysterious command to return home. For, what is asked of him is more than an outward return to his native city. The "return" has a deeper meaning: Francis is being urged to go back to his inner origins, to the primordial affective powers of the soul and the elemental images in which these powers speak to him. He must re-immerse himself in his own archaism and in that of his cultural milieu; he is being sent on a journey to those underground springs from which flow the images and symbols that constitute what might be called the waking dream of a historical group. He is being referred to the images and symbols that nourished his soul in the epics and love-songs. In them he had hitherto seen only reflections of his own desires. Now he is being urged to question and decipher them, to look beyond the archaic shapes of desire, and hear in them the voice of Being, calls to authentic spiritual growth.

The remarkable thing about Francis is that his spiritual conversion does not require a break from the images and themes that have inspired him until now, but rather a reinterpretation of these same images and themes and thus a continuation, in a new form, of their dynamic power over him. The new supernatural inspiration of his life purifies and renews these great images, but in turn it receives from them an astonishing vitality, youthfulness, and creative power.

Thanks to these images, then, Spirit and life, *eros* and *agape,* can meet in a fruitful way. Father Damien Vorreux rightly observes:

> The *Chanson des Chêtifs,* the *Qûete du saint Graal,* and *Tristan et Iseut* are more than a simple background or poetic accompaniment to the life of St. Francis, for these compositions fostered in the thirteenth century an enthusiastic vision of which the Poverello was a worthy representative. In his view, each of his communities was to be a "court of love," where the highest kind of charity would be taught and practiced, a "round table" where valiant knights would plan their future conquests for the honor of God and the love of his people. [38]

And Scheler writes:

> The self-styled "troubador of God," who kept to the end of his life the habit of humming his beloved French songs to himself, was never to lose hold of this strand of his past life; it can be seen, even in the rigorous and heroic asceticism of his later career, in the almost indescribable tenderness of his relations with St. Clara. And yet, with incomparable spiritual artistry, as unself-conscious as it was undersigned, he succeeded, for all his early absorption in the historic emotional attitude of the Provençial cult, in so divesting it of all substance, all worldly or amorous import, that virtually nothing but its serene and ethereal rhythm was left behind and

> Francis was able to link it fruitfully with "the spiritual love of God, of Christ and of persons."[39]

In Francis, eros is spiritualized and christianized; it turns into a marvelous capacity for love that embraces the whole of nature and utters a creative assent to all of reality.

It is impossible, in dealing with any man's life, to separate the great mystical images that enchant him, from the destiny of his primordial affective powers. Thus we are brought back to the vital image of fire that stands like a beacon in the heart of Francis' universe. How can we help but connect the saint's deeper affective experience with the extraordinary love he had for fire, and with the engaging, idealized image he had of this element?

The fire Francis imagined and loved was a fire from which he no longer had anything to fear, a fire whose terrible power to destroy had been transformed into an unquenchable energy of light. This fire was no longer a cause for fear or anxiety. It was "Brother Fire, through whom you brighten up the night. How beautiful he is, how gay! Full of power and strength." Such a fire could only symbolize a life of immense energy, but a life purified and spiritualized and itself transformed into light. "If you are to stay seated before the fire," writes novelist Ernst Wiechert, "you must first chase the demons from your heart; otherwise they will snap their fingers at you in every leaping flame."[40] Francis could calmly let the fire consume his garments; he himself had nothing to fear from it. And when the doctor decided to cauterize his temples as a cure for his blindness, he "offered himself joyfully and eagerly to the iron"; when it was over, his only comment was: "I did not feel either the heat of the fire or any pain in my flesh."[41]

The secret rapport in Francis' life between "Brother Fire" and deeper affective powers is picturesquely shown in two stories in the *Fioretti.* We may, of course, be doubtful about the historical value of the stories, but in any event they have profound symbolic value as expressions of a psychic and spiritual truth. In that sense, they are certainly true. The first of the stories concerns an incident that occurred on Francis' travels in the East when he went to meet Sultan Malik al-Kamil. Here is how the author of the *Fioretti* tells it:

> With one companion he [Francis] chose a certain district, and he went into an inn where he had to rest overnight. And there he found a certain woman who was very beautiful in face and body but very foul in mind and soul. That cursed woman solicited St. Francis.
>
> St. Francis answered her: "If you wish me to do what you want, you must also do what I want."
>
> "I agree," she said. "So let's go and prepare a bed." And she led him toward a room.
>
> But St. Francis said to her: "Come with me and I will show you a very beautiful bed." And he led her to a very large fire that was burning in the house at that time. And in fervor of spirit he stripped himself naked and threw himself down on the fire in the fireplace as on a bed. And he called to her, saying: "Undress and come quickly and enjoy this splendid, flowery, and wonderful bed, because you must be here if you wish to obey me!" And he remained there for a long time with a joyful face, resting on the fireplace as though on flowers, but the fire did not burn or singe him.
>
> On seeing such a miracle that woman was terrified and felt remorese in her heart. And she not only repented her sin and evil intention but was also perfectly converted to the faith of Christ. and through the merits of the holy Father she became so holy in grace that she won many souls for the Lord in that region.[42]

The story is evidently quite marvelous though not so credible from the historian's viewpoint. The truth it expresses is, however, of different order, for it concerns the innermost life of the spirit, giving symbolic form to an interior experience. From this viewpoint, the most remarkable thing about the story is Francis' attitude to the woman who urges him to sin and who embodies desire in an almost animal form, eros in its savage state. He does not reject her; he does not withdraw in fear; he does not condemn her. Instead, he takes her as she is, with her desire. Since she wants to be united to him, he invites her to join him where he lives, where his real existence is lived out, that is, in his vital depths that are here symbolized by a great, beautiful, alluring fire in which he can throw himself naked without being burned. This fire to which Francis offers himself with complete self-abandonment and which does not burn him is an image of a profound affective life in which the ardor of passion has fused with the fervor of the spirit. Francis no longer has anything to fear from the dark forces of desire; he can open himself to everything. This "very large fire" symbolizes the reconciliation of *eros* and *agape* in Francis' soul.

The second incident takes place in the friary of St. Mary of the Angels, near Assisi. Francis has decided to yield to St. Clare, now cloistered at San Damiano, and grant her wish to take a meal with him and his brothers at St. Mary of the Angels.

> St. Francis had the table prepared on the bare ground, as was his custom. And when it was time to eat, St. Francis and St. Clare sat down together, and one of his companions with St. Clare's companion, and all his other companions were grouped around that humble table. But at the first course St. Francis began to speak about God in such holy and profound and divine and marvelous way that he himself and St. Clare and her companion and all the others who were at that poor little table were rapt in God by the overabundance of divine grace that decended upon them.
>
> And while they were sitting there, in a rapture, with their eyes and hands raised to heaven, it seemed to the men of Assisi and Bettona and the entire district that the Church of St. Mary of the Angels and the whole Place and the forest which was at that time around the place were all aflame and that an immense fire was burning over all of them. Consequently the men of Assisi ran down there in great haste to save the Place and put out the fire, as they firmly believed that everything was burning up.
>
> But when they reached the Place, they saw that nothing was on fire. Entering the Place, they found St. Francis with St. Clare and all the companions sitting around that very humble table, rapt in God by contemplation and invested with power from on high.

> Then they knew for sure that it had been a heavenly and not a material fire that God had miraculously shown them to symbolize the fire of divine love which was burning in the souls of those holy friars and nuns.[43]

Once again, the historical value of the story is doubtful; the first biographers do not record such an incident. But who can doubt the psychological and spiritual value of the tale? Certainly it would be impossible to better express the power and exquisite beauty of the friendship between Francis and Clare, for the story is told in a symbolic language that is far more eloquent than any abstract analysis.

The great symbol which the writer spontaneously uses is fire: an immense fire, but one that does not burn.[44] We are in the presence once again of the great Franciscan image of fire, with all its wealth of meaning. The story is also parallel in certain respects with the earlier story we reported. In both, the main theme is Francis' relation to women. In Clare's case, however, the "very great desire" she had of meeting Francis and taking a meal with him is a desire that has been purified. She is at one with him at the highest level of his calling, for she has followed him in a profound conversion, in humility and self-detachment, and in his assent to reality in its entirety and to the following of Christ. In other terms, Clare and Francis meet in that fire that symbolizes the love, both divine and deeply human, which unites them.

After having attempted to bring out the inner meaning of the image of Brother Fire in Francis' life, we turn now to the place of the image in the overall movement of the *Canticle.* As we saw earlier, this movement is essentially that of the soul's ardent quest of the Most High, a quest which begins with openness to and communion with creatures. The soul that has seen and acknowledged the Most High to be inaccessible turns with great humility to creatures, takes its place among them, and, united with them as brothers and sisters, seeks to praise God along with them. At the same time and at a deeper level, creatures and their archetypal images enable the soul, in its quest of the sacred, to return to and accept itself, its inner depths, and its obscure roots in the unconscious. Why should it do so? Because the Most High awaits the soul where its roots are.

In this movement of descent from heaven to earth, each creature to which appeal is made can be regarded as a great symbol that helps the soul relate to its own archism and that of mankind. The succession of symbols represents an increasingly complete self-opening of the soul to its own totality, and this means to the great primordial affective powers that link it, in the unconscious, to the very well-springs of life and being and to the mystery the latter embody. At the same time, the succession of images also represents an ascent to the light that shines in these hidden powers. By means of symbols the obscure affective forces achieve expression in language and join in the praise of God. They raise the soul toward its ultimate goal, the Most High, but as a soul now reconciled to itself and to the immensity of being.

The reconciliation is expressed in the *Canticle* beginning with the very first image, that of Brother Sun who symbolizes union and plenitude. In this great fraternal image of the sun, all the vital, psychic, and spiritual energies of the soul shine forth, transfigured and redeemed. Then come the humbler cosmic images; Sister Moon and Stars, Brother Wind, Sister Water. Each of them enables us to grasp a different aspect of reconciliation. They also reveal the secret of reconciliation: an increasingly radical detachment from self.

The image of Brother Fire must be located within this whole. By reason of its brilliance and energy, Brother Fire resembles Brother Sun. Like the latter, Brother Fire is an image of the father and of God, an image of life-giving and creative power. It is really the same basic psychic energy that is symbolized by Brother Fire and Brother Sun. There is this difference however: Brother Fire is expressly linked to night; the image of fire and the image of night go together: "through whom you brighten up the night."

This last point is an important one. The sun is celebrated as the light that shines in the day, the fire as the light that shines in the night. Like Brother Sun, Brother Fire expresses the integration of the soul, but it shows this to us from what we might call a nocturnal angle of vision. We should bear in mind that the man who, in the evening of his life, sings of light in the *Canticle,* is a man who spent part of his life in the dark recesses of caves, where he begged God, amid the soul's inner night, that he might be "cleaned and enlightened interiorly and fired with the ardour of the Holy Spirit."[45] Peter Lippert rightly observes:

> Francis lived a life of all-embracing love, but we should not think of that life as have been one long enthusiastic song of praise or the dreamlike ecstasy of a man who never stopped smiling. No: if his life was any one thing, it was a life of bitter suffering. His love spread limitless light and sweetness to all around him, but that love rose out of the soul's dark and sober depths. It sprang from a mind that was austere, a mind that trembled as it thought on God, and the world, sin and judgment, time and eternity.[46]

In his *First Life,* Celano relates an incident which reveals its full significance only in our present context and which sheds special light on the *Canticle.* The incident occurred in the early days of the Franciscan brotherhood. One night Francis was absent and the little community was left on its own.

> And behold, about midnight, when some of the brothers were resting and some were praying in silence with great devotion, a most splendid fiery chariot entered through the door of the house and turned around two or three times here and there inside the house; a huge globe of light rested above it, much like the sun, and it lit up the night. The watchers were dazed, and those who had been asleep were frightened; and they felt no less a lighting up of the heart than a lighting up of the body. Gathering together, they began to ask one another what it was; but by the strength and grace of that great light each one's conscience was revealed to

the others. Finally they understood and knew that it was the soul of their holy father that was shining with such great brilliance.[47]

This vision and its interpretation are of great psychological interest. Here we have two symbols of the *Canticle,* fire and sun, closely associated in "a passage of the night." The fiery chariot that crosses the night is topped by a sun. The image of the fiery chariot or solar chariot is very ancient, being part of mankind's basic mythology. In the course of history we find it reappearing, in an almost identical form, in quite different cultural contexts. Elijah, for example, was taken to heaven in a fiery chariot; so was Mithras. Ezekiel saw the glory of the Lord departing in a chariot ringed with fire. And in his *Metamorphoses* Ovid tells how young Phaëthon asked his father for permission to drive his chariot, the chariot of the sun, and how the inexperience charioteer was not strong enough to keep the horses from running wild and setting fire to the universe.[48]

The fiery chariot is an archetypal image whose full significance and meaning are supraindividual. The image of the fiery chariot or the solar chariot originates in the collective unconscious and contains a universal message. The appearance of such an image in the first fraternal community, of which Francis is the leader and inspiration, undoubtedly relates to the basic course of the community, its basic vocation in our world; its meaning is spiritual and prophetic.

Speaking in general terms, we can say that the image of the fiery chariot as the horse-drawn bearer of the sun symbolizes a whole in which animal nature with its dark, wild forces, is associated with the luminous and divine element, that is, the soul and its loftiest aspirations, and thereby transfigured and illumined. The image is a symbol of the integration of the vital and the spiritual, of our obscure beginnings and our call from God. It is understandable, that the fiery chariot should often be seen as ascending to heaven, as the hero, himself transformed into a sun, is carried aloft in the fiery chariot.

There are some details in the brothers' vision that deserve special attention. It is through the little door that the great splendid chariot enters the house: *per ostiolum domus currus igneus splendidissimus intrans.*[49] The sun it carries emits its rays at the very heart of night: *fere media noctis hora.* Its light does not remain external to those who perceive it but is felt deep within: *non minus cordis senserunt quam corporis claritatem.* And,when the vision had disappeared, this interior light remained, enabling each to read the consciences of the others: *ex vi et gratia tantae lucis, unius alteri erat conscientia manifesta.* Thus, far from crushing the brothers, the irruption of superhuman power that had first frightened them brought them a heightened awareness. It made each of them transparent to the others, so that all achieved communion with one another in one light.

Now we can see the full meaning of the vision. It symbolizes a total integration and reconciliation that can only be effected in a passage through the night and specifically by a passage through the little door. This midnight sun is surely basically the same as the divine "sun" of which St. Teresa speaks in her *Interior Castle:* a sun that remains "in the interior of the soul" but manifests itself in all its splendor only at the end of the journey when its "great light. . .is transmitted to the faculties in the interior part of the soul."[50]

The most instructive part of Celano's account is its conclusion. "Finally they understood and knew that it was the soul of their holy father that was shining with such great brilliance: *Intellexerunt denique ac noverunt animam sancti patris exstitisse fulgore tam maximo radiantem.*" In this recognition we see the outcome of the vision itself. Students of mythology have noted that the myth of the sun developed quite naturally into a myth of the "well-beloved" solar hero as the understanding of the myth became more profound.[51]

We can also note in the conclusion of the story the admirable sureness with which the brothers interpreted the vision, seeing in the passage of the solar chariot an image of the soul's pilgrimage. It seems clear that the world of symbols and their deeper meanings was open to these men. In fact, when we read the Franciscan sources generally, we are surprised at the number of symbolic dreams and visions that accompanied the growth of the early brotherhood, and at the decisive role these played in their spiritual development. Moreover, if the brothers unhesitatingly recognize the soul of their Father in the vision of the fiery chariot that bore the sun, the reason is probably that they themselves, in their following of Francis, were making the same "pilgrimage" and undergoing the same transformation of soul. They were initiates and "pilgrims," as Francis liked to tell them. What they saw in this vision of light in the depths of darkness they were also experiencing intensely in their own interior depths.

The great integration and reconciliation had begun in them; they now saw it to be fully accomplished in their leader and father. Consequently, Francis took on for them the appearance of a solar hero. To all of them he was a sensible symbol of what they too were to experience; he was a prophecy of their future. St. Bonaventure comments on this incident:

> They were sure God had shown him [Francis] to them in this glorious chariot of fire, radiant with the splendor of heaven and inflamed with burning ardor, so that they might follow him as loyal disciples. Like a second Elias, God had made him a "chariot and charioteer" (cf. 4 Kgs 2, 12) for all spiritual people.[52]

The disciples help us to a better understanding of their master. In the difficult art of awakening and guiding souls Francis was not simply a past master, but an artist in the fullest sense of the word. He was a poet of the soul as well as of nature. In fact the two are inseparable. His dialogue with the visible was also a dialogue with the invisible, and his esthetic contemplation of things was a journey of the soul into its own sacrality and symbolized an interior transformation. St. Bonaventure sums up: "In everything beautiful, he saw him who is beauty itself, and he followed his Beloved everywhere by his likeness imprinted on creation; of all creation he made a ladder by which he might mount up and embrace Him who is all-desirable."[53]

His contemplation of the world was thus also a way of educating his own desires, and it began precisely with those great images of human desire which things become when they are dreamt of with a certain depth. This is a point we must constantly bear in mind in interpreting the *Canticle.* Readers have too often seen in the *Canticle* only an esthetic vision of things. They have failed to realize that the vision was in turn a language of the soul, a "poetics" of the spirit and its transformations, and that it had to be interpreted as such. The *Canticle* is the unconscious, symbolic expression of an interior journey, the journey Francis was making all his life long and in which an affective union with the humblest created things was joined with a spiritual ascent to the heights.

Chapter 9

Sister Earth, Our Mother

All praise be yours, my Lord, through Sister Earth, our mother,
Who feeds us in her sovereignty and produces
Various fruits with colored flowers and herbs.

Francis began his praise in the heights of heaven and gradually descended to earth. Now the Canticle changes to a song of earth.

The first thing that strikes us in this stanza is the title given to the latter: *Sora nostra matre Terra.* The expression "the earth, our mother" is certainly very old. M. Eliade, in his *Patterns in Comparative Religion,* notes that while the very earliest religious experiences of men "earth" still meant simply the entire cosmic environment (soil, rocks, trees, waters, shadows, etc.) as a repository of diffuse sacred forces, "one of the first theophanies of the earth as such, and particularly of the earth as soil, was its 'motherhood,' its inexhaustible power of fruitfulness. Before becoming a mother goddess, or divinity of fertility, the earth presented itself to men as a Mother, *Tellus Mater*."[1]

Francis makes his own this archaic image of the Mother Earth and celebrates the earth accordingly: She "feeds us" as a mother does her child, and her fertility is evidenced in "various fruits." But Francis adds a significant detail: in addition to fruits there are "colored flowers and herbs."[2] The earth is not satisfied simply to feed her children, but like a truly concerned mother, surrounds with beauty all who belong to her. The grass and flowers are the earth's adornment; they create a realm of gracious beauty and are a joy to eye and soul; they are the mother's smile stretching across the cosmos.

The point that is new and surprising in Francis' naming of the earth is the designation "Sister" which he combines with that of mother: "Sister Earth, our mother." To his eyes the face of Mother Earth is also the face of a sister, and it is as a sister that he sings of her, conferring new youth upon her thereby. At a deeper level, he establishes a new relation between himself and the earth. The name "sister," when given to the earth, neither destroys nor weakens her motherhood, but it does set limits upon it. The name "sister" says that though the earth is our mother on whom we depend for our lives, she is not the absolute and ultimate source of being and life. Rather, she is herself a creature as are all the other things that make up the cosmos.[3]

The earth is part of the great family of creatures. She and we alike depend, when all is said and done, on the same transcendent source: the Father who has created all things. She is our sister. This understanding engenders a new affective attitude to Mother Earth, since the sense of dependence and piety we feel toward her as Mother is colored by affection for her as a Sister. The veneration and gratitude Francis has for the maternal earth is directed through her to a higher source: "All praise be yours, my Lord, through Sister Earth, our mother."

"Through" is the appropriate word here, for though the earth is put in the ranks of creatures, she does not on that account lose her mysterious quality for Francis. Her maternity manifests to him a higher source of life and beauty. But it is important for us to understand that this capacity for manifestation or revelation is bound up, in Francis' case, with a deep affective communion with the cosmic reality. We would be taking a very superficial and extrinsicist view of things were we to approach Francis' image of "Sister Earth, our mother" from a purely esthetic point of view or even to regard it as merely a pretext for praise. No, Francis truly communes with the earth and with God through the earth. His celebration of the earth in the *Canticle* echoes this profound inner experience.

To convince ourselves of this we need only examine the part the earth played in Francis' religious life and loftiest spiritual experiences, and to consider his close relationship with the earth. We will thereby gain a concrete understanding of his communion with the earth and will be able to perceive the full meaning of the hierophanic image of "Sister Earth, our mother."

Francis' mystical experience is closely linked to the earth. We shall turn our attention here to three types of very meaningful facts: Francis' repeated and prolonged stays in caves, his dream of the tree, and the desire of the dying Francis to be laid naked on the bare ground *(humi positio).*

1. Sojourning in Caves

As we reflect on a life that of Francis, especially in its relation to nature, we will do well to recall these words of Gaston Bachelard:

> The imaginative powers of the human spirit develop along two quite different lines. Some are stimulated by novelty and take delight in the picturesque, in variety, in the unexpected. The images awakened are always images of spring, and the imagination produces flowers, already full-grown, in nature distant from us. The other imaginative powers delve downward to the depths of being, seeking there both the primordial and the eternal. They rise above seasons and history. In nature, within us and outside us, they sow seeds in which form is buried deep in substance, seeds in which *form is internal.*[3]

It must be admitted that the first kind of imagination has too often been brought to bear on St. Francis' life. The result has been a pretty story of the birds and the wolf or the rabbit, with the hero becoming creation's superficial prince.

Francis lived in the midst of creation with a vast soul open to its every form and every breath. That is perfectly true. But what kind of nature did he seek out and love in a special way? Let us follow him, and we shall see him climbing the foothills of the Apennines that enclosed Rieti Valley or the lofty rocks of Mt. Alverna. What drew him to these heights? Was it the sun-dazzled surface of things? By no means, for, once he attained the heights, he did not rest until he had found some deep cave or cleft where he might bury himself. "*In the clefts of the rock* he would build his nest," says Celano.[4]

It is noteworthy that this external practice of Francis gives expression to the same interior movement that may be seen in the *Canticle:* a great energetic thrust toward the heights (toward the Most High), linked to a descent into the depths and to a communion with all that is most lowly. Francis spent a good deal of his life searching on the heights for caves or caverns wherein to hide his fervent life. This repeated pattern shows an inclination of the soul: a need for immersion. It is this need that we must now explore.

The cave or cavern has always awakened profound echoes in the human soul. Since time immemorial it has been one of the privileged places to which man has linked his earthly lot. To begin with, it offers him a natural shelter against all sorts of dangers. Then it continues to attract him by its very mysteriousness. The world of the cave is an interior world that has its depths and is full of echoing shadows: a world that casts a spell through the basic images it evokes.

The cave is a maternal symbol, and to enter its depths and remain there is to return to the mother. But in this case the mother is not reducible to the stature of her human embodiment. "To abide in the cave," says Bachelard, "is to share in the earth's life, within the very womb of Mother Earth."[5] In the form of the cave or cavern we rediscover our Mother, the earth, and it is to her that the contemplative relates when he withdraws into a cave. The cave represents for the solitary more than simply a defense against the gaze of the curious or against outside distractions; it also represents inwardness and depth. It provides a secret room, but only for the kind of thought that penetrates beneath the surface.

Mother Earth is only a symbol of an inner totality, the totality of those origins and unconscious roots that sustain and nourish us in the form of basic psychic energies and structures. To enter the cave in order to abide there symbolizes an entering into relation with this subterranean, archaic world of the soul and allowing ourselves to be drawn by the mystery that is within us. In the depths of the cave some glittering priceless treasure always lies.

Entering the cave also means confronting a world that inspires fear because of its very ambivalence. In the depths of the cave there is also a monster: the dragon with whom man must do battle if he is to possess the treasure. To bury oneself in the cave is thus to accept struggle, fear, and death. Jung writes: "The cave is the equivalent of the grave."[6] And: "sunk in his own depths, he is like one buried in the earth; a dead man who has crawled back into the mother."[7]

The cave is not only a place of conflict and death, but a place of resurrection as well. Its darkness, as the eye slowly accustoms itself to it, becomes a dawn rising over an inner, hidden world. The cave is thus the place of great initiations and great gestations. There man gains access to the mystery that is within him. When the contemplative leaves his deep-delved retreat and returns to the light of day, this light dazzles his eyes like the light on the world's first morning. The cave, then, is always waiting for the sun.[8] It effects a new birth and is a cosmic womb.

It is a striking fact that all the great spiritual experiences of Francis' life, from his conversion to an evangelical life to his stigmatization on Mt. Alverna, required this sort of cosmic womb. The first of these experiences, his conversion, was a dramatic rebirth in the womb of Mother Earth. Young Francis had until this point lived on the surface of reality and of himself, amid worldly bustle and dreams of martial glory. Suddenly he discovered the emptiness of his life and began a slow descent into the depths. Here is how Celano tells the story:

> Since there was a certain man in the city of Assisi whom he [Francis] loved more than any other because he was of the same age as the other, and since the great familiarity of their mutual affection led him to share his secrets with him, he often took him to remote places, places well-suited for counsel, telling him that he had found a certain precious and great treasure. This one rejoiced and, concerned about what he heard, he willingly accom-

panied Francis whenever he was asked. There was a certain grotto near the city where they frequently went and talked about this treasure. The man of God, who was already holy by reason of his holy purpose, would enter the grotto, while his companion would wait for him outside; and filled with a new and singular spirit, he would pray to his Father in secret. He wanted no one to know what he did within. . . .He prayed devoutly that the eternal and true God would direct his way and teach him to do his will. He bore the greatest sufferings in mind and was not able to rest until he should have completed in deed what he had conceived in his heart; various thoughts succeeded one another and their importunity distubed him greatly. . . .Consequently, when he came out again to his companion, he was so exhausted with the strain, that one person seemed to have entered, and another to have come out.

One day, however, when he had begged for the mercy of God most earnestly, it was shown to him by God what he should do. Accordingly, he was so filled with joy that he could not contain himself, and, though he did not want to, he uttered some things to the cars of men. But, though he could not keep silent because of the greatness of the joy that filled him, he nevertheless spoke cautiously and in an abstruse manner. For, while he spoke to his special friend of a hidden treasure, as was said, he tried to speak to others only figuratively; he said that he did not want to go to Apulia, but he promised that he would do noble and great things in his native place. People thought he wished to take to himself a wife, and they asked him, saying: "Francis, do you wish to get married?" But he answered them, saying: "I shall take a more noble and more beautiful spouse than you have ever seen; she will surpass all others in beauty and will excel all others in wisdom." [9]

In this account by Celano, we find all the characteristic themes associated with the symbol of the cave: the "precious and great treasure" that gives the cave its element of mystery and fascination; the penetration of the cave's depths by the hero who is the only one to descend into it; the theme of struggle and death, with the hero risking his life in the passage through darkness ("He bore the greatest sufferings in mind. . . .When he came out again to his companion, he was so exhausted with the strain, that one person seemed to have entered, and another to have come out").

We must observe that, inside the cave, it is within Francis' own soul that the struggle takes place. The dark depths that the hero must confront are those of the soul. In his struggle with them, Francis goes through a kind of agony so long as he is unable to master the depths: "He. . .was not able to rest until he should have completed in deed what he had conceived in his heart." The struggle is between the superficial ego and the deeper plan which involves the real development, the true calling, of the hero: "He prayed devoutly that the eternal and true God would direct his way and teach him to do his will."

The most remarkable point is that in order to emerge into the light, this spiritual plan should require the soul's descent into the darkness of the cavern. The cavern which contains the "precious and great treasure" is here an archetypal image that relates the soul to its own "archeology," to the whole of past history: its own and that of mankind. The function of the great symbols is to open us to the fundamental experiences that bring a man face to face with his own mystery and that of being itself. It is by exploring this archaic depth of the soul in the light of the "eternal and true God" that man discovers what he is called to be, his vocation. We see here the truth of Paul Ricoeur's statement: "Re-immersion in *our* archaism is no doubt the roundabout way by which we immerse ourselves in the archaism of humanity, and this double 'regression' is possibly, in its turn, the way to a discovery, a prospection, and a prophecy concerning ourselves."[10]

The symbolism of the cave reaches its successful outcome in the rebirth of the hero. The latter discovers the "precious and great treasure"; he manages to wrest it from the darkness, keeps hold of it, and brings it up into the light of consciousness: "One day. . .when he had begged for the mercy of God most earnestly, it was shown to him by God what he was to do." We should not interpret this "what he was to do'' as referring to a specific, passing action; it refers rather to a new direction for the whole of life. The revelation here given to Francis is the revelation of a new life and a new love. He cannot contain himself for joy. It is truly a new man that emerges from the cave.

When asked about the joy that radiates from him, he is able to answer, says Celano, only "cautiously and in an abstruse manner," "figuratively." His recent experience cannot be put into clear, conceptual terms; symbols alone provide a language for expressing the deeper experiences. Francis tells others that he is cancelling his departure for Apulia where he planned to join the army of Gauthier de Brienne and win glory in battle; he will indeed do great and noble deeds, but in his native place. Here we have highly symbolic language, for Francis is saying that henceforth he will pursue his highest goal, not outside of himself, but in his native place, within himself.

The theme of the betrothed comes as a fitting crown to this spiritual experience, for it gives symbolic expression to the soul's new union with its deepest self and its sacrality. The maternal symbol of the cave is transformed into the symbol of the betrothed and the bride. The hero who has discovered his full, real calling accepts it without reserve.

Such was Francis' first great spiritual experience in connection with Mother Earth. It was soon to be followed by another just as decisive in his life. He had begun to conduct himself as a changed man, and his angered father finally gathered some friends and neighbors and went in search of him. At this point Francis took refuge in a hiding place he had prepared for himself at San Damiano.

> But he, the new athlete of Christ, when he heard of the threats of those who were pursuing him and when he got knowledge of their coming, wanting to *give place to wrath,* hid himself in a certain secret pit which he himself had prepared for just such an emergency. That pit was in that house and was known probably to one person alone; in it he hid so continuously for one month that he hardly dared leave it to provide for his human needs.

> Food, when it was given to him, he ate in the secrecy of the pit, and every service was rendered to him by stealth. Praying, he prayed always with a torrent of tears that the Lord would deliver him from the hands of those who were persecuting his soul. . . . And though he was in a pit and *in darkness*, he was nevertheless filled with a certain exquisite joy of which till then he had had no experience; and catching fire therefrom, he left the pit and exposed himself openly to the curses of his persecutors. He arose, therefore, immediately, active, eager, and lively.[11]

In this episode the subterranean pit is first of all a place of refuge; it acts as a maternal shelter for the novice against his father whom he does not dare face. But then it becomes a tomb in which the hero is buried "in darkness."

Here, once again, a man has a profound experience of Mother Earth; specifically, an experience of return into the mother. On this occasion, the return which is symbolically experienced in the form of a subterranean hiding-place, does not mean a simple repetition of the hero's sojourn in the maternal womb. It is a passage through darkness to a far vaster and more elemental totality; concretely, it expresses a death to self and an insertion into the universality of being through an adherence to a higher will. In this experience, the hero acquires a new power that enables him to scorn his empirical self and accept his true calling. In this contact with the earth he encounters the Invincible One who resides in the depths of his being. Eliade writes:

> The "return to the origin" prepares a new birth but the new birth is not a repetition of the first, physical birth. There is properly speaking a mystical rebirth, spiritual in nature—in other words, access to a new mode of existence (involving sexual maturity, participation in the sacred and in culture; in short, becoming "open" to Spirit). The basic idea is that, to attain to a higher mode of existence, gestation and birth must be repeated; but they are repeated ritually, symbolically. In other words, we have here acts oriented toward the values of Spirit, not behavior from the realm of psycho-physiological activity.[12]

After a month of this subterranean life, Francis emerges from his hiding place fully resolved to confront threats, blows, and mockery, and to follow his call. He was a novice when he took refuge in the underground pit; he is a man when he leaves it, no longer afraid to assert himself. "From that cavern, that was a furnace of glowing gratitude and humility, there came forth one of the strongest and strangest and most original personalities that human history has known."[13]

Such experiences of Mother Earth left a deep mark on Francis. He could never forget them, and the cave would always be connected in his mind with the discovery of the "precious and great treasure." It had an unbroken fascination for him, and it was always his delight to bury himself in some subterranean depth with the eagerness of those who mine the earth in search of gold. This trait is remarkable since Francis loved the light beyond any other created thing. As the author of the *Mirror of Perfection* says, "Above all creatures unendowed with reason he [Francis] had a particular love for the sun and for fire."[14] Matter that was fiery and filled with light was matter as Francis loved it most.

What unconsciously drew him into the dark depths of the earth, was the archetypal image of Mother Earth with all that it represents. When he buried himself in caves and caverns, he was consenting to return to his own profoundly hidden sources and to enter into contact with his own "archeology" and that of mankind. It was an act of deep humility, detachment from himself, and reconciliation. In performing it, he was entering into a fraternal union with Mother Earth and all that she symbolizes. The maternal earth became his "sister": a "sister" very dear to him and closely associated with his highest calling, his search for the Sacred.

We are beginning to see why Francis speaks as he does to the Most High when he comes to "Sister Earth, our mother," in the course of the *Canticle.* His poetic celebration of the earth and its motherhood does not stop at the surface of things. Rather, when he calls Mother Earth his sister and praises her for inexhaustible fruitfulness, he is unconsiously giving expression to the radical communion between his soul and all those inner, obscure energies and powers that link it to being and life in all their immensity.

At the same time, Francis is also expressing the transfiguration that has occurred within him. We must bear in mind that during the night before Francis composed the *Canticle* he received from the Lord assurance of his entry into the kingdom; it came in the imaged form of a transfiguration of the entire earth into "an immense and precious treasure."[15] The *Canticle* and especially the stanza on "Sister Earth, our mother," celebrate this transfiguration which itself is in turn a symbol for a radical transformation of the soul. Francis' praise of Mother Earth is the song of a man who "with great humility" has loved God even in all those obscure forces that sustain and nourish us, so that he sees these transformed into an eternal treasure of light and glory.

There is another event of Francis' life that reveals its full meaning when we look at it in this perspective. This event also takes place in a cave. Three years before his death, Francis wanted to express in a sensible fashion the memory of the Child-God's birth at Bethlehem. By so doing, he would unite himself as fully as possible with this great mystery of our faith. To this end he had a manger put in a cave on the mountainside near Greccio, and had an ass and an ox brought there. When Christmas night came, Francis "stood before the manger, uttering sighs, overcome with love, and filled with a wonderful happiness."

Here, for Francis, was palpable renewal of the mystery of a God being born, amid animals, in the depths of the earth. One witness, says Celano, "saw a little child lying in the manger lifeless, and he saw the holy man of God go up to it and rouse the child as from a deep sleep."[17] St. Bonaventure recounts the same incident: "A knight called John. . .claimed that he saw a beautiful child asleep in the crib, and that St. Francis took it in his arms and seemed to wake it up."[18]

Readers have generally focused their attention on the element of the marvelous in this incident without seeing its deeper meaning. And yet, if one were to try to give symbolic expression to Francis' spiritual experience, one could not do better than to repeat this story, for Francis was a man whose very actions were a language that showed clearly what he was. Celano himself did not miss the point, when speaking of Greccio in an other connection, he comments: "Here is that place where he brought back to memory the birthday of the Child of Bethlehem, becoming a child with that Child."[19]

For Celano the outward celebration points to an interior process: "becoming a child with that Child (*factus cum Puero puer*)." The creche in the cave and Francis taking the beautiful child in his arms and waking it in the night: these are a symbol of the hidden birth of the eternal divine Child in the depths of the soul of a man fully reconciled to his own "archeology." The outward celebration is the sensible expression of an approach to God along the way of deep humility and total humanness, the way of the Incarnation.

Rudolf Bultmann, the Protestant theologian, is quoted as saying: "I want Christ without the crib." But to want Christ without the crib amounts to wanting him without his links to the natural world, without his having entered the cosmic and human womb. Then the event of faith has nothing to do any longer with "Mother Earth." This kind of faith in Christ expresses a relation to transcendence, but one that involves a break with all that links us to the cosmos and to life itself. The perspective is idealist: Salvation has nothing to do with our fleshly condition; it does not touch our vital, psychic roots; it does not affect man in his total destiny as a being who "is rooted in his animal nature and reaches out beyond the merely human toward the divine."[20]

Francis' spiritual journey takes him along quite different paths. He achieves a relation to the transcendent God, but by travelling the humble road of the Incarnation, meeting the most high Son of God down in the depths of our human "archeology." St. Paul says of Christ: " 'He ascended' —what does this mean but that he had first descended into the lower regions of the earth? He who descended is the very one who ascended high above the heavens, that he might fill all men with his gifts."[21] If God is to be born in man, he needs the whole of man, his hidden, obscure roots. In one of his Letters, Francis writes: "Look at God's condescension, my brothers, and *pour out your hearts before him* (Ps. 61:9). Humble yourselves that you may be exalted by him (cf. 1 Pet. 5:6). Keep nothing for yourselves, so that he who has given himself wholly to you may receive you wholly."[22]

2. THE DREAM OF THE TREE

Francis' relation to the earth, our mother, and to all that she symbolizes does not find expression only in events or actions of his external life. It also manifests itself in his dreams. This becomes quite clear from some dreams in which the earth exercises a real fascination. Celano reports one of these:

> One night after he had given himself to sleep, it seemed to him that he was walking along a certain road, at the side of which stood a tree of great height. The tree was beautiful and strong, thick and exceedingly high. It happened as he drew near to it, and was standing beneath it, admiring its beauty and its height, that suddenly the holy man himself grew to so great a height that he touched the top of the tree, and taking hold of it with his hand, he bent it to the ground (*eamque manu capiens facillime inclinaret ad terras*).[23]

Celano explains the dream by connecting it with the steps Francis was about to take in order to win from Pope Innocent III, "the highest and loftiest tree in the world," the approval of his Rule. The providential dream was meant to encourage Francis by assuring him of the success of his efforts: Innocent, the Lord Pope, would let himself be bent as easily as the mighty tree of the dream and would stoop to grant Francis' request.

The fact that the dream did relate to Francis' approach to Pope Innocent in no way lessens its profound mystical significance. This great dream is one that emanates from the archetypes. For the image of the tree that is at the center of the whole dream is an archetypal image, one of those basic symbols that are found in myth and in the art and dreams of every age, and that played an important role in the archaic religions. M. Eliade writes:

> The cosmos was imagined in the form of a gigantic tree; the mode of being of the cosmos, and first of all its capacity for endless regeneration, are symbolically expressed by the life of the tree. . . .The image of the tree was not chosen only to symbolize the cosmos but also to express life, youth, immortality, wisdom. In addition to cosmic trees, like the Yggdrasil of Germanic mythology, the history of religions records trees of life (*e.g.*, in Mesopotamia), of immortality (Asia, Old Testament), of knowledge (Old Testament), of youth (Mesopotamia, India, Iran), and so on. In other words, the tree came to express everything that religious man regards as *pre-eminently real and sacred*, everything that he knows the gods to possess of their own nature and that is only rarely accessible to privileged individuals, the heroes and demigods. This is why myths of the quest for youth or immortality give prominent place to a tree with golden fruit or miraculous leaves, a tree growing "in the distant land" (really in the other world) and guarded by monsters (griffins, dragons, snakes). He who would gather its fruits must confront and slay the guardian monster. This in itself tells us that we have here *an initiatory ordeal of the heroic type;* it is by violence that the victor obtains the superhuman, almost divine condition of eternal youth, invincibility, and unlimited power.[24]

In some tribes, the Karadjeri, for example, the climbing of a tree is itself an initiatory ceremony: the tree symbolizes the axis of the cosmos, the World-Tree, and by climbing it the initiate enters heaven.[25] The ascent of the tree thus symbolizes a new and supernatural birth. According to Jung, the tree is essentially a maternal symbol.[26] But the return to the image of the mother is likewise a preparation for a new birth: "The entwining trees are at the same time birth-giving mothers."[27] On the Wiesbaden bas-relief that depicts the legend of Mithras, the latter can be seen being born at the top of the tree.

Back now to Francis' dream. One point in it strikes us immediately: the tree stands beside the road Francis is travelling. It does not seem, at first sight, to be in any sense the goal of his journey. Yet the encounter with the tree will be most important.

This tree is not any ordinary tree, but is "of great height . . .beautiful and strong, thick and exceedingly high." Its beauty, height, and vigorous growth draw the eye and exercise a real fascination. As a manifestation of life, power, and beauty, this tree is a mystery and the manner in which it is described reminds us of the great tree in Nebechadnezzar's dream: "I saw a tree of great height at the center of the world. It was large and strong, with its top touching the heavens."[28] We will remember too how Daniel at the king's bidding interpreted the dream: he saw in the gigantic tree that was destined to be cut down an image of the king's fate: "This large, strong tree that you saw, with its top touching the heavens. . . .you are that tree, O king, large and strong!"[29] In Francis' dream, the tree is related to his destiny at a deeper level, the tree is part of a language in which the depths find voice. With this in mind, we must pay close attention to the twofold movement of Francis in relation to the tree of his dream.

The first movement is that of Francis' yearning toward the heights into which the tree towers. Fascinated by the beauty and great height of the tree, Francis finds himself literally drawn upward, raised up to the loftiest branches, "to so great a height that he touched the top of the tree." What is the significance of this irresistible movement to the highest part of the tree? Trees which attract and which entwine their branches are, as Jung has remarked, a maternal symbol; they are "birth-giving mothers." When Celano sees in the tree of Francis' dream an image of Pope Innocent III from whom Francis was seeking approval of his Rule, he is correct. But we must realize that to Francis the pope was the personification of *Mater Ecclesia.*

If we bear in mind the intense and impatient desire of the young founder to have his way of life approved by Mother Church, to feel himself united to her in a close communion of life and outlook, and to be deeply involved in the life of the Church, we will readily become convinced that the irresistible pull which emanates from the tree of his dream and draws him to its top, represents "a return to the mother," a return to the maternal womb. But it is a return for the sake of a new birth, a birth from on high and to a higher life. It is the top of the tree that attracts Francis, and the top of the gigantic tree melts into the heavenly vault; thus it is a symbol of the sacred, of the Most High.

The powerful attraction that lifts Francis to this superhuman height expresses the deep-seated desire of his being in its entirety to live the highest kind of life, even a divine life, as he goes in quest of his own highest self. We find in this dream the same vertical movement that marks the opening of the *Canticle.* The latter, in its opening two stanzas, is a hymn to transcendence before becoming the *Canticle of Creatures.*

In Francis' dream, as in his *Canticle,* this first movement is followed by another that, in paradoxical fashion, links the invocation of highest heaven with a descent to the earth and a communion with it. When Francis reaches the top of the tree, he grasps it and effortlessly bends it to the ground. This second movement also has an important symbolical point. In grasping the top of the tree, the hero is in a sense taking the initative away from the power that has picked him up and raised him to such a height. He thereby affirms his own vocation; he triumphs over the "mother." Far from remaining suspended from the tree and entwined in its branches as a bird in its nest is, he goes his own way. He reverses the situation and subjects the tree to the movement he decides on. He bends it to the ground, implants it in the earth again.

We return to Mother Earth. Francis leaves the heavenly heights to which the first movement of his soul has carried him and, in his dream as in his *Canticle,* returns to Mother Earth. The point is not that he renounces his quest of the Most High, but rather that his quest of the sacred and his birth into divine life must be effected through a humble communion with Mother Earth and all the interior, hidden forces she represents.

Francis' religious way is all-embracing. Because it is one of deep humility and acceptance, it lays hold of man with all his roots. It reconciles man with his own totality as it reconciles him with god, and it does so in one and the same movement. Pierre Emmanuel writes in his *Le goût de l'Un:* "I am convinced that the vertical dimension of transcendence passes through the obscure regions of our being; that the heights of the spirit coincide with the depths of the soul; and that the exploration of that darkness is the road to the supreme light which, in our unknown depths, bids us set out into the night."[30] We think Francis voices the same conviction in his own way when he praises the Lord "through Sister Earth, our mother, who feeds us in her sovereignty."

3. The Last Wish of the Dying Francis: To Be Laid Naked on the Bare Ground

We are trying to grasp as fully as possible the significance of the celebration of "Sister Earth, our mother" in the *Canticle,* by relating it to various incidents of Francis' life which were really experiences of Mother Earth, both at the cosmic and at the psychic and spiritual levels. The *Canticle* flowed up from the depths of Francis' soul and cannot be unrelated to these important experiences; it must give unconscious expression to them.

Among the events and actions of Francis' life that can be connected with his celebration of Mother Earth, there is one that is specially deserving of attention. Celano tells it thus:

> He [Francis] spent the few days that remained before his death in praise, teaching his companions whom he loved so much to praise Christ with him. He himself, in as far as he was able, broke forth in this psalm: *I cried to the Lord with my voice: with my voice I made supplication to the Lord.* He also invited all creatures to praise God, and by means of the words he had composed earlier, he exhorted them to love God. . . .Then to the brothers: "When you see that I am brought to my last moments, place me naked upon the ground just as you saw me the day before yesterday; and let me lie there after I am dead for the length of time it takes one to walk a mile unhurriedly."[31]

According to this account of Celano, the dying Francis sang his *Canticle of Brother Sun;* then he told the brothers his wish to be laid naked on the bare ground when the moment of his passing came. It is difficult to avoid seeing a connection between Francis' desire and his *Canticle.* When he sang, "All praise be yours, my Lord, through Sister Earth, our mother," and when, a little later, he expressed a wish to be laid on the ground so that he might die resting on it, was not the same basic inspiration at work in both actions? Was he not seeking to express the same thing in languages that, though different, were equally symbolic?

But what did it mean for Francis to be laid naked on the bare ground at the moment of death? What significance did he attribute to this action? If we are to understand it, we must see it in the context of all the acts that were connected with his dying and made of this a real liturgical celebration.

As his death approached,

> while. . .the brothers were weeping very bitterly and grieving inconsolably, the holy father commanded that bread be brought

to him. He *blessed and broke it* and gave a small piece of it to each one to eat. Commanding also that a book of the Gospels be brought, he asked that the Gospel according to St. John be read to him from the place that begins: *Before the feast of the Passover.* He was recalling that most holy supper which the Lord celebrated as his last supper with his disciples.[32]

In all this, Francis was indicating the meaning he intended his death to have; he saw his death as a passover, celebrated in close communion with the paschal mystery of him whom he had been imitating all his life long. He accepted his death as a way of entering more deeply in the mystery of Christ and of passing with Christ to the Father. It is in this context that Francis' last wish shows its significance. A few days before, he had already had himself placed "naked on the naked ground, so that in that final hour when the enemy could still rage against him, he might wrestle naked with a naked enemy."[33]

This act of supreme self-stripping undoubtedly shows Francis' determination to be identified as full as possible with Christ as he died on the cross in utter destitution. Celano expressly says as much when he ends his account of Francis' death with the words: "The hour therefore came, and all the mysteries of Christ being fulfilled in him, he winged his way happily to God."[34] St. Bonaventure makes the same point:

He had acted as he did in his anxiety for poverty, and he was unwilling even to keep a habit unless it was on loan. Christ hung upon his Cross, poor and naked and in great pain, and Francis wanted to be like him in everything. That was why at the beginning of his religious life he stood naked before the bishop, and at the end he wished to leave the world naked.[35]

His action thus represents the climax of his union with and likeness to Christ.

And yet this interpretation, with its emphasis on destitution for the sake of likeness to Christ, seems to leave unmentioned an essential aspect of Francis' action. We are referring to the element of adherence to and communion with the earth itself. The wish to be put in direct contact with the earth, to be returned to it as it were, at a moment so important in the soul's life, cannot be regarded as either accidental or without significance. It has its own deeper meaning and must be related to what Francis is saying in the *Canticle* when he praises God "through Sister Earth, our mother."

We must recognize that in Francis' action there are two things which are closely linked, but do not spring from the same level of the soul. First, there is the determination to be like Christ and to enter into deeper communion with him and his mystery. This determination is expressed here in a ritual of communion with the earth, a ritual that is not specifically Christian in origin. Francis is unconsciously repeating a very archaic rite that is heavy with meaning.

Among many ancient peoples, direct contact with the earth was obligatory at birth and at death; it was customary to lay a newborn child and a dying person on the bare ground. Thus

> in ancient China "the dying man, like the newborn infant, is laid on the ground. . . .To be born or to die, to enter the living family or the ancestral family (and to leave the one or the other), there is a common threshold, one's native Earth. . . .When the newborn infant or the dying man is laid on the Earth, it is for her to say if the birth or the death are valid, if they are to be taken as accomplished and normal facts". . . .Just as the infant is placed on the ground immediately after birth so that its true Mother shall legitimize it and confer her divine protection on it, so, too, infants, children, and grown men are placed on the ground—or sometimes buried in it—in case of sickness. Symbolic burial, partial or complete, has the same magico-religious value as immersion in water, baptism. The sick person is regenerated; he is born anew. The operation has the same efficacy in wiping out a sin or in curing a mental malady.[36]

The purpose of the rite is to put a man in communion

with a whole that is greater than he and that sustains and nourishes him, and thus to rescue him from his particular situation and throw open to him a new and all-embracing life. The individual is resituated within the totality of being; he is brought into harmony with his own mystery and thus with the totality of his own soul. Mother Earth is an archetypal image of the unconscious and symbolizes the whole obscure psychic life of the soul. Through renewed contact with Mother Earth, the individual symbolically renews his ties with the sphere of his soul that is hidden from him with his own "archeology" and with the "archeology" of mankind. But this redescent into the prehistory of the soul is not a retrogression but the path to a new birth. A man is now born into a life that transcends that of the individual as an empirical entity; he participates in the totality of being and in its sacrality.

The remarkable thing about Francis is that he renews this archaic rite with its inherent meaning and closely links it, in an utterly spontaneous fashion, with a mysticism of union with Christ. The closest kind of personal communion with Christ is here achieved by following the path of the great human symbols, by a redescent into "Mother Earth" and all she stands for. A loving, unreserved adherence to Jesus finds expression in a fraternal communion with "Sister Earth, our mother." We cannot but think here of what Teilhard de Chardin says in his "The Mass on the World":

> The man who is filled with an impassioned love of Jesus hidden in the forces which bring increase to the earth, him the earth will lift up, like a mother, in the immensity of her arms, and will enable him to contemplate the face of God. . . .The man who is filled with an impassioned love for Jesus hidden in the forces which bring death to the earth, him the earth will clasp in the immensity of her arms as her strength fails, and with her he will awaken in the bosom of God.[37]

We can now better understand the joy Francis experienced in his final moments. "He accepted death singing," says

Celano,[38] and his song was his own song of sun and earth. There is a scene in Dostoyevsky's novel *The Brothers Karamazov* which can help us comprehend Francis' joy as he lay dying on the bosom of Mother Earth. The aged starets, Zossima, has just died. During his last hours he had reminded his favorite disciple, Alyosha, of the Gospel words: "'Except a corn of wheat fall into the ground and die, it abideth along: but if it die, it bringeth forth much fruit.' Remember that."[39]

During the wake, the monks, gathered around the dead man as is their custom, listen to the reading of the Gospel by one of their number. Alyosha, weary and emotionally drained, dozes. In his half-sleep he hears the account of the marriage feast of Cana being read and sees Zossima alive again, walking toward him and commenting on the Gospel. Alyosha awakes; the monk's body lies cold and stiff in the coffin. Alyosha gazes at it for a moment, then suddenly turns, leaves the cell, and goes rapidly down the steps, driven by a thirst for freedom and unlimited space.

> The fresh, motionless, still night enfolded the earth. The white towers and golden domes of the cathedral gleamed against the sapphire sky. The gorgeous autumn flowers in the beds near the house went to sleep till morning. The silence of the earth seemed to merge into the silence of the heavens, the mystery of the earth came into contact with the mystery of the stars. . . .Alyosha stood, gazed, and suddenly threw himself down flat upon the earth.
>
> He did not know why he was embracing it. He could not have explained to himself why he longed so irresistibly to kiss it, to kiss it all, but he kissed it weeping, sobbing and drenching it with his tears, and vowed frenziedly to love it, to love it for ever and ever. "Water the earth with the tears of your gladness and love those tears," it rang in his soul. What was he weeping over? Oh, he was weeping in his rapture even over those stars which were shining for him from the abyss of space and "he was not ashamed of that ecstasy." It was as though the treads from all those innumerable worlds of God met all at once in his soul, and it was trembling all over "as it came in contact with

> other worlds." He wanted to forgive everyone and for everything, and to beg forgiveness—oh! not for himself, but for all men, for all and for everything, and "others are begging for me," it echoed in his soul again and again. But with every moment he felt clearly and almost palpably that something firm and immovable, like the firmament itself, was entering his soul. A sort of idea was gaining ascendancy over his mind—and that for the rest of his life, for ever and ever. He had fallen upon the earth a weak youth, but he rose from it a resolute fighter for the rest of his life, and he realized and felt it suddenly, at the very moment of his rapture. And never, never for the rest of his life could Alyosha forget that moment. "Someone visited my soul at that hour!" he used to say afterwards with firm faith in his words.[40]

"The mystery of the earth came into contact with the mystery of the stars": the two came into contact in the soul of Francis as they did in the soul of Alyosha. Do we not see in both men a single basic spiritual experience in which the evangelical demand for utter detachment is united to and fused with a profound love and communion with the earth? "Except a corn of wheat fall into the ground. . .": Far from eliminating the natural journey of the soul in quest of its sacrality, the Gospel words borrow the obscure language of myth in order to lead man to his own full truth and ultimate destiny. The Gospel's words tell of a need to return to the earth, the need for the soul to be immersed in its hidden, unconscious origins, in its cosmic and psychic "archeology." Such an immersion is inevitably experienced initially as a death: a death to the world of the "I," with its false claims, its illusory power, its ambitions and desires. Do we perhaps have here the very meaning of evangelical humility and poverty? That is how Francis understood them.

The immersion and death are not an end in themselves, but the starting-point for a rebirth of man into a universe marked by communion. Here is where the conversion proper to the Gospel transcends myth and symbol, even while using them. Because evangelical conversion is characterized by faith in the dead and risen Christ, it actually gives what myth and symbol can only glimpse and aim at, without truly experiencing it.

The phenomenology of religion has brought to light the ultimate intention that shapes the very structure of myth. The latter, says Paul Ricoeur, "indicates. . .the intimate accord of the man of cult and myth with the whole of being; it signifies an indivisible plenitude, in which the supernatural, the natural, and the psychological are not yet torn apart."[41] But, as Ricoeur also observes, "this intuition of a cosmic whole, from which man is not separated, and this undivided plenitude, anterior to the division into supernatural, natural, and human are not *given,* but simply *aimed at.* It is only in intention that the myth restores some wholeness."[42]

The conversion proper to the Gospel opens up to man new depths of existence and thus satisfies the deeper intention of myth, but it does so while giving this same intention a new meaning and content. Francis' celebration of the earth as our mother is not a return to paganism; it is not a return to archaic man, the man who lives in darkness, fascinated by a lost unity that he seeks vainly in the past, in some primordial time. Francis celebrates rather a dawn that shows the whole order of nature to be permeated and illumined by him who is a life-giving Spirit. The soul looks for the "great beginnings" not in the past but in the future and in the light of the risen Christ. The lost paradise has now become the promised land, as eschatology absorbs and transforms archeology. Myth means not only the "memory of innocence" but also the "hope of pardon."

The full meaning of Francis' celebration of Mother Earth and of his desire to commune with her even in his dying are undoubtedly summed up in "reconciliation of the supernatural, the natural, and the human." It is quite understandable that such an experience should be accompanied by an intense will to forgiveness. At the high point of his ecstasy, Alyosha "wanted to forgive everyone and for everything, and to beg forgiveness—oh! not for himself, but for all men, for all and for everything." The earth he embraces and drenches with his tears is an earth streaming with mercy, an earth that is reconciled, a sacred earth whose mystery fuses with the mystery of the stars.

Francis has the same experience. It is striking that immediately after the stanza on Mother Earth in the *Canticle* come two stanzas in celebration of forgiveness, stanzas praising God "through those who grant pardon for love of you." Though composed at a later time, these two stanzas are an integral part of the *Canticle,* and their meaning is not circumscribed by the particular circumstances that stimulated their composition.

As Francis sings these next stanzas shortly before dying, he regards them as the logical continuation of his praise of creatures and especially his praise of Mother Earth. For, Mother Earth is no longer simply the reality his ancestors knew, the Mother with the torn womb. She has been made new, and her face is the face of a sister: "Sister Earth, our mother," This is a reconciled earth that has been visited by the grace of limitless forgiveness. It is not an idyllic earth on which trials and sickness are no more, but it is certainly an earth filled with hope. "Pardon is the hope of glory,"[43] and already an encounter with the Most High.

Francis, like Alyosha, is a man risen from the dead. He is such because he has accepted the Incarnation, because even in his most spiritual flights he has accepted the heavy burden of earth and has welcomed necessity itself as a sister: "A Franciscan knowledge of necessity: I am 'with' necessity, 'among' creatures" (Paul Ricoeur).[44]

Chapter 10

Pardon and Peace

All praise be yours, my Lord, through those who grant pardon
For love of you; through those who endure
Sickness and trial.

Happy those who endure in peace,
By you, Most High, they will be crowned.

The *Canticle of Creatures* proper ends with the stanza on "Sister Earth, our mother." Nonetheless, Francis decided to add four more stanzas. These were a later inspiration and sprang from special situations. The first part of the *Canticle* (Stanzas 1—9) dates from the fall of 1225, the two stanzas on pardon and peace were composed in July, 1226, in the palace of the bishop of Assisi, as Francis sought to end a dispute between the bishop and the mayor of Assisi.[1]

Are these two stanzas to be regarded as a simple appendix that owes its existence to a limited occasion and has no connection with the basic inspiration of the *Canticle?* There seems to be no connection between these stanzas and those that precede it. The themes and concerns are different. Up to this point the entire poem was focused on the natural world and on praise of God through the cosmos. Now it suddenly turns to the world of men, and to man's destiny as he attempts to cope with his fellows, with illness, and with trials of every kind. The tonality of these stanzas is quite different. The praise of the cosmic elements unfolded entirely under the sign of an unclouded and unshadowed spirit of brotherhood. In these two stanzas, however, we find ourselves in a world of tension, conflict, and suffering.

Despite these various differences, Francis incorporated the stanzas on pardon and peace into his *Canticle* and this forces us to reflect more carefully on them. He evidently felt that the stanzas fitted into the poem as a whole and that they were of the same basic inspiration. And so we must ask: Is it not one and the same spirit of fraternal presence to the world that is expressed here and in the earlier stanzas? Is it not the same will to reconciliation that is expressed in both parts, first in a fraternal celebration of the cosmic elements and now in the praise of pardon and peace? Do we not find simply two different ways of voicing the same spiritual experience?

We may go even further. Are not these two stanzas, which are devoted to specifically human brotherhood under the sign of pardon and peace, to be interpreted as the emergence, after a period of slow maturation, of the ultimate purpose of the entire cosmic praise itself?

To find an answer, we must turn again to Francis' life and try to determine what relations there were, in his interior life, between cosmic brotherhood and human brotherhood, between his affective communion with all subhuman creatures and his love of persons, who are beings endowed with a spiritual soul.

It is impossible to overestimate the importance of relationships with other people for a man like Francis. As the son of a merchant and himself an able businessman who became used to trade when quite young, Francis soon acquired a taste for contacts with others and an ability to deal with them. He took spontaneously to social intercourse, being naturally agreeable and courteous, "a very kindly person, easy and affable."[2]

The grace that converted him in no way eliminated this natural openness and receptivity; on the contrary, it gave them even greater scope. Throughout his life, Francis was very sensitive to others. We see him preferring the company of the lowliest and most outcast, but he remained open to all, even the great ones of this world. Thus he went unhesitatingly to Pope Innocent, became the friend of Cardinal Ugolino, and crossed the Mediterranean to bring the Good News to the Sultan of Egypt, whose respect he won by his own great nobility of spirit. His *Letter to All the Faithful* and his *Letter to the Rulers of the People* combine to give us an idea of the breadth of his interest in and concern for people. However, it was with the brothers the Lord had given him that Francis' relationships were most numerous and intimate.

What we must be aware of is not the scope and extent of these human relationships as their quality. From this point of view, two traits characterize them. The first is their *personal* or individual aspect. Chesterton makes the humorous comment that Francis was a man who could not see the woods for the trees. He saw not the crowd or mankind in general but the individual, the unique person with his special history and calling. Each individual was, in his eyes, unique and the object of a unique love. He concerned himself with each individual as though that individual were the only one in the universe. His sympathy for the individual enabled him to adapt himself to widely varying characters and found an expression appropriate to each. Peter Lippert rightly observes that the most precious heritage Francis gave his religious family and the Church was "the sense of and feeling for the living person, for the individual and singular, and for the special quality of each person."[3]

The second trait marking Francis' relations with men is that these relations are always conducted under the sign of peace. In his Testament he writes: "God revealed a form of greeting to me, telling me that we should say, 'God give you peace.'"[4] The greeting is not to be taken as a conventional formula but expresses a deeply rooted attitude of and desire for reconciliation.

Francis gives the greeting its full biblical and evangelical meaning. The peace he wants for each and all is the divine favor, forgiveness, a return to grace, the recovery of divine friendship: in short, a complete reconciliation with God. Inseparable from this is the reconciliation of men with each other and with themselves under the same sign of mercy. The peace Francis wishes men is the peace Christ came to give the world. According to Celano, Francis "did not consider himself a friend of Christ unless he loved the souls that Christ loved."[5] All his relationships with others were permeated by an intense desire for mercy and reconciliation. It was a desire that sprang from the depths of his being.

"Since the strength of Francis' love made him a brother to all other creatures, it is not surprising that the charity of Christ made him more than a brother to those who are stamped with the image of their Creator."[6]

There is no better expression of the tender, merciful love for all men that filled Francis' heart to overflowing than the advice he gave to a Minister of the Order:

> I should like you to prove that you love God and me, his servant and yours, in the following way. There should be no friar in the whole world who has fallen into sin, no matter how far he has fallen, who will ever fail to find your forgiveness for the asking, if he will only look into your eyes. And if he does not ask forgiveness, you should ask him if he wants it. And should he appear before you again a thousand times, you should love him more than you love me, so that you may draw him to God.[7]

One day Francis told Brother Riccerio, who was tormenting himself interiorly: "Let no temptation disturb you, son; let no thought exasperate you; for you are very dear to me. Know that among those who are especially dear to me you are worthy of my affection and intimacy. Come to me with confidence whenever you wish and talk to me with great familiarity."[8] This incident makes it clear that Francis offered others his friendship: a friendship compounded of affection and respect; a friendship that helped others realize they were loved by God and saved; a friendship that helped them to be at peace with themselves and all other human beings.

Such was Francis' love for human beings. This love was inseparable from a more general attitude of tenderness, compassion, and mercy toward the whole of reality and its every manifestation, even the most natural and material. The desire for reconciliation that inspired and characterized all of his relationships with other men was matched by a deep sense of brotherhood and affective communion with even the lowliest of the cosmic elements. It is important that we grasp the connection between these two kinds of relationship in Francis' soul, if we wish to understand the connection in the *Canticle* between the properly cosmic section and the stanzas on pardon and peace.

The connection between the two kinds of relationship is close and profound. We do not do it justice by saying that in Francis the desire for reconciliation with his fellow men was accompanied by a sense of cosmic brotherhood. It is rather the case that his will to reconciliation was somehow mediated by his sense of humble brotherhood with the realities of the natural world. Such a statement may surprise many people of our day, and it requires explanation.

To modern man only man is "brother" to man; all other creatures belong to a world of "objects" which we men are free to manipulate, use, and dominate as we please. Science has limited our vision of the world to what is quantitative and measurable in the latter and has accustomed us to thinking of nature as a field of "objects." In consequence, our presence to the world is shot through with a dualism: on the one hand, we deal with persons; on the other, with the "objects" that comprise nature. We build an absolute barrier between the two realms by invoking the transcendence that is ours as spiritual beings. Modern man believes that by so doing he can reconcile two contradictory affective attitudes: an attitude of respect, receptivity, and sympathy toward his likes, an attitude of aggressiveness, conquest, and domination towards nature in its entirety; he thinks of himself as infinitely superior to all of it. This means that his love of men has nothing to do with the bonds that link him to the natural world.

The mistake men make in cultivating this dualist outlook is that they fail to realize that nature is not only outside us and around us but within us as well. We are, indivisibly, body and soul, necessity and freedom. Man is not a pure self-awareness having accidental relations with the cosmos but nonetheless lays hold of himself in his pure subjectivity in relation to other pure subjectivities. Modern man thinks that by identifying himself with consciousness and freedom he can take a position above and beyond his natural being and simply eliminate his own "archeology" and the whole dark area of his being that has its roots in nature and the necessity that marks nature. Yet when he attempts to do this, he simply thrusts down into the darkness forces that belong to him and that he does not recognize.

Despite man's rejection, these forces continue to operate within his being and his soul since his soul contains far more than consciousness. When these biophysical forces are not integrated into the conscious personality but instead are left uncontrolled, they live their own muted, clandestine, and anarchic life in the unconscious, a life that is then completely archaic in character and terribly dangerous to the personality as a whole. The dualist outlook of modern man, who opposes the human to the natural, thus leads to a division within man and makes impossible a complete reconciliation with himself and his fellow human being.

According to Jung, it is these obscure, unacknowledged forces that give rise to obsessions, individual neuroses, and collective forms of possession that are far more destructive than natural cataclysms. The will to power and the aggressivity which man directs toward nature finally turns back on him and his human dignity by suddenly rousing him to a frenzied violence against his fellow men that leaves him astonished and dismayed. It is a painfully evident fact that, despite the lofty idea modern man has of himself and his fellows and all his professions of faith in the transcendent dignity of the human person, we live in a human universe that is constantly threatened by unforeseeable outbursts of violence. In these outbursts, all the archaic forces of the soul that man has been unwilling or unable to integrate with his lofty ideal of human existence rage out of control.

The universe of Francis of Assisi was an utterly different kind of place. In it we do not find any radical division between the world of men and the rest of creation. Men are the object of a special love, but the love of men is part of vast piety toward the cosmos that makes all creatures man's friends. Francis thinks of himself as a brother not only to his fellow men but to all creatures. Even when he gives the name of brother or sister to the material elements, he is not simply indulging in allegory. He really has a sense of brotherhood with regard to these humble realities, and there is a real affective communion between himself and them.[9]

We must be sure that we understand this "communion." It is not reducible to a vague sentimentality, for it corresponds to a profound and absolutely basic intuition: "By the power of his extraordinary faith he tasted the Goodness which is the source of all in each and every created thing, as in so many rivulets."[10] In Francis' eyes, all creatures have their being because of the same creative love; they are the varied expressions of that love. It is this common origin that is the basis of the great cosmic brotherhood. This intuition does not remain theory for him. In fact, it is not even in the first instance a theory at all, but is something he feels in every fiber of his being; it gives rise to a constantly renewed feeling of love for the cosmos and an ever fresh sense of wonder.

In thus opening himself to the world and setting himself among creatures and "dreaming" of these, at a profound level, as his "brothers" and "sisters," Francis also opens himself to that obscure part of his being which has its roots in nature; he fraternizes, unconsciously, with his own depths. In dealing with the elements as brothers and sisters, his soul is coming to grips with itself and with all that is unexplored within it and seeking to emerge into the light. Francis has opened himself to the world, and now the world opens itself to him.

The great cosmic images of Brother Sun, Sister Moon, Brother Wind, Sister Water, and so forth, express a communion not only with the elements themselves, but also through them (once they have been properly imagined and assigned a value) with the soul's own "archeology" and that of mankind in its entirety. Out of what abyssal past do these images come? The soul which contemplates them and adheres to them in an ingenuous, loving way, lives in a past that is not only its own personal past, but the past of the human soul as such. It relives the primordial affective experiences of mankind and the fraternal world of which it dreams is still the world that Genesis calls good.

These archetypal images of Sun, Water, Fire, etc., do not express simply a return to the past. They are also the privileged means that enable the soul to gain possession of itself in its entirety and with all its depths. They are a path to a renewal of the whole being, starting with a conversion of the primal forces of the soul. By expressing and symbolizing these forces, the images of Sun, Water, Fire, Earth, etc., we give them a new dimension that is cosmic and universal. They liberate these forces from their archaic sphere, that of instinctual satisfaction, and enable them to achieve a higher destiny. They transform them into forces for progress. They open them to the life of the spirit.

When man is thus reconciled to his own vital powers and his own affectivity in its entirety (under the guise of the great fraternal cosmic images), he is reborn to a new personality that is as big as the world, open to the whole of being, and receptive to the mystery of the Other in all its fullness. As brother of the sun and all other creatures, Francis walks among beings and things as a man liberated from all defensiveness and egoism. He lives in a violent medieval world that bristles with turrets and crisscrossed by moats, but his own universe is empty of fortresses and walls, and knows no frontiers. His gaze, so full of sun and stars and water and wind, has become marvelously human.

No one exemplifies better than Francis what Jung says of the liberating power of the great cosmic symbols:

> The empirical truth never frees a man from his bondage to the senses; it only shows him that he was always so and cannot be otherwise. The symbolical truth, on the other hand, which puts

> water in place of the mother and spirit or fire in place of the father, frees the libido from the channel of the incest tendency, offers it a new gradient, and canalizes it into a spiritual form. Thus man, as a spiritual being, becomes a child again and is born into a circle of brothers and sisters: but his mother has become the "communion of saints," the Church, and his brothers and sisters are humanity, with whom he is united anew in the common heritage of symbolical truth.[11]

In the light of these remarks, we see the profound connection in Francis' *Canticle* between the cosmic praise and the stanzas on pardon and peace. The latter can no longer be regarded simply as an addition inspired by a special occasion and therefore by external circumstances. On the contrary, they emerge from and are a fuller development of the work as a whole. In them the deeper meaning of the entire poem comes to light; in them the symbolic truth contained in the cosmic praise is unveiled. The *Canticle* shows itself to be the song of a man who is fully reconciled and at peace in his relations with others and with himself, even in "sickness and trial."

It is indeed remarkable that this hymn to the great cosmic brotherhood should continue with a celebration of pardon and heroic patience. The Franciscan vision of a fraternal universe is not an ingenuous, nostalgic evocation of a lost paradise. It is rather a world vision in which reconciliation takes priority over separation and unity over division. The vision undoubtedly does look beyond separation and sin and beyond the struggle between freedom and nature to a complete unity of the supernatural, the natural, and the human. But this unity is not to be sought in the past or in a return to some primal sleep. It is to be sought in a deeper presence to self and other beings. That is the meaning of the stanzas celebrating pardon and peace.

There is a final point to be noted about these stanzas. It is that the praise ends with a beatitude: "Happy those who endure in peace, by you, Most High, they will be crowned." We will recall that what Francis has in view in his *Canticle* is nothing less than the Most High himself. That image dominated the opening two stanzas where it occurred twice. It appeared again in the second set of two stanzas, in connection with the cryptic image of "my lord Brother Sun." After this it disappeared from the *Canticle.* Now it reappears when the *Canticle* is close to its end.

Francis has not given up for even a moment on his invocation of highest heaven. He has simply recognized that "no mortal lips are worthy to pronounce your name" or speak the mystery of the Most High. We noted earlier that these words in the second stanza are an expression of a decisive experience in Francis' spiritual life: the experience of a self-stripping before God and the renunciation by the soul of the attempt to take possession of God and his mystery. Before God, Francis ranks himself among creatures; he acknowledges himself to be their brother, "with great humility," thanksgiving, and a sense of wonder. His quest for the Most High becomes associated with a quest for communion with visible things. Visible things become, as he praises God through them, the path of reconciliation with himself and others.

It is this humble detour through creation and in opening itself to a desire for universal pardon and peace that the soul truly encounters God. The man who acknowledged that he was unworthy to pronounce the name of the Most High and who "with great humility" agreed to be brother to all creatures and to praise God with them see himself crowned by the Most High: "By you, Most High, they will be crowned."

The image of the Most High does not point to an abstract transcendent Being cut off from creatures, nor does it symbolize the imaginary refuge of a soul permeated with resentment of its earthly condition and of the obscure, unconscious links that bind it to the natural world. The image expresses a Transcendence that is to be encountered in an ever more intimate presence to the humblest of created realities. This Transcendence waits for man down at the roots of being. The Most High thus appears here as the crowning fulfillment of this humble love of creatures, to which the soul has opened itself by becoming reconciled to its own mystery in its fullness, and which manifests itself in a boundless desire for pardon and peace.

The man whom the Most High crowns is solar man who is filled with mercy for every creature. Like the sun, such a man sheds his splendid rays on all. Like the sun, he is a symbol of the Most High, because he offers to all "his entire attention and the gift of his whole self; for these [are] an analogy of the presence and of the gift God makes of Himself at all times and to all creatures."[12]

Chapter 11

Sister Death

All praise be yours, my Lord, through Sister Death,
From whose embrace no mortal can escape.

Woe to those who die in mortal sin!
Happy those She finds doing your will!
The second death can do no harm to them.

These last two stanzas of the *Canticle* were composed at the beginning of October, 1226, when Francis was close to his final agony.

> Then he spent the few days that remained before his death in praise, teaching his companions whom he loved so much to praise Christ with him. . . .He also invited all creatures to praise God, and by means of the words he had composed earlier, he exhorted them to love God. He exhorted death itself, terrible and hateful to all, to give praise, and going joyfully to meet it, he invited it to make its lodging with him. "Welcome," he said, "my sister death."[1]

These stanzas are the author's welcome to his own death. What they express is not a spiritual meditation or exhortation on death in general, but the existential encounter of the poet with his own death, an encounter with the very "event of dying." They are a celebration of this encounter.

Francis wishes to link his celebration of death with his celebration of all other creatures: sun, moon, and stars, wind and water, fire and earth. Again, as in the preceding stanzas on pardon and peace, we cannot but ask: What internal links bind this celebration of death to the rest of the poem? How can a *Canticle of Brother Sun* shift into a canticle of death? How can the expression of fervent communion with things turn into an expression of the experience that removes us completely from things? The question cannot be evaded. We may venture to say that the failure to see how the *Canticle of Brother Sun* is also, in a profoundly true sense, a canticle of death, has often led to superficial interpretations of the poem as a whole.

The stanzas begin, as do the previous sets of stanzas, with a burst of praise. But here the basis is no longer one or other creature but what Francis calls his "Sister Death." The expression has the same simplicity as for example "Sister Water," and this we can hardly help find surprising, especially since Francis makes no effort to hide the true face of this final "sister." His description goes straight to the point: "Sister death, from whose embrace no mortal can escape." A strange sister indeed, whose face is that of inevitable necessity! No one can escape her! But in this description the real meaning of the expression "Sister Death" is revealed: it expresses a fraternal encounter with necessity, with the hard and inexorable necessity of dying; an encounter that is experienced and celebrated, in the open-endedness of praise, as a path leading to the Sacred.

We do not have an experience, in the strict sense of the word, of death and its inevitability. "The idea of death actually penetrates into me from the outside; I learn it through the elementary biology which intercourse with other human beings and the observed event of their death teach me. In them I discover an empirical law without exception."[2] But, although I grasp the necessity of the law, my grasp is not grounded in any awareness of my own being; admission of the necessity is rather forced upon me from without, as the necessity of a brute fact. Even when the necessity applies directly to me as an individual face to face with the event of dying, the necessity continues to be impenetrable by my self-consciousness.

The idea which I have of death and its necessity at this moment can of course affect me deeply. My idea remains, nonetheless, the idea of something completely opaque, something I cannot in any way lay hold of and explore. I know that I cannot indefinitely avoid death, but death itself eludes me, even when it is right at hand and has me by the throat. "I have. . .no means of anticipating the actual event of dying itself."[3] My only experience is of life, even if it be life at its last gasp. The "event of dying" always lies beyond the direct grasp of consciousness, and remains something wholly other which I can in no way assimilate or dominate. I can conceive of it only as the negation of my conscious existence, death comes as a threat of annihilation. Thus, the necessity of death may force itself upon me from outside as a sheer fact, but it is not for that reason acceptable to the conscious self; it can give rise within me only to anxiety and rebellion.

Yet it is to this opaque necessity that Francis declares himself a brother, just as he declared himself earlier to be brother to the sun. His assertion is not marked by anxiety; it is just as straightforward and simple as his earlier assertions. He greets death as a sister. We might regard the words "Sister Death" as merely the effect of poetic enthusiasm were it not for the fact that Francis speaks thus when faced with the event of dying.

Were we ignorant of Francis' real sentiments, we might also regard the fraternal greeting as the appeal of a dying man for deliverance from intolerable suffering. After all, do not many men think of death as a "sister" who liberates them by depriving them of all self-awareness? But that is certainly not Francis' meaning. Far from voicing the distressed cry of a consciousness that longs for the end of its existence, the words "Sister Death," in Francis' mouth, are a profound and heartfelt acceptance of the very necessity of dying, an acceptance that gives his existence access to its fullest possible dimensions.

To greet death as a "Sister" is to acknowledge a close relationship between her and the self; it is to discover in the total otherness of death something really not alien to us but a further dimension of ourselves. The dimension is one which I cannot comprehend and to which I can open myself only by an act in which I completely surrender my separate, individual self in an astonishing gesture of the greatest possible poverty.

We must situate the fraternal salute to death within the *Canticle* as a whole, as we have thus far seen it. The *Can-*

ticle is not simply an expression, albeit religious, of esthetic emotion when confronted with the spectacle of nature. It is rather a hymn of praise of God out of the midst of humble fellowship with the entirety of creation. By that very fact, it is also the expression of a far-reaching act of self-stripping and openness to the whole realm of the involuntary or "necessity from below," an act whose context is the wonder-filled celebration of things.

This self-stripping or self-dispossession reaches its climax in the celebration of the earth, in the fervent communion with "Sister Earth, our mother." The earth "is only the surrounding of my absolute involuntary."[4] It is upon the earth that Francis asks to be laid when he comes to die. Here we can see the full truth of what Paul Ricoeur calls "a Franciscan knowledge of necessity: I am 'with' necessity, 'among' creatures."[5] The *Canticle* thus culminates in the total stripping of self. Francis is no longer locked up inside his narrow individuality; no longer does he crouch protectively over the self as over a treasure. He has been completely freed of all possessiveness with regard to himself, and has made his own the advice he had given to others: "Keep nothing for yourselves, so that he who has given himself wholly to you may receive you wholly."[6]

Being thus stripped of self, Francis is completely open to Being. Henceforth he exists more truly in Being than in himself; he is at home there, and his song is a song of Being. When Francis sings his hymn of creation, he is no longer able to enjoy creatures himself, for even the least ray of sun burns his eyes. What he praises in them is the creative splendor of Being, which exists beyond anything he himself can see or touch. His *Canticle* is a "unique affirmation of the value of the life and existence we receive from the hands of God."[7]

All this amounts to saying that the *Canticle* is the expression of a truly radical conversion. Characteristic of this conversion is an increasing lack of interest in anything that has to do with man's limited conscious individuality, and a growing concern with all that has to do with Being in its fullness. The existential center of gravity has been displaced: it is now to be found not in the self and its exclusive interests, however spiritual, but in the mystery of Being.

The man who has thus put himself into the hands of Being now sees everything, including death, in the positive light of Being. Death is for him no longer the alien destroyer; she is that only to a man who clings to his ego. "Woe to those who die in mortal sin," says Francis immediately after greeting Sister Death. Mortal sin, sin that brings death to the soul, is precisely the closing in of the conscious self upon itself and its individuality; it is self-possession at any price, a protective withdrawal into the self that turns being into having.

A man who thus cuts himself off from Being is spiritually dead. For him, the greatest evil is bodily death, for it means the breakdown and destruction of the self. Pierre Emmanuel writes:

> Death terrifies us because it takes everything from us, including, first and foremost, our very selves. At my death, my egocentric energies cease to exist, and with them the ego to which I link my identity. This change in direction, this biological shattering, seems to me to be the annihilation of my very being. As I observed certain deaths and the violence that was indistinguishably the work of the dying person and of an Other, I seemed to be watching the final act of a struggle in which a self, in the name of the person's entire being, was vainly rejecting the obvious.[8]

Francis of Assisi had long meditated on the bitter death of the man who seeks to retain possession of himself, as we can see from the example he gives in his *Letter to All the Faithful,* where he draws the moral: "All the talent and ability, all the learning and wisdom which he thought his own, are taken away from him."[9] Such a death, says Francis, causes "such anguish and distress that only a person who has experienced it can appreciate it."[10] No possessiveness, however ardent, can resist the destructive power of death. Consequently, in the eyes of a man whose being has degenerated into a having and has become an object to be possessed, death is the path of despair, a road that leads nowhere. For such a man, death cannot be transfigured; it is the symbol of nothingness; it is the totally opaque other, it is nothingness.

We must acknowledge at least one manner of conceiving immortality is in fact a way for the self to ward off the destruction death brings. According to this conception, the individual will continue to possess himself after death. Such an idea of immortality is, however, simply a creation of our proprietary instinct projecting itself from time into eternity. But as Pierre Emmanuel remarks:

> Immortality and eternity are radically different kinds of concept and spring from contrasting worlds of thought. We must give up immortality if we are to rise to the level of eternity. In this surrender we commit the self to Being. . . .Eternity is a mode of existing, but one opposed to the mode of existing proper to Being. Eternity is not *my* mode of existing but that of Being.[11]

If the creature is to bless death and its inevitability, he must ascend to the mode of being proper to the Eternal One: "Happy those She [Death] finds doing your will! The second death can do no harm to them." He who has accepted the loss of the self and has entrusted himself to Being and Being's creative plan is already immersed in him who is eternal. He no longer lives the life of an isolated individual but shares the life of Being itself. Consequently, he is capable of the supreme hope. The Eternal himself is his hope: "You are our haven and our hope. . . .You are our eternal life," sings Francis in his *Praises of God.*[12]

Francis can confront both the sun and death with the brotherly spirit and the same joy of heart. The same mystery of Being speaks to him and draws his praise. But he can look at death in this fashion only because he has first consented, "with great humility," to be brother to the sun and all other creatures and has learned, through his wonder-filled contact with them, to see in "necessity from below" a reflection of the Most High.

It is in this light that we can now see the profound but hidden link between these final two stanzas of the *Canticle* and the rest of the poem. These stanzas put the seal of the Eternal God on the cosmic praise that has preceded. The road that passes through creatures proves to be a road into eternity.

This is one aspect of the relation between "Sister Death" and the praise of creatures. The *Canticle* leads logically to the supreme detachment manifested in the fraternal welcome given to death, it is evidently only in the light of that welcome that the poem can be sung with its full depth of meaning. For Francis, existence itself is a source of delight, and "every moment renews the joy of an encounter with the Eternal that takes place in familiar objects."[13]

The delight is the delight of total poverty. Francis has entrusted himself without reserve to Being in his fraternal welcome of death and its inevitability. Such a radical self-commitment to Being is the only way for a human being to be fully present to the world in a truly openended fashion.

> In renouncing all these things [the good things of the world and the flesh], he [Francis] destroyed at the same time all the barriers separating him from the creative act, the source of infinite beauty that is always available to us . . . .The work of creation continued to unfold itself before his eyes.[14]

It is in the light of "Sister Death," that the *Canticle* reveals its full splendor. It is not to be confused with a simple exercise of enthusiastic piety, but is rather the direct expression of Francis' interior self-opening to Being. Here, in Rilke's phrase, "song is existence." Within Francis' being, creation continues to unfold; there it manifests its inexhaustible plenitude and is transformed into "an immense and precious treasure" of eternity.[15]

For song, as taught by you, is not desire,
not wooing of something finally attained;
song is existence. . . .[16]

Praising, that's it! As a praiser and blesser
he came. . . .
He is a messenger always attendant,
reaching far through their gates resplendent
dishes of fruit for the dead to praise.[17]

These verses from Rilke's *Sonnets to Orpheus* could have been written of Francis. Like the song of Orpheus, Francis comes from beyond the threshold of death; it originates in a profound receptivity that embraces everything, even death. On his return from the abode of the dead Orpheus cries out: "Being here's glorious!" (*Hiersein ist herrlich!*).[18] Similarly, it is from the depths where he has welcomed death as a sister that Francis celebrates the splendors of creation.

Only by him with whose lays
shades were enraptured
may the celestial praise
faintly be captured.[19]

Here we are worlds removed from a *Canticle* to be interpreted as a pastoral poem of religious inspiration. And yet, if we want to grasp the real meaning of Francis' celebration of the world, we must link the poem with the great inspiration represented by Orpheus. The *Canticle of Brother Sun,* an Orphic hymn? Yes, but we must understand such a claim properly! We are not at all saying that the myth of Orpheus exerted even the slightest conscious historical influence on Francis. We are simply indicating the experiential depths out of which the poem was created, and the great unconscious archetype who speaks in the *Canticle.*

Only such a reading of the *Canticle* can lead us to a solution of the problem we raised at the beginning and that has presided over the whole of this study: the problem of the bond that links in a single celebration Francis' love of the invisible and his enthusiastic praise of the created universe, the powerful impulse of his soul toward the Most High and his closeness to material things, his spiritual experience that was characterized by utter detachment and his profound communion with the earth. Given such a problem, it is not a matter of indifference for us to understand that in Francis' poem Orpheus is the singer. For, Orphic poetry is essentially a poetry of reconciliation. By his singing Orpheus reconciles heaven and earth, life and death:

> Does he belong here? No, his spreading
> nature from either domain has sprung.[20]

The two domains also meet in Francis' poem. But are there two domains? No, for this man who, in his ardent movement toward the Most High, has submitted, "with great humility," to make simple things his companions and to deal as a brother with the earth and even with necessity from below and with death, there are no longer two domains? No, for this man who, in his ardent movement toward the Most High, has submitted, "with great humility," to make simple things his companions and to deal as a brother with the earth and even with necessity from below and with death, there are no longer two domains. There is no longer a world above and a world below, a luminous world of the spirit and a dark world of nature. The Most High himself is present at the roots of reality and flourishes in all things. The kingdom of God is no longer another world set over against our present world, but is at the heart of even the most ordinary, humdrum existence; it is a transforming power dwelling at the core of our present life.

The *Canticle of Brother Sun* wells up out of Francis' joy when he becomes certain that the kingdom is his. The remarkable thing is that the kingdom thus guaranteed him presents itself in the form of an immense and precious transfiguration of the present world:

> Suddenly he heard a voice in spirit: "Tell me, Brother: if, in compensation for your sufferings and tribulations you were given an immense and precious treasure: the whole mass of the earth changed into pure gold, pebbles into precious stones, and the waters of the rivers into perfume. . . .would you not rejoice?. . . . Be glad and joyful in the midst of your infirmities and tribulations: as of now, live in peace as if you were already sharing my kingdom."[21]

Such a transformation of the world takes place only in the person who is open: open to all things, even to the point of welcoming death as a sister. Rilke is not deluding himself when he invokes the figure of the little Poor Man, who in death is invisibly united to all things, while all things are transfigured in him.

> When he died, so light as to be nameless,
> he was scattered; his seed flowed
> in the brooks and sang in the trees
> and gazed at him calmly from the flowers.
> He lay and sang. And when his sisters came
> they wept for their beloved spouse.
>
> Oh! where has the clear echo of him gone to?
> Why do the poor who wait not feel
> from afar his presence, his rejoicing and his youth?
> Why do they not see rising in the east
> the great evening star of poverty?[22]

Rilke answers this last question in one of his *Sonnets to Orpheus:*

> Raise no commemorating stone. The roses
> shall bloom every summer for his sake.
> For this is Orpheus. His metamorphoses
> in this one and that. . . .
> Could you but feel his passing's needfulness.[23]

Chapter 12

The Sun and the Cross

Our analyses have shown that Francis' *Canticle of Brother Sun* is the poetic expression of a man's reconciliation with his total destiny in the world. The originality and depth of this poetic vision will perhaps emerge even more clearly if we compare it with that of another singer of the sun.

We have had occasion in the earlier chapters to refer to Neitzsche's *Thus Spoke Zarathustra.* A fuller comparison between that work and Francis' poem may prove surprising to us. But we must forget for a moment the philosophical theories voiced by Zarathustra; our only interest is in the poetry of the work and more especially in those great direct images of matter which inspire the work and have their own value and significance apart from the ideas expressed and the writer's intentions.[1] From the viewpoint of its major images, must we not say that Nietzsche's *Zarathustra* is also a *Canticle of Brother Sun*?

At the heart of Zarathustra's poetic universe, as in that of Francis of Assisi, stands the image of the resplendent sun. It is not accidental that Nietzsche's hero bears the name of the ancient prophet of sun, flame, and pure fire. Zoroaster or Zarathustra means "Golden Star." The prologue of Nietzche's work is dominated by the image of this great star. It is the sun that Zarathustra addresses himself first and foremost, as to a guide and a model:

> One morning he rose with the dawn, stepped before the sun, and spoke to it thus:
>
> "You great star, what would your happiness be had you not those for whom you shine?
>
> "For ten years you have climbed to my cave: you would have tired of your light and of the journey had it not been for me and my eagle and my serpent.
>
> "But we waited for you every morning, took your overflow from you, and blessed you for it.
>
> "Behold, I am weary of my wisdom, like a bee that has gathered too much honey; I need hands outstretched to receive it.
>
> "I would give away and distribute. . . .
>
> "For that I must descend to the depths, as you do in the

> evening when you go behind the sea and still bring light to the underworld, you overrich star.
>
> "Like you, I must *go under*—go down, as is said by man, to whom I want to descend."[2]

This image of the sun, like that of "my lord Brother Sun" in the *Canticle,* speaks not only to the eyes but to the soul as well. For the soul, it is the symbol and exercises the attraction of Being and its creative generosity. It is both an epiphany and an invitation: an invitation to participate in the world's grandeur. Moreover, by communing through imagination with this lofty image of light and its generous outpouring, the soul discovers its own destiny: "Like you, I must *go under*. . . ." Here we have an image that pervades the whole work and plays a basic role for it inspires Zarathustra's activity at every point:

> I want to go to men once more; under their eyes I want to go under; dying, I want to give them my richest gift. From the sun I learned this: when he goes down, overrich, he pours gold into the sea out of inexhaustible riches, so that even the poorest fisherman still rows with golden oars. For this I once saw and I did not tire of my tears as I watched it.
>
> Like the sun, Zarathustra wants to go under.[3]

Zarathustra's dream is to become "like the sun," "a self-propelled wheel. . .a sacred 'Yes,'"[4] so that he may play the divine game of creation. To this end, he must descend from his mountain and bring the light into the depths. Zarathustra is willing to leave the solitary heights to which the inner impulse of his being had driven him, he can no longer be satisfied with a transcendence apart. That kind of transcendent God is dead. This movement of descent to earth in order to commune with beings there reminds us of the similar movement we observed in Francis' *Canticle.*[5]

But does Zarathustra really descend to the earth? Does he succeed in truly becoming a brother to the beings of earth? Does his Canticle of Sun turn into a Canticle of Creatures as well? It might seem at first that the answer to these questions is Yes. We see Zarathustra rushing down the mountain path, seeking out the village in the valley, and mingling with men. Yet, strange to say, his imagination, at its deeper levels, continues to dwell on the heights and soar over the peaks like the eagles who are "neighbors of the snow, neighbors of the sun."[6]

The material of his dreams is neither earth nor water nor fire, but air: the thin, biting air of the glaciers, the air men breathe in the freezing, wild alpine heights. It is matter that is subject to no pull of gravity. Zarathustra's imagination communes with none of the other elements but remains in this narrow cosmic circle, a prisoner of this "azure bell."[7]

In his book *L'air et les songes,* Gaston Bachelard has a chapter on the images of matter in Nietzsche's poetry. He writes:

> Nietzsche is not a poet of the *earth.* Leaf mold and loam and tilled open fields provide him with no images. The metals, minerals, and gems which the "poet of earth" loves for their inner riches stir in him no *reveries of inwardness.* Stone and rock often appear in his pages, but only as symbols of hardness; they have none of the slow life—the slowest of all lives, life extraordinary for its very slowness—that they possess in the reveries of the "poets of stones."[8]

As for the *soft earth,* Nietzsche feels only revulsion toward it.[9]

Nor is Nietzsche a poet of *water.* "Images of water are certainly to be found, since no poet can entirely do without metaphors of liquidity. But in Nietzsche's work these metaphors are fleeting and casual; they do not shape his *reveries concerning matter.*"[10] There are a few exceptions. One is a poem in which Nietzsche voices "a need of sweetness, shadow, and water":

> Ten years have slipped away—
> no drop of water has reached me,
> no moisture-laden wind, no dew of love—
> a land deprived of rain. . . .

Today I draw them, bid them come:
create a shadowed space around me with your breasts!
—I want to milk you,
cows that graze upon the heights!
Wisdom warm as milk, sweet dew of love,
I pour you out in floods upon the land.[11]

It must be observed that this maternal, nourishing water does not spring from the earth but falls from heaven; it belongs to a "world of heights." "The place where this soothing water collects is the heavens."[12] Does not Nietzsche say of the sea: "It *wants* to be kissed and sucked by the thirst of the sun; it *wants* to become air and height and a footpath of light, and itself light"![13] The image once again betrays "a psychism focused on ascents"; it also shows the attraction the image of the sun has for the poet.

The same kind of observation can be made of Nietzsche's images of fire. The flame that burns in his imagination is the kind associated with Jupiter. It is fire from heaven, it is lightning and thunder. The poet's imagination always carries him back to his favorite place. We may even say it never leaves that place, but with the strong beat of eagle wings seeks to rise ever more deeply into it: "O heaven above me, pure and deep! You abyss of light! Seeing you, I tremble with godlike desires. To throw myself into your heights, that is *my* depth. To hide in your purity, that is *my* innocence."[14]

Neitzsche is thoroughly fascinated by this "heaven pure and deep" that precedes sunrise and reveals to him a superhuman purity and innocence he yearns to share:

> Gods are shrouded by their beauty; thus you conceal your stars. You do not speak; thus you proclaim your wisdom to me.[15]
>
> And when I wandered alone, for *whom* did my soul hunger at night, on false paths? And when I climbed mountains, *whom* did I always seek on the mountains, if not you? And all my wandering and mountain climbing were sheer necessity and a help in my helplessness: what I want with all my will is to *fly,* to fly up into *you.*[16]
>
> O heaven over me, pure and light.[17]

Nietzsche's song, like that of Francis, is dominated by and focused on the *image* of the "Most High." "We embrace the heavens ever more longingly. . . .the fatality of the heights, *our* fatality," he says of himself.[18] Nietzsche is the very model of a poet of the vertical dimension, a poet of the summits, a poet bent on ascending."[19] Unlike Francis, Nietzsche's path to the highest heavens does not pass through communion with the humble things of earth. His sensibility and imagination reject the possibility of regarding these things as brothers and sisters. In one of his poems Nietzsche goes so far as to disdainfully refuse such brotherhood:

> Not by land,
> not by sea
> runs the road that takes you
> to the country that is always bright.[20]

Not by land or sea: not by earth or water. Here is a rejection of the elements that are female and can bear fruit; a rejection of maternal images; a rejection of elements that can mediate: "And whom did I hate more than drifting clouds. . . .? I loathe the drifting clouds, those great stealthy cats. . . .We loathe these mediators and mixers, the drifting clouds."[21]

The only cosmic element with which Nietzsche's imagination feels true brotherhood and in which his reveries find satisfaction is the air: the pure, icy air of the heights:

> Verily, we keep no homes here for the unclean: our pleasures would be an ice cave to their bodies and their spirits.
>
> And we want to live over them like strong winds, neighbors of the eagles, neighbors of the sun: thus live strong winds. . . .
>
> Verily, a strong wind is Zarathustra for all who are low.[22]

As Michel Mansuy aptly notes, "the air, in Nietzsche, can turn into a gale or become filled with butterflies."[23] Nietzsche's poetry does have certain favorite images linked with the earth. Consider this image of a tree: "It is with man as it is with the tree. The more he aspires to the height and light, the more strongly do his roots strive earthward, downward, into the dark, the deep—into evil."

But we should not let ourselves be misled here. This image of the tree does not signify any communion with necessity from below, any needs for roots that reach into the depths. The fact that the depths are equated with evil shows Nietzsche's image of the tree is quite different from Francis. It expresses the danger a man runs when he seeks to pursue his highest desires. The danger comes precisely from the man's roots for he feels himself being drawn downward by the subterranean action of all that links him to the earth. The more he seeks to rise, the more his roots seek to draw him down into the abyss.

The only action of the roots is a negation of any heroic resolution. It is the work of a sapper who can make the noble individual fall back into sceptical mockery of his own highest hopes and indeed of all high hopes. In such an atmosphere, we are far removed indeed from an mystical communion with the depths of the earth. Nietzsche's image of the tree brands such a communion as an evil that can make the noble man fail in the pursuit of his highest hopes.

There is an essential difference between the poetic vision of Nietzsche with its proud self-limitation to a cosmos consisting solely of air and sun, and the poetic vision of Francis who, while remaining open to the radiant image of the Most High, also enters into communion with the lowliest elements of the cosmos and feels himself a brother to our Mother Earth. Nietzsche's *Canticle of Brother Sun* never turns into a *Canticle of Creatures,* that is, of all creatures without exception.

This difference of vision has a notable impact on the poet's interior development. The images which determine a poet's style have their own special destiny, and the poet who experiences these images intensely comes to share that destiny. We may not with impunity allow ourselves to become intoxicated with any images for we are always the children of our imaginations.

Nietzsche and Francis of Assisi: two types of poet, two kinds of presence to the world, two destinies. We know the destiny to which Nietzsche was led by the magic hand of his own poetry. His mystical enthusiasm for images of air and of the highest, iciest solitudes inevitably fostered a style of thought characterized by arrogance and a penchant for aloneness. His ideal being was one enamored of the superhuman and of a higher divine state in which man would at last be delivered from the pull of gravity, from all that binds him to earth, from all that constitutes his "archeology," and in which he would be like God:

> Cast down into the abyss that weighs upon you!
> Learn, man, to forget! Learn to forget!
> The art of forgetting is something divine!
> If you want to rise,
> if you want to be at home in the heights,
> cast down into the sea all that weighs upon you!
> Yonder is the sea, throw yourself into it!
> The art of forgetting is something divine.[25]

As Bachelard notes, there is no question here

> of plunging oneself into the sea in order to find rebirth in its waters. The point rather is to cast from us all that weighs us down. . .to throw all that is heavy in us into the sea so that it may disappear forever. Thus we annihilate our ponderous, sluggish other self: everything in us that is earth and interior secret past. Then our other air-like self will shine forth in splendor; we will be "free as air,". . .and experience the decisive about-face that will mark us with the sign of the more-than-human. We will be airy-light and rise directly up into the freedom of the heavens.[26]

We have the great transvaluation of all values that Nietzsche dreamed of while intoxicating himself on images of the air: "He who will one day teach men to fly will have moved all boundary stones; the boundary stones themselves will fly up into the air before him, and he will rebaptize earth—'the light one.'"[27] Such a man will owe nothing now to Mother Earth. He will be delivered from necessity from below and freed from all that is "other." He will be a man without a past, without father and mother, and will be his own beginning. He will be the totally transparent being: God.

Sustained by his reveries of the air, Nietzsche believed, in certain moments of poetic intoxication, that his dream had become a reality and he had reached a state of divine consciousness: "Now I am light, now I fly, now I see myself beneath myself, now a god dances through me."[28]

These words give us a glimpse of the spell cast on Nietzsche by images of the air. "The native country where a being truly belongs to itself is the air of heaven. Nietzsche is constantly returning to it.[29] "The pure air symbolizes the consciousness of the moment of freedom."[30] But this divine consciousness of airy lightness, which Nietzsche here claims as his very self, cannot represent the whole reality of man who is both god and animal. Sooner or later, such a consciousness will feel the stirring beneath it of the "dark monster," the unconscious forces which link the consciousness to earthly life and which it too readily believes it has sloughed off:

> Everything is still asleep now. . .; even the sea is asleep. Drunk with sleep and strange it looks at me. But its breath is warm, that I feel. And I also feel that it is dreaming. In its dream it tosses on hard pillows. Listen! Listen! How it groans with evil memories! Or evil forebodings? Alas, I am sad with you, you dark monster, and even annoyed with myself for your sake. Alas, that my hand does not have strength enough! Verily, I should like to deliver you from evil dreams.[31]

"I am. . .even annoyed with myself for your sake": here speaks the tragic fate of a split person, trapped in its own reveries of the air, divided within, and incapable of becoming reconciled to the subterranean levels of its being and thereby open to its own totality. Nietzsche has rejected the symbols that could serve as mediators, the great maternal images of water and earth: "Not by land, not by sea." Consequently, the lines of communication are cut between the conscious part of his being (symbolized by the image of the sun) and the "other," the "dark monster" who is beset in its dreams by "evil forebodings."

Shut off from his own "archeology" and that of mankind, Nietzsche was condemned to ignorance of the path that leads through authentic communion with life and other beings; interior division and even madness lay ahead. He turned from what was at hand and looked for what was far off, seeking an impossible encounter amid the solitude of the glaciers and the ceaseless winds. On the heights, "six thousand feet above mankind and time," he waited for a friend, but the only friend who came was his air-wrought double, Zarathustra.

In the heaven created by his reveries of the air, Nietzsche communed with no one: not with men and not with the Most High." "Bird-wisdom speaks thus: 'Behold, there is no above, now below!"[32] As Paul Ricoeur rightly observes, "to refuse necessity from below is to defy Transcendence."[33] Nietzsche was really playing the solar hero who replaces the god. He identified himself with Transcendence. "I live in my own light; I drink back into myself the flames that break out of me. I do not know the happiness of those who receive. . . .They receive from me, but do I touch their souls?"[34]

Quite different indeed was the life and destiny of Francis of Assisi. His destiny was expressed in a poetry of the sun, but it was a poetry also open to all the basic cosmic images. Francis saw in the sun a symbol of the Most High, but he judged himself unworthy even to pronounce the name of that Most High. To the very depths of his being he acknowledged the fact that God alone is God; far from identifying himself with God, he took his place among creatures and unhesitatingly described himself as their brother. His attitude drew him to an esthetics that was dominated by humility and preserved his religious life from any tinge of idealism.

Though he was an enthusiastic brother to the sun, Francis did not spurn Sister Water, "so useful, lovely, precious and pure." He was friend to Brother Wind, but did not give less praise to "Sister Earth, our mother, who feeds us in her sovereignty." Francis was filled with a heartfelt willingness to be carried and nurtured by Mother Earth. His path to the Most High led through communion with all these humble realities. It was a path that opened him to all that exists, and first and foremost to himself: to the dark region of his being, to his roots that were sunk deep in the whole past of man and indeed of life itself.

The esthetics of humility did not simply carry Francis to the heart of sensible things. Through these, once they were interiorly felt and imagined, he was brought into contact with his own depths: not by way of narcissistic introversion but by way of detachment from self and entrusting of himself to Being. He was able to accept within a larger vision the obscure primordial forces of the soul. Liberated from egocentric concentration on themselves, they could develop freely in an intimate communion with all other creatures and with the author of all creatures. The praise of material things thus became the language of an authentic spiritual ascent that involved and transfigured the whole order of nature.

Francis' *Canticle of Brother Sun,* unlike that of Nietzsche, is truly a canticle of all creatures. It does not lock man up in an icy, arrogant solitude but opens him to a sharing in and love of all beings; it sets him on the road of reconciliation, mercy, and peace, a road that leads to a real encounter with him whose name no mortal lips are worthy to pronounce: the Most High himself.

Francis in his *Canticle* is the best illustration of a remark by Martin Heidegger: "Anything true and authentic reaches maturity only if the person is open to the call of highest heaven, while at the same time remaining under the protection of the earth that supports and produces him."[35] How did Francis manage to combine these two states of soul? What was the secret of his success? We emphasized earlier the humility that led him to take his place among creatures. But this attitude in turn was grounded in a profound and far ranging vision. His capacity for looking humbly and tenderly at all things, however material, was intimately connected with his discovery of the human, suffering face of Christ. We cannot insist too much on the fact that this man who sang of Brother Sun and all other creatures was the stigmatic of Mount Alverna who carried in his soul no less than in his body the burning image of Christ crucified.

Malraux has the splendid sentence: "It was in the shadow of the crucifixion, not in the splendor of the Pantocrator, that Christian Rome discovered the child's eyes that would so obsess Dostoyevsky, and the mute eyes of ox and ass, so dear to Francis."[36] The words are those of a philosopher of art, but they expressed in imaged form a historical and existential truth. The dazzling image of Christ the Pantocrator that so fascinated the soul of Byzantium and later that of the Christian West reflected an imperious type of religious consciousness that held it over created things rather communing with them or feeling a brotherly sympathy with them. Such a consciousness was somewhat remote from the lowly ways proper to the Incarnation; in fact, it ignored both the infancy and the agony of Christ.

The *Canticle* introduced a new way of looking at things. But the new outlook of wonder and brotherly feeling cannot be separated from a particular image of the Son of Man. There is a close relation between Francis' praise of the world and his contemplation of Christ. Celano tells us that "many times, as he went along the way meditating on and singing of Jesus, he would forget his journey and invite all the elements to praise Jesus."[37] And what did Francis contemplate in Christ? The humility of the Transcendent One which revealed to him the mystery of *agape.* The Most High Son of God entering our world, not simply assuming our fleshly nature but becoming part of the web of sensible reality that included even the humblest material things—*that* is what kept the soul of Francis in a state of constant wonder.

It would take us far afield to elucidate fully this aspect of the Incarnation, Christ's communion with the things of creation. We can only remind the reader of a few essential points. The first public act of Jesus, the act with which he began his mission, was to descend into the Jordan, to the great astonishment of John the Baptist. It was in this humble communion with the water that he received the Spirit. Water and Spirit! Jesus himself tells us we must be born again of both if we are to enter the kingdom of God.

We should also reread the discourses of Jesus, especially the parables. In them, the images of the most humble everyday realities abound: the light from the lamp, the way, the tree, the house, the field and its treasure, the seed, the red sky at evening, the wind whose voice we hear without being able to tell where it comes from or where it is going; all these are there, and much else. But these are only comparisons made to appeal to an essentially rural audience? No, there is more than this to it.

All these images reveal a man who humbly stays close to created things. He has the ability to look at them, accept them, imagine and dream them in a profound way, to the point of finding them strangely like the kingdom of heaven. "The kingdom of heaven is like. . ." is a favorite expression of Jesus. It is as though he were telling us that the kingdom is not somewhere beyond the clouds or in another world, but has come to us and is to be found at the very heart of everyday life; that the surest way for us to draw near to it is to stay close to the simplest things of our experience. Because he himself is in communion with the inexhaustibly fascinating reality of things and can make us see them as he sees them, Christ is able to introduce us to the mystery of the kingdom. In the process, the Gospel of the kingdom becomes a canticle of creatures.

A great deal has been written on the teaching of Jesus from the moral and doctrinal viewpoints, but the poetry of the Gospel has largely been overlooked. It is usually thought of as simply a matter of expression, as the outward garment of the message proper, or as something accidental. It has not been approached as a manner of living on this earth and being present to our world. Above all, it has not been thought of as a way of being present to the kingdom by being present to the world.

Christ does not defend himself against reality. He has no fear, no distrust, of nature. On the contrary, he is filled with wonder at the things of the world and gives himself completely to them. Isn't nature, after all, the Father's work? By approaching nature in this fashion, Christ opens himself to the "grace" of the imagination. "When the spiritual development is intense, the concrete or esthetic sense of visible things tends sometimes, as with St. Bernard, to become dulled, but we do not have to lament any such defect in our Lord,"[38] That is Father de Grandmaison's judgment and the point he is making is important with regard to the very message of Jesus.

"Man lives poetically on this earth," when he reaches the point of living there fully and authentically.[39] Only the "grace" of the imagination makes it possible for man not simply to commune with things but also, and above all, to come in contact, through the basic images of things, with his own deep psychic roots and those of mankind. When Christ opened himself to this "grace," he became present to the whole of our "archeology." He went down into the great river of the human psyche, just as he went down into the water of the Jordan. He thereby accepted and made his own all the dark forces in man and transfigured them. What was darkness in us became light in him. He made himself the archetype of our own transfiguration.

But Christ went even further. In a mysterious fashion he

linked material things and their images with the supernatural life he came to bring. He made them the means of man's divinization; consequently, man is to receive the very life of God by giving himself over to things. The sacramental economy of salvation which Christ established reveals to us the hidden meaning of things. It reveals by fulfilling it. It shows us that "the world serves man's *body,* but especially does it serve his *soul;* it helps him preserve and develop his *life,* but especially does it help him achieve *wisdom.*"[40]

When Jesus wishes to cure the man born blind and thereby to tell the world that he is its Light, he begins by stooping to the ground in a gesture of love filled with fervent humility. With his saliva he makes a little mud and smears it on the blind man's eyes, then tells him: "Go, wash in the pool of Siloam."[41] Through this humble communion with earth and water Christ gives the man a new birth into the light of the invisible God.

Have we really understood and fully accepted this dimension of the salvation Christ brings us? It is doubtful that we have. Fearing a revival of pagan naturalism, we have played down Christian sacramentalism and emptied it of all affective and mystical communion with the elements it uses. Christ had no such fear of putting men in contact with Mother Earth and with the water that is the source of life. He took the archetypal images and gestures of natural religious man and revived them. Undoubtedly he gave them a new meaning, but the new meaning did not eliminate the old; it fulfilled it in the highest degree.

By assuming the archetypal images and giving them a new meaning, Christ also took over the power these images have to transform the depths of the human psyche. Louis Beirnaert writes:

> By their [myths and symbols] mediation, salvation, first communicated to the fine point of the soul, penetrates all the depths of the psyche. Christ and the Church, by taking up and using the great images of sun, moon, wood, water, mother, etc., have brought the message of grace to the affective powers for which

these symbols stand. We must not reduce the Incarnation to a taking of flesh in the narrow sense. God has entered even into the collective unconscious to save it and to fulfill it. Christ went down into hell. And how can the salvation so won take hold on our unconscious minds unless it speaks their own language and accommodates itself to their own categories![42]

It was part of Francis of Assisi's mission to remind us, by means of his *Canticle of Brother Sun* with its celebration of "Sister Earth, our mother," that the Gospel has been preached even to the pagan depths of man and that the pagan and the Jew that lie dormant in every man are now reconciled in the new man.[43] Francis received the grace to do this when he received the grace of contemplating and imitating Christ crucified. This statement may seem a paradox but, when all is said and done, does not the full reality of the incarnation emerge most strikingly and completely in the suffering and death of Christ? Is it not in his suffering and death that Christ abandons himself most unreservedly to things and through them places himself in his Father's hands? Like the grain of wheat, he falls into the earth, and does it willingly.

It is not surprising, that Francis' humble, loving attitude to things should find its purest source in contemplation of the crucified Jesus. It is from the depths of the suffering he shares with Christ that he looks at created things and sees them to be his brothers and sisters. They no longer amount to a mere external spectacle; they are now part of him. It is as though they were living a transfigured life within his soul with its unlimited horizons. It is as if he himself had become sun, stars, wind, water, fire. All these things sing their song within him at the very moment when the image of the crucified Jesus transforms his whole being with its splendor. Francis can say with utter truthfulness that Violaine says in Claudel's *The Tidings Brought to Mary:*

Violaine. I have no longer any eyes.
The soul lives alone in the ruined body.

Mara. Blind!
How then are you able to walk so straight?
Violaine. I hear.
Mara. What do you hear?
Violaine. I hear all things exist with me.[44]

Chapter 13

Man Redeemed

The *Canticle of Brother Sun* and of all creation is the song of redeemed man. Francis composed it when the Lord had assured him of his kingdom, the first biographers tell us.[1] The information is of great value for it tells us the joy being expressed in the *Canticle* is the joy of salvation and the praise of the cosmos is the language this joy creates for itself. When properly understood, may not this praise give us an insight into the experience of redeemed man and into the full dimensions of that experience?

Our aim is to grasp the originality and full extent of the religious process that finds expression in the *Canticle.* We are struck by the fact that in it two attitudes, two movements of the soul that seem contrary to each other, meet and join. One movement is toward the Most High, the transcendent God who is beyond the reach of any creature and whose name "no mortal lips are worthy to pronounce"; this vertical movement finds forceful expression in the first two stanzas. The other movement is toward communion with all creatures and with the cosmic elements, even the humblest and most material.

It is by no means to be taken for granted that these two movements should meet and join. In fact, their union is quite exceptional. It seems that each should exclude the other? The first, if left to itself, tends to beget an acosmic religious attitude, characterized by a breaking of the ties that link us to the world of nature, for it is inspired by a keen sense of God's transcendence and therefore rejects any representation of him that is drawn from the natural world as being inadequate and even idolatrous. The second movement, on the contrary, tends to beget a pantheistic sense of communion with the divine as felt and perceived in all the manifestations of nature. It yields the discovery that "all creation seems to rest with God in a profound mystery"[2] and that creation itself is something sacred.

The surprising thing is that two such opposite movements should here be in perfect harmony. Max Scheler observes that

> if St. Francis had been a theologian and philosopher. . .if he had attempted an exact formulation of that vision of God and the world, which he simply intuited, lived and perfected, he would certainly never have become a pantheist, but might well have had to admit an element of "panentheism" into his scheme.[3]

The German philosopher sees Francis' affective identification with nature as a sacred reality that in no way lessened his sense of the spiritual and transcendent character of the mystery of God, but, on the contrary, became the basis on which he built a new and original relation to God in his transcendence.[4] His *Canticle* shows this new relation, since it is by celebrating creatures and entering into fraternal communion with them that he rises up to the Most High and relates himself to the One whom no human words can express. What a paradox!

This extraordinary union of movements and attitudes deserves our attention all the more since we live in a world in which a powerful current of religious thought is promoting a faith that is completely free of any and every image of the world. This outlook has some solid arguments on its side. One is that the image of the world which prevailed when God's word was spoken to men and which influenced its presentation has been unable to stand up against the impact of science. Another, and more radical, is that any image whatsoever of the world, be it mythological or scientific, tends to objectify and reduce to the dimensions of this world the transcendent reality it claims to meditate; it thereby reduces the transcendent to the level of the created.

When, we try to translate transcendent reality into images of this-worldly reality, we quite naturally represent God's power and action as the kind of power and action proper to this world. Consequently, we must reject the image if we are to penetrate to its transcendent meaning. The word of God has to be stripped of its cosmological wrappings if its truth, its existential meaning, is to be grasped. Once the word is thus purified, it proves to cast an intense light on human existence and reveals the inmost meaning of our personal history.

Men must therefore be willing to live their relation to God and his word in a faith that rejects all images of the world and all support in the natural order. In short, if faith is to be authentic and reach its true object, it must be lived in independence of all that connects us with nature; it must be lived by an act of sheer freedom. Rudolf Bultmann claims that "the man who desires to believe in God must know that he has nothing at his own disposal on which to build this faith, that he is, so to speak, in a vacuum. . .Man before God always has empty hands."[5]

Given this contemporary current of thought, we think it is of exceptional interest to meditate on Francis' poetic approach to the transcendent God. If ever a man accepted to stand before God with empty hands and to receive from God his assurance of salvation, it was the Poor Man of Assisi.[6] But at the same time his assurance finds expression in cosmic praise that lays whole of the natural world in its entirety and thus enables the world to act, within certain limits, as mediator for man and the thrust of his faith toward transcendence.

First of all, let us summarize the various aspects of Francis' celebration of the world as these have emerged from our analyses. A first point is quite clear: that the celebration is an act of authentic brotherly communion with all the cosmic elements. Creatures in the *Canticle* are not simply an excuse for praise, but the objects of a profound affective communion. A second point is that the communion is implemented in a descending movement: from the noblest elements to the lowliest, from the heavenly to the earthly. From glorious "Brother Sun" it descends as far as "Sister Earth, our mother," and even the "colored flowers and herbs" of the field. This descending movement mirrors a radical self-stripping. In the sight of him whose name "no mortal lips are worthy to pronounce," Francis acknowledges himself brother to all creatures and deeply united to them: not just to the noblest of them but to the lowliest and most hidden.

A careful examination of the way in which Francis celebrates these various elements has led us to think that through them Francis is entering into a fraternal communion—unconsciously, to be sure—with something further. For, in a sober yet very intensely felt way, Francis attributes values to the cosmic elements; they are the object, in depth, of his imagination and his dreams. The images he presents of them in the *Canticle* are laden with unconscious interior values. They express more than mere physical realities; they relate to something more radical, something to do with the inner sources of man's being, something Francis discovers himself to be in obscure, hidden communion with. The cosmic images become symbols of the primordial forces at work in the soul.

In communing with the cosmic images Francis is pursuing his fraternal relationship with a whole range of reality that lies within him. The various cosmic elements he celebrates are a code for the depths of the psychic life; they are images of libido, desire, and eros, but a libido, a desire, and an eros that have been liberated from their anarchic forms and transfigured and integrated with the life of the spirit. Here the process of self-stripping of which we spoke a moment ago manifests its full extent, for it involves a profound openness and acceptance of necessity from below. Beneath the discourse concerning the cosmos we must therefore read a more radical discourse that has to do with the reconciliation of the soul with its own "archeology" and that of mankind.

Yet it would surely be a mistake to stop at a purely psychological interpretation of the *Canticle* and to see in it only a symbolic expression of reconciliation with the self and of a search for psychic balance and integrity. To be satisfied with this would be to mutilate and even distort Francis' brotherly communion with the elements of nature. Such a communion certainly does lead to a real reconciliation of man with his own psychological depths, but we must remember the properly ontological and religious dimensions of this reconciliation.

The *Canticle of Brother Sun* is, above all else, a celebration. As such it expresses a basic attitude. Francis's originality, even within the Church, is that he discovered, with the instinct of a genius, that the most important thing is not to manage or administer reality but to celebrate it. The element of celebration protects the Christianity of Francis from any taint of juridicism and dogmatism, and gives it its radiant, solar character. In speaking of "celebration," we must not think of this solely in cultural or liturgical terms; we must think of it as operating at a deeper level and implying a way of being in the world, accepting, intuiting, and living the world.

We made the point earlier that for Francis singing is a mode of existence. To put it another way, existence itself is "en-chanted," and this in its every manifestation, even suffering and death, because existence in its entirety has been touched and permeated by the mystery of salvation. The mystery of salvation does not unfold in a sphere separate from the realities of this world. There is not, on one side, a purely supernatural world, and on the other a natural, profane world that is left to its own laws and inherent necessities. Nothing that exists falls outside the mystery of salvation. The very earth has drunk the blood of the Savior as it dripped from the cross. In fact, the mystery resides precisely in the fact that salvation unites heaven and earth. This is the point Francis is making in his Office of the Passion:

> The Father of heaven, most holy, our King, sent his beloved Son from on high before all the ages, the doer of saving deeds on earth.
>
> Let the heavens be glad and the earth rejoice; let the sea and what fills it resound; let the plains be joyful and all that is in them.
>
> Sing to the Lord a new song; sing to the Lord, all you lands.[7]

We can see now the connection between the praise of creatures and that joy at salvation which, according to the early biographers, inspired Francis' hymn. The *Canticle* is truly the song of redeemed man. The redeemed man who expresses himself in the poem is not reducible to a pure subjectivity that has arbitrarily been cut off from the world of nature; he does not despise the whole realm of the involuntary or his own earthly eros. No, it is the whole man who encounters the transcendent God, and he encounters him precisely by accepting his own totality and that of the world: a totality he refuses to possess and dominate but chooses to celebrate as the locus in which the mystery of salvation unfolds.

The salvation of which the *Canticle* sings is a salvation that lays hold of the very depths of man's being. We must bear in mind that the proclamation of salvation out of which the Canticle *arose* used as a symbol "the whole mass of the earth changed into pure gold."[8] A sentence we quoted earlier from Pierre Emmanuel finds its full application here: "The vertical dimension of transcendence passes through the obscure regions of our being." God waits at the roots of things and it is there that Francis meets him and recognizes him. This recognition, which requires a profound self-dispossession, changes his darkness into light, his night into the sun's splendor.

It is here that heaven discloses its mystery. This experience of salvation takes the form of an experience of God in the soul's depths, an experience in which the movement from the highest to the lowest, from the Creator to the creature, from the Holy One to the sinner, proves to be the mark of the transcendent God himself.

Conclusion

The Poetry of Salvation

> Whatever be the relation of the human soul, in even its boldest and most rarefied dreams, to the economic and social system, the soul also moves beyond its human milieu, out into the vast cosmos. Contact with the universe sets profound and mysterious forces resonating within it, the forces of that eternal life that precedes the societies of men and will outlast them.[1]

Does the man who dies at daybreak have any interest in the sun that will not rise again for him? Yet Francis of Assisi, blind and dying, still sings of the sun and all other creatures! This paradox has impelled us read the *Canticle of Brother Sun* once again and to inquire into its real meaning. What is it that Francis is really calling his "brothers" and his "sisters" in this poem? What lies behind expressions like "Brother Sun," "Sister Moon and Stars," "Sister Water," and so on?

It is evident that when Francis sings of "Sister Water, so useful, lowly, precious and pure," he has in mind something far more important, meaning-filled, and elemental than what the chemist designates as H_2O. The same holds true of all the other cosmic realities celebrated in the *Canticle:* none of them is limited to what clear concepts can grasp. On the other hand, rising out of darkness and extreme suffering, the *Canticle* cannot be regarded as expressing straightforward emotion roused by the spectacle nature affords. This is not to deny the poetic and cosmic dimensions of the work. It is simply to say that the poetic discourse is an echo of another discourse at a deeper level. Each of the elements celebrated refers to something both near and distant, transparently clear and inexhaustibly meaningful, exterior and interior, something that is mirrored in the clear eyes of the child and found in the bottomless depths of the soul.

On examination, the poem has proved to be the symbolic, and probably unreflective, language of an experience that takes place in the night of the soul and that involves the whole man. The *Canticle of Brother Sun,* far from being simply an accompaniment or decorative embellishment of an existence, celebrates an interior process directed toward the full reconciliation of man with the world, with himself, and with God. In fact, it is not even enough to say that the poem gives expression to such a reconciliation; we must go further and say that the poem is part of the spiritual experience and plays a determining role in it. Here, if anywhere, "song is existence."[2]

Francis believed in the power of his *Canticle* to effect reconciliation not only in himself but in others as well. The author of the *Mirror of Perfection* tells us Francis derived so much consolation and sweetness from his poem that he wished to send Brother Pacificus and some other friars to go about reciting and singing it, for "we are God's minstrels. . .who must inspire the hearts of men and stir them to spiritual joy."[3] On another occasion, a dispute had arisen between the bishop of Assisi and the mayor of the city; seeing that no one was intervening to make peace between them, Francis told some of the friars: "Go and sing *The Song of Brother Sun* before the Bishop, the Mayor, and those who are with them. I trust that the Lord will at once humble their hearts, and that they will return to their former affection and friendship."[4] A naive notion? But experience proved that Francis' belief was justified. His *Canticle* did have power to reconcile.

Down the centuries, the *Canticle of Brother Sun* has illuminated and transformed many a human journey. It has taught men a new presence to the world and to themselves.

By leading them to a fraternal communion with the things of nature, "with great humility" and a profound sense of wonder, it has enabled them to accept themselves and their own "archeology." It has reconciled them to the obscure regions of their souls and brought them to fulfillment by causing them to open themselves completely to the light of the Most High. Dante was justified when he wrote:

> . . .Bursting from this slope [Monte Subasio] where most the
> steep is broken, earth saw such a sun's [Francis'] ascent. . .
> Let him who names the place not rest content,
> then, with *Ascesi* [Assisi]—that's too weak a word;
> who'd speak aright should say *the Orient.*[5]

Does the *Canticle of Brother Sun* have the same value today? Can it touch the soul of contemporary man in the same fashion and play the same reconciling and transforming role? Our age has good reason to be proud of its scientific and technological conquests. In the microscopic world of the atom and in the immensity of space, man is constantly building an ever more extensive network of knowledge and power. When for the first time he walked on the surface of the moon, he not only opened up a new field of exploration but attained a new level of self-awareness. Now he has proof that he is not forever limited to earth but is in fact a citizen of space. And he continues to look even further and higher, as though fascinated by the image of the "most high," by which he measures himself and with which he secretly identifies himself.

Before the tribunal of a self-esteem that has thus grown beyond all measure, what value does the *Canticle of Brother Sun* still have? Surely the temptation is great to see it simply as the expression of a world view that was too simple and narrow and is now outmoded and infantile. There is something to say, it seems, for such a judgment. In the age of atomic energy, what is the point of stopping to contemplate the four "basic" elements of the ancients: earth, water, fire, and air, as though they were still to be regarded as the roots of being? Now that the moon has become accessible to us and will soon have revealed all its secrets to us, how can we still think of it as something "precious" that can put us in touch with the Sacred? As for the sun: we know now that it is only one star—and by no means the largest—among countless others.

If the *Canticle* were indeed only a poetic celebration of an archaic world system, it would indeed by difficult to pay it much attention. At most, we could admire its ingenuousness; it would provide no help in living our lives. But, as a matter of fact, we have shown in our earlier chapters that what the *Canticle* expresses is not so much a cosmology as an interior, spiritual experience. The vision of the cosmos is only the surface form of a discourse being carried on at a deeper level.

It is the properly anthropological dimension of the *Canticle* that is still important for us and calls for our attention. The real human problems are the same despite all our scientific and technological achievements. They are the problems that arise from man's relations to his fellow men, to himself, and to the mystery of existence. We must admit, moreover, that it is easier for men to set foot on the moon than to accept the "Other" and open themselves to Being in its totality. It is in relation to these problems that *Canticle of Brother Sun* still has something to say to us, something of vital importance.

This hymn to man's brotherhood with all the elements that make up the cosmos is the poetic expression of his reconciliation with the totality of his own being and with Being itself in all its fullness; in this reconciliation man opens himself to the mystery of the world, a mystery that is dark with the darkness caused by excessive light. In short, Being in its entirety is here encountered and celebrated as light.

The *Canticle* tells us the secret of such a reconciliation. The latter is possible "only if the person is open to the call of highest heaven, while at the same time remaining under the protection of the earth that supports and produces him."[6] "Under the protection of the earth": in a fraternal communion with the lowliest realities, those which are a vital part of our lives and are everywhere at hand and sensible: water, fire, air, light, tree, house, and so forth.

To grasp the full significance of such a message, we must keep in mind the real meaning of Francis' communion with nature. This communion has nothing in common with the romantic vision of the world. It does not seek out nature as a reflection of the self or as a decorative embellishment for human life. Nature's mission is not to turn the attention of man to himself or to enable him to contemplate the succession of his inner states, but rather to open a way for him toward what lies outside and beyond him and ultimately to Being in its fullness.

Francis' communion with nature is, first and foremost, the expression of a profound detachment from self. Standing before the Most High whose name "no mortal lips are worthy to pronounce," Francis deliberately puts himself at the side of other creatures; he takes his place among them and enters into a fraternal communion with even the least of them. Far from concealing himself in the consciousness of his own spiritual dignity, he cultivates a genuine communion with his own dark and hidden origins, with "Sister Earth, our mother."

Such a way of acting is for Francis not the result of a mere intellectual attitude or of mere sentimentality. It is because he is following the poor, humble Christ that Francis effectively gives himself over to material reality and its rough touch: to the burning sun, the icy wind, the water, the bare ground. This man of the town, accustomed to refinement and delicacies, willingly lives a life of poverty amid the things of nature: close to them, without protection against them, and without the least intention of dominating and possessing them. He learns to know them by submitting to them. Thus there is a rough, austere side to the Franciscan experience of nature and we often tend to forget this. It is through this obedience to things that Francis intends to strip himself of all self-will,[7] and it is in this frame of mind that he enters into the brotherhood of creatures and becomes a man of the sun, wind, and water, a man whose existence takes on, even in his highest aspirations, the coloring of the humblest material things.

A second point to be noted about Francis' communion with nature is that it is sustained and permeated by a spirit of praise. Francis is not satisfied merely with living in close contact with things. He also wants to express them, to celebrate them in a hymn which is one of praise of the Most High. His song gives voice to an experience of the world that is shot through with wonder. This is a very important point: things stir no echo in us except to the extent that we allow ourselves to be gripped by wonder at them. Man cannot free himself of his own self-will by a simple act of his will. If he depended solely on the power of his will, he would be hopelessly turned in upon himself, with the self as the determining agent of his destiny; he could not truly consent to allow anything else to dispose of him. Only wonder can break through the barrier and effect the miracle. For, by drawing a man outside himself, wonder detaches him from himself and opens him to a profound communion with the world.

In this context, Paul Ricoeur rightly observes: "It is the incantation of poetry which delivers me from myself and purifies me."[8] The Franciscan humility that brings the spiritual man so close to the things of nature and, through them, to his own obscure inner roots, would be impossible without the spirit of poetry and praise that sustains it. "The discipline of reality is nothing without the grace of imagination."[9] This grace is fully operative in Francis' *Canticle of Brother Sun;* our analyses have shown with what depth and yet what delicacy the things of nature are therein imagined and celebrated. No covetousness, no slightest desire to possess and dominate taints Francis' vision of them. His imagination even seems to cease acting in their presence, but in fact it is at work bringing to light their most important dimension, it reveals their openness to the Most High. In that light they prove to be "precious" in their very bareness and simplicity; no additions, no embellishments are needed. There they are for all to see, yet everyone of them, the lowliest as well as the noblest, the water on the earth as well as the star in the sky, though dressed in its everyday colors, is an epiphany of Being. In each of them shines forth

> [the] never nowhere without us: that pure,
> unsuperintended element one breathes,
> endlessly knows, and never craves.[10]

That is what rouses profound wonder in Francis' soul and causes him to take his place in the great brotherhood of creatures.

Francis' communion with nature involves exploration and leads to gratitude, since the universe he celebrates has a treasure concealed in it. It is this treasure that his hymn of praise endeavors to draw forth into the light. A living presence, mysterious and inward, dwells in all these "precious" things. By entering into a wondering fraternal communion with sun, moon, and stars, wind and water, fire and earth, Francis finds himself, paradoxically, exploring his own inmost depths. Under cover of the great cosmic images with which he discovers himself to be in close kinship. Francis comes in contact with his primordial affective experiences. What then awakens in him and makes him so young and freshly senstive before the things of nature is his own deepest being. The light that shines in his wondering gaze is the light of man's first awakening, the light given to a being as it first enters the world and receives uniquely new impressions from all things. Unconsciously, Francis rediscovers the enchanted world of childhood.

But does not this return of the soul into itself contradict what we said just above, when we remarked that in the experience of wonder a man is detached from himself? What then is the meaning of this reimmersion in his most archaic past? We need only observe that, far from leading to a turning inward on itself, this reimmersion is the path of liberation and openness to the light of Being. The humble descent into the dark depths by means of the enchantment exercised by poetry ends in a transfiguration of the soul's primordial forces. The grace of wonder and praise is a grace of renewal.

Here childhood comes alive in a man, but not for the sake of re-experiencing the past. The individual does indeed rediscover the past, but it is a past that has been stripped of everything non-essential, and purified of all that was related only to some particular desire or state of soul. In the rediscovery, things now speak the language of the essential and the eternal; the esthetic and the ontological fuse, and in the splendor of simple things the light of being shines forth. This light is the dawning of the sacred, as the humblest realities become annunciations. A man has the experience which Romano Guardini felicitously describes in his book on the stages of life:

> Existence then takes on the character it has in a Cézanne still life. There we see a table, and on the table some apples; nothing more. Everything is there, out in the open, unconcealed. There are no questions to be asked, and therefore no answers to be given. And yet, there is mystery everywhere. Things are more than what their immediate presence makes manifest. We are led to think henceforth that the real mystery is the mystery resident in this very clarity.[11]

There are poets who grapple with things and color them with all the fires of their own passions, distorting them in the service of their own desires. For such poets, things have no real existence of their own but are simply a reflection of the poet's self. Other poets, on the contrary—the really great poets—see things as they objectively exist, untainted by anything man might project upon them. For such poets, things are vitally alive and bathed in an intense light unique to each. The lowliest and most everyday reality, like the kitchen chair of Van Gogh's painting, restores the poet's sense of the miracle of existence and its enchantment.

If things lay hold of our being in such depth as this, it is certainly not in order to turn that being in upon itself but in order to renew it completely by the mysterious clarity that surrounds them. They become the means by which the being moves beyond itself toward complete, universal being. Thanks to them, man rediscovers the house of his childhood, but the house is now as large as the universe. He then comes to know the supreme, innocent joy of existing; he can live like a child, and with a child's trustfulness, in the presence of the ultimate secret of reality. It comes as no surprise, therefore, that his song should have the radiance of "a morning resplendent with light, the kind of morning on which to be forever a child." This canticle of creatures, over which shines a great fraternal sun, is also a song of childhood, and indeed of an eternal childhood.

The humble reimmersion of man in his own archaic depths, a reimmersion accomplished under the sign of cosmic images lovingly celebrated, proves to be the path of an authentic spiritual ascent along the way of praise. Francis has nothing more to fear from the wild forces within his soul, for he has won them over and they have become his brothers and sisters. It is really they who sing in his *Canticle* through the images of "Brother Sun," "Brother Wind," "Sister Water," "Brother Fire," and the others.

Each of these fraternal images, in its own way, points to a unity that is not to be sought in the past by a return to some lost paradise, but in man's own heart by the meeting and reconciliation of flesh and spirit, *eros* and *agape,* nature and freedom, creature and Creator. We must go a step further and say that the images already make the poet share that unity. They have power over the soul's depths, and they participate in the power of the reality they symbolize. Then, by a kind of incantation or enchantment, they inspire what they signify; they enter the heart and there break out into praise. The song itself, when it attains this level of intensity, leads out into existence in its totality. It carries the soul and all its vital powers toward their highest destiny: the Most High.

The *Canticle,* uniting as it does the thrust toward the Most High and a fraternal communion with all creatures, represents a unitive grasp of reality. This is a point that is surely essential to the Franciscan message. The spiritual life cannot be built above, and in abstraction from, nature; neither can it be built in independence of the obscure region of our being and in contempt for our cosmic and psychic roots. Authentic spiritual life can only be a rounded growth, marked by an openness to all reality. The man who wishes to be reborn of the Spirit must accept fraternal communion with water—and not only with water, but with fire, wind, earth, and the other cosmic entities as well. He must enter, with a marveling and singing soul, into fraternal communion with all creatures, and even with the night and its darkling light. He must be willing to go beneath the rocks into the sunless hidden cave where he may see the divine Child awaken between the ox and the ass. The *Canticle of Brother Sun* celebrates this divine birth in the depths of man himself.

We should not be surprised, therefore, to see the cosmic praise changing finally into a celebration of pardon and peace. The brother of the sun, the wind, the water, and all other creatures has become a marvelously human person: "All praise be yours, my Lord, through those who grant pardon for love of you; through those who endure sickness and trial. Happy those who endure in peace." Pardon and peace—sure signs of the new birth. No more contempt for others, no more aggressiveness, no more disturbance of soul. We know that for Francis disturbance of soul or irritation were signs of secret clinging to self; they were proofs that in his inmost self a man was being led by something other than the Spirit of God.[12]

The man in whom the Spirit of the Lord really dwells is

not disturbed or irritated by anything, even the faults of others.[13] His life is not without its human tensions, but in the midst of them he preserves his peace. A limitless will to peace and pardon possesses him and guides him. That will, however, is not a surface activity of the soul, nor is it to be had on command by a simple act of the will. It comes instead from the depths and it is what makes a man be truly an image of God: patient toward every creature, merciful, solar.

The most striking thing about all this is that this pacification of man in his relations with his fellow men and with himself is inseparable from a very humble fraternal communion with material things themselves; the latter is the means of the former. Francis of Assisi was convinced that man has no access to genuine spiritual wisdom unless he travels the road of simplicity whereon he will meet his brothers and sisters, the lesser beings of creation: "Hail, Queen Wisdom! The Lord save you with your sister, pure, holy Simplicity."[14]

We cannot avoid asking here: Is such a communion with nature still possible in the modern world? Man's relations with material things and the lower orders of creatures are defined today in terms of power and conquest, not of sympathy and communion. The whole of our Technological and industrial civilization rests on man's power over nature. Our civilization is an expression of reason seeking to dominate the world and being able to achieve its goal with the help of science. There is hardly any place now for singing of and celebrating the things of nature. What our civilization sings of and celebrates is the power of man and his rational mind.

Man's very success in this enterprise is the reason why man also finds himself caught today in a web of social relationships that cannot serve to express what is deeply human in him. We have to realize and accept the fact that when the technological and industrial exploitation of nature is triumphant, the very reality of man himself is also seen in purely functional terms: How can we *use* it? The "rational" ferocity with which modern man treats nature is thus turned against man himself and begins to operate in his relations with his fellow men. It forbids him any deep communion with others as well as any access to his own depths. Existence is flattened out; we are in the age of "one-dimensional man."

Under such conditions, how can man seek an existence marked by peace in St. Francis' sense of the word? He cannot do it by renouncing his power over nature, for he needs that power if he is to struggle against illness and poverty and to alleviate the sufferings of men. But, there is perhaps a way of using that power so that instead of nature being destroyed or denatured, it will be put at the service of man, as it can be if man is able to liberate nature from the power of sheer blind forces. Marcuse rightly points out that "cultivation of the soil is qualitatively different from destruction of the soil, extraction of natural resources from wasteful exploitation, clearing of forests from wholesale deforestation."[15] They are qualitatively different in regard not only to nature which undergoes these operations but also for man who performs them.

Modern man must realize that in his dealings with nature he is also dealing with himself at the unconscious level: dealing with that which is most hidden in him, but also that which exercises the determining influences on him. Depending on how he treats the things of nature, he either opens himself or closes himself to his own depths. For him, there can be no genuine and complete reconciliation with himself and with his fellow men unless he communes as a brother with nature as well.

What we are urging here is not mere sentimentality but a different attitude that involves the whole man, from his unconscious depths up to his relationship with the transcendent God. To be brother to all creatures, as Francis was, is in the last analysis to choose a vision of the world in which reconciliation is more important than division. It is to overcome separation and solitude and to open oneself to a universe of sharing, in which "the mystery of the earth [comes] into contact with the mystery of the stars"[16] in a vast movement of pardon and reconciliation. Such a spiritual experience is in the strict sense ineffable as far as its inner reality goes. It can be expressed only in symbols: in a celebration of the world in which the soul, in its fraternal communion with all created things, itself becomes radiant sun.

Epilogue

The Language of the Soul's Night

April, 1945: The Allied armies are penetrating deep into the heart of Germany. A lengthy freight train is moving slowly along the line from Passau to Munich, with thousands of exiles packed into its cars. They have been shut up there for twenty-one days now. Hundreds have already died; hundreds more are at death's door, delirious from hunger. The train started from Buchenwald and has made a long detour through Czechoslovakia and the mountains of Bohemia; now it is heading for Dachau near Munich. Suddenly, incredibly, singing can be heard from one of the cars; it is Francis of Assisi's *Canticle of Brother Sun*! "All praise be yours, my Lord, through all that you have made, and first my lord Brother Sun. . . .All praise be yours, my Lord, through Sister Earth, our mother."

What can such a song mean in circumstances like these? The men who sang were hardly more than ghosts themselves, surrounded by the dead! What was going on in this railroad car?

Now that we have finished our study of the *Canticle,* we ask the patient reader to let us insert here a few pages of the diary we kept during the time of our deportation from France. We can think of no better illustration of the thesis we have been developing in this book: that Francis of Assisi's *Canticle of Brother Sun* is not simply an expression of esthetic, or esthetico-religious, emotion at the spectacle of nature, but the expression of an experience that takes place in the night of the soul.

Yet, as we open this diary, we feel a scruple. Who, after all, can claim to have had an experience really like that of the Poor Man of Assisi. There has been only one Francis of Assisi, and he alone has sung, with identical fraternal feelings, of both the sun and death. Well, we are not claiming to have imitated him, even from afar. But is it not amazing that we were given the grace of singing the praises of the sun while the shadow of death hovered over us?

* * * * *

April 7, evening: night has fallen, the train rolls on. In what direction? We do not know. One thing is certain: we are on our way—ninety to a hundred men in each car, crouching, crushed against one another, a fellow prisoner between one's legs, like skeletons packed one upon another. The horrible nightmare is beginning. (Could we possibly have thought at that moment that it would last, not three, four, or even five days, but twenty-one days and twenty-one nights?)

No room to stretch out a leg. And we are so exhausted! And so full of despair, too! This very morning, we were still in Buchenwald, waiting for a liberation that seemed very near. We had waited all through the winter, amid hunger and cold, hard work, and death. Many had died. At last, we had survived all that. Then, suddenly, liberation was at hand. It had lifted its head only a few miles away, as real and as powerful as the spring sun that had defeated the long winter. From the hilltop at Buchenwald we could see the flames from the mouths of the American guns. It was only a matter of days now, perhaps even of hours. The cannon were thundering, and hope was leaping in our hearts.

But the SS decided to evacuate a section of the camp. Several columns of prisoners had already set out, under heavy guard, on the preceding days. Today it was our turn. With death in our hearts, we walked the few miles from the heights of Buchenwald to the station at Weimar. We were turning our backs on hope, this long column of four to five thousand condemned men. Really, we were no longer among the living. Some comrades, their strength drained away, fell during the march, and the SS put a bullet through their heads. In some spots, the path was spattered with blood and brains.

At Weimar station, they put us on board.

Now we are rolling onward into the unknown. Two SS guards to each car. Some cars are covered; others, like ours, still black from coal dust, are open to the sky. A few comrades were able to bring a blanket; lucky for them, since the nights are still cold in Germany at this time of year when winter is barely over. A deathly silence reigns among us. Rocked by the swaying of the train, we sink into a boundless sadness.

Next morning, Sunday, April 8: we stop at a small station. The train stands there all day, then all night. We are forbidden to stand up, even to restore circulation to our legs. We are forced to remain crouching, day after day. For food, a few potatoes and a bit of bread; nothing hot, of course. Meanwhile, a very cold fog descends.

There are people from all over Europe among the hundred or so packed into our car. From all social classes, too. Most are between twenty and thirty years old, but all look like very old men. Some know why they were arrested and deported: they were part of a resistance movement. Others are there simply because they were caught in a random sweep in Paris or Warsaw or some other city. But we speak as little as possible of such matters. In extreme wretchedness such as this, what is there to know about a man except the suffering that now fills his being? Here the suffering is limitless and everyone shares it. All differences fade away in the face of the common destiny. Lost in this mass of men, there are five of us who are sons of St. Francis.

Monday, April 9: The train starts moving again shortly before noon. While we are under way, the SS relax their vigilance. We take advantage of this to stand for a moment and take a look at the countryside through which we are passing. During the afternoon the train stops in the extensive suburbs of Leipzig, and the SS have those who have died during the journey brought out of the cars. These are quickly and unceremoniously buried beside the track. During the night and throughout Tuesday morning, we continue on eastward. We travel along the Elbe for a while and are only about thirty miles from Dresden. But now the train turns southward.

At this time the SS were probably intending to take us to the concentration camp at Flossenburg in the Oberpfalzer Wald, on the Czechoslovakian frontier. For reasons unknown to us they had to drop this idea.

Wednesday morning, April 10: We are at Pilsen in Czechoslovakia. Groups of Czechs immediately gather along the tracks. They are deeply moved at the sight of our striped garments and skeletal figures. They begin to throw bread to us. The SS fire a few shots at them. The train rolls on slowly and passes under a bridge in the city. Some people who have gathered on the bridge drop food into the cars. We knock each other over trying to get a morsel of bread. More than ever, we are forbidden to stand up, but our hunger is too strong to resist. The train stops at a little station in the countryside, not far from Pilsen. There we are shunted to a siding. In the evening, they give us a little food: one ration-loaf of bread for ten men. The day ends with the departure of the dead whose number increases each day. The corpses are no longer buried beside the track but piled in great open wagons at the rear of the train. The corpses are hardly more than skeletons now; they are seized by the arms and legs, shoved upwards, and tipped over into the car.

Next morning, Thursday, April 11: The train stands all day in this little station. In the evening, the dead are removed; nothing else happens all day long. The same thing the next day; we spend all day without food, and in the evening they remove the dead. Life is tragically simplified for us now. We have only one occupation to fill our time: watching others die, while we ourselves wait for death. On the average, two men died each day in each car; that means about a hundred deaths a day for the whole train.

These days spent motionless seem endless to us. But the nights bring a further torment. Alongside the dying, who are at their last gasp, some of the living fight for a bit of space in which to sleep; others go mad and pound their heads against the sides of the car in order to finish their nightmare. Over us, an SS man rains down blows with a club in order to restore quiet. But even all this is not the worst. The terrible, awful thing is to find oneself watching for a neighbor to die and telling oneself that tomorrow there will be more room to stretch out in.

During the night between Friday and Saturday, attempts are made to escape from several of the cars. This act of despair will cost all of us dear. In the morning, an SS officer climbs into our cars and fires into the mass of prisoners. Two of our comrades are hit; they will spend a long time dying.

Only on Monday, April 16, does the train set out again. We have the impression the SS do not know what to do with us and will be forced to kill us all. But the weather is marvelous. Everything is a call to life: over our heads, a wide blue sky; the larks tumble about up there, drunk on the freedom of space; in the fields men and women are working at the harvest; yonder a few small churches lift their steeples. The train stops again at evening, on a plateau. Once again we wait, face to face with death. There we are, completely cut off from everything that is going on in the world. Where are the Allies? What is happening in France just now? These big questions seem irrelevant to us now. For many of us, it is already too late.

During the night between Tuesday and Wednesday, the train starts up again. It travels toward the southeast. Now we are entering the mountains of Bohemia. The scene is full of grandeur. From the floor of our car we can watch the forests on the upper slopes. The new light-green foliage of the birches stands out against the dark green of the giant firs. Here and there the gold of flowering bloom catches the eye. Spring is bursting out. Nature, ignorant of what men are doing to each other, continues to produce greenery and flowers once again. From the moist warm earth the sun draws the good smells of a forest in the spring.

In some places the slopes narrow into a rocky, precipitous ravine. Our train with its five thousand condemned men moves slowly through these wild ravines. The idea comes to us that we have been brought there for some barbaric celebration. Then suddenly, fear. Above our heads, over the side of the car, appears "the killer," an SS officer. We have called him that because he has already killed several among us. He stares at us the way a bird of prey stares at a nestful of creatures he is going to kill. His rifle is pointed at us; the monster fires into the heap of men. Two comrades are now dying. One has been shot in the stomach and blood is pouring from his mouth. We are all spattered with blood. A terrible anxiety grips body and soul. There can be no doubt now, we are doomed to be exterminated. At this thought, we feel our hearts jumping wildly, like a bird that has been mortally wounded and flutters around in its own blood, unwilling to die.

We have been traveling all day. This evening, the train has halted in a little station at the edge of the Bohmerwald. The railroad bridge across the Danube at Passau has just been cut. We are forced to stay there on a siding several days, six to be exact. Long, terrible days. To crown our wretchedness, the good weather is followed by rain. It falls, cold and steady, for three days and three nights. We are paralyzed by the cold. There is nothing hot for us to eat. Some of us, coming back from removing the dead, have managed to pick up some pieces of wood and a few bricks along the track. On the bricks we light a fire in the car. It's really more a ghost of a fire. We crowd around it to get dry and warm, but the flame is too weak. Besides, skeletons can't get warm. Most of these days pass without any food at all being given to us, and we must be satisfied with a few dandelions hastily picked beside the track as we return from fatigue duty with the dead.

The dead! There are more and more of them. Many of our comrades die of dysentery; many of exhaustion. Others have contracted erysipelas and are the most horrible spectacle of all. Within a night or a day, these men become unrecognizable; their swollen fiery faces are completely distorted. Delirious with fever, these unfortunates fill the night with their yelling; they scream for water, but in vain. In the morning, their bodies lie stiff in death. Sometimes the corpses remain in the car throughout the day, washed by the pools of water that have formed here and there on the flooring.

These extremities of suffering plunge us into acute anxiety. It is no longer simply the anxiety that grips any living thing as death approaches. Amid our terrible distress there arises in us a strange feeling that eats away at those inmost certainties which till now had sustained us. We have a growing impression that we have been handed over to some blind, savage power. There we are, thousands of men abandoned to hunger, cold, vermin, and death. The human being is completely crushed. Man, whom we had till now believed was made in God's image, now seems laughable: worthless, helpless, hopeless; a being caught up in a whirlwind of forces that play with him, or rather, pay absolutely no attention to him. That is how we see ourselves now—that, and nothing more. Among the corpses that lie in the water of the car, eyes turned back, is a companion or a friend. Everything we can see, every experience we must undergo, tells us we are in the grip of an iron law, handed over to the play of blind forces—and that this, and this alone, is reality.

Reality where the Father has no place! Experience that once in your life, and you will never again speak lightly of the "death of God." It is an atrocious experience. When the Father is absent, the Son is in agony. The Son's agony is always due to the Father's silence, the Father's absence. And where can the least sign of the Father be found in this hell? Now we understand the words: "My soul is sorrowful enough to die."

Black night fills our souls. And yet, on the morning of April 26 when one of us[1] is in his last moments and the light has almost left his eyes, what rises from our hearts to our lips is not a cry of despair or rebellion, but a song, a song of praise: Francis of Assisi's *Canticle of Brother Sun*! Nor do we have to force ourselves to sing it. It rises spontaneously out of our darkness and nakedness, as though it were the only language fit for such a moment.

What brings us in such circumstances to praise God for and through the great cosmic brotherhood? Theories have no place in our utter confusion of spirit; they offer no shelter against the storm. The only thing that remains and is priceless in our eyes is the patience and friendship this or that comrade shows you. Such an act by someone who, like yourself, is immersed in suffering and anxiety, is a ray of light that falls miraculously into the wretched darkness that envelops us. It re-creates you, makes you a human being once again. Suddenly we learn all over again that we are men. And when such an act of friendly help has been done to you, you in turn are able to do it for another and thus respond to the reign of brute force with a freedom and love that bear witness to another kind of reality. Men have assisted him who is a murderer from the beginning and have thus succeeding in creating a world without God. But they have not succeeded wholly. In this dark world, the brilliant rays of divine love are still to be seen. The man who acts as a brother is always a witness to the Father. Anyone who sees him sees the Father as well.

At such a moment, astounding though it seems, we experience wonder before the world; we experience the sacred in the world. Such an experience is possible only in extreme deprivation of soul and body. Only in utter distress and need can we fully appreciate a mouthful of bread, a sip of water, a ray of sunlight, and now and then, like a visitor from another world, the warm greeting of a passerby. The tiny drops of rain that tremble on the telephone wires in the evening light after a storm are filled, to the selfless eye, with a boundless innocence. And the broad rain-washed heaven shows us—how luminous, how pure it is! All these lowly things that we can contemplate from the floor of our car are not the result of passing chance. They speak sweetly to the soul.

Where do they come from, this purity and innocence that suddenly lay hold of us through these humble realities? Whence the limpid radiance that bathes the world but is perceptible only amid extreme poverty? How innocent things are. Do you smile? Yet this experience can be matched by no other. Nietzsche said: "One must. . .have chaos in oneself to be able to give birth to a dancing star."[2] We certainly have not been spared chaos. Devastation is everywhere, around us and within us. History has swept like a cyclone across our lives. And yet, over this heap of ruins, there now shines "the great evening star of poverty."[3]

Surely, through this changeless transparency of things, it is the most primitive level of being that communicates with us; it is that indomitable, eternal reality that remains unchanged through the course of history. The man with the rifle can spread death and keep thousands of men in the thrall of fear; he cannot destroy a great deal. But he is powerless against this hidden spring of purity and innocence. Man's arm cannot reach to these depths.

The purity and innocence do not originate in us. They do, however, well up within us, at the deepest level of the soul, and when they do, they restore childhood there. It is not our gaze that brings them into being; on the contrary, it is they that enable us to see things once again as children do. But this purified vision is attained only through a kind of agony, when we have become poor enough to welcome such purity and innocence. What chaos we must have within us if we are to see the world born once again into the light! It is always in the shadow of the crucified Christ that the Christian, at the end of his journey, recovers the vision of a child. His selfless gaze is then no longer fixed on some lost paradise. Rather, even at the heart of devastation and death, it expresses an immense will to peace and mercy. And, despite the seeming power of evil, it is such a man who is the stronger. He is capable of defeating the most monstrous onslaughts of barbarism. Amid the furor of history, his eyes speak of the end. They do more than that: they sing of it.

Because this vision was given to us, we were able, on an April morning somewhere in Germany, to gather round our dying brother and sing of the sun and the stars, the wind and the water, the fire and the earth, and also of "those who grant pardon for love of you." "When he died, so light as to be nameless,"[4] there was no flight of larks overhead, but a supernatural peace had filled our hearts. That evening, we carried his body away, accompanied by blows from the SS who felt we were not moving quickly enough. His was the last death in our car.

How could we forget such an experience when we reread today Francis of Assisi's *Canticle of Brother Sun?*

Canticum Solis[1]

Altissimu, omnipotente, bonsignore,
tue sono le laude,
la gloria elhonore
et omne benedictione.

Ad te solo, Altissimo, se Konfano
et nullu homo enne dignu
te mentovare.

Laudato sie, misignore, cum tucte le tue creature,
spetialmente messor lo frate sole,
loquale iorno et allumini noi par loi.

Et ellu ebellu eradiante cum grande splendore:
de te, Altissimo, porta significatione.

Laudato si, misignore, per sora luna ele stelle:
in celu lai formate clarite
et pretiose et belle.

Laudato si, misignore, per frate vento,
et per aere et nubilo
et sereno et omne tempo
per loquale a le tue creature
dai sustentamento.

Laudato si, misignore, per sor aqua,
laquale e multo utile et humile
et pretiosa et casta.

Laudato si, misignore, per frate focu,
per loquale ennalumini la nocte:
edello ebello et iocundo
et robustoso et forte.

Laudato si, misignore, per sora nostra matre terra,
laquale ne sustenta et governa,
et produce diversi fructi
con coloriti flori et herba.

Laudato si, misignore, per quelli ke perdonano
per lo tuo amore
et sostengo infirmitate
et tribulatione.

Beate quelli kel sosterrano in pace,
ka da te, Altissimo,
sirano incoronati.

Laudato si, misignore, per sora nostra
morte corporale,
da laquale nullu homo
vivente poskappare.

Gai acqueli ke morrano
ne le peccata mortali!

Beati quelli ke trovarane
le tue sanctissime voluntati,
ka la morte secunda
nol farra male.

Laudate et benedicite, misignore,
et rengratiate et servaite li
cum grande humilitate.

Notes

Introduction

1. 1C 47, pp. 268-69.
2. LP 43, p. 1020.
3. *Ibid.*
4. 2C 213, p. 532.
5. LP 43, pp. 1020-21; cf. 2C 213, pp. 532-33.
6. 2Reg, ch. 6, p. 61.
7. Paul Ricoeur, *The Symbolism of Evil,* trans. Emerson Buchanan (New York: Harper & Row, 1967), pp. 12-13.
8. Cf. 1C 47, pp. 268-69.
9. Max Scheler, *The Nature of Sympathy,* trans. Peter Heath (New Haven: Yale University Press, 1954), p. 87.

Canticle of Brother Sun

1. *Omnibus,* pp. 130-31. At the end of this book we shall offer the reader, as the original text, the oldes known form of the *Canticle,* the one in Assisi Codex 338 (now in the municipal library of Assisi).
2. The original Umbrian word *mentovare* is not easy to translate. It can be compared with the Old French word *mentevoir,* which means "have in mind, call to mind." The idea being expressed here is surely that which we find in 1Reg, ch. 23: "We are all poor sinners and unworthy even to mention your name" (p. 51).
3. Literally, "he bears your meaning, Most High" (*de te, Altissimo, porta significatione*).
4. Philologists disagree as to whether *per* here means *by* or *through* (*by means of*). As a matter of fact, "at a time when a verbal distinction has not yet been established by the use of two different words, men do not make a mental distinction between the two ideas. For Francis and his hearers, *per* meant both *by* and *through*" (Thêophile Desbonnets and Damien Vorreux [eds.], *Saint François d'Assise: Documents* [Paris: Editions Franciscaines, 1968], p. 196, n. 3).

Chapter 1

When Creatures Speak

1. Friedrich Nietzsche, *Beyond Good and Evil; Prelude to a Philosophy of the Future,* trans. Walter Kaufmann (New York: Vintage Books, 1966), p. 2.
2. Jean Lacroix, "Désir et langage," *Le Monde,* June 6-7, 1965. Cf. Paul Ricoeur, *Freud and Philosophy: An Essay on Interpretation,* trans. Denis Savage (New Haven: Yale University Press, 1970), p. 25.
3. Ricoeur, *op. cit.,* p. 27.
4. Test, p. 69.
5. Gilbert K. Chesterton, *St. Francis of Assisi* (New York: Doran, 1924), p. 132.
6. Raphael Brown, Appendix VIII, "The Canticle of Brother Sun," in Omer Englebert, *Saint Francis of Assisi,* trans. Eve Marie Cooper (second ed., rev. and augmented by Ignatius Brady, O.F.M., and Raphael Brown; Chicago: Franciscan Herald Press, 1965), pp. 441-58.
7. Michel Mansuy, *Gaston Bachelard et les éléments* (Paris: Corti, 1967), p. 354.
8. Gaston Bachelard, *La terre et les rêveries de la volonté* (Paris: Corti, 1948), p. 5.
9. 2Let, p. 101.
10. 5Let, p. 113
11. Test, p. 67.
12. Bachelard, *op. cit.,* p. 291.
13. Mansuy, *op. cit.,* p. 354.
14. René Descartes, *A Discourse on Method,* Part VI, in *A Discourse on Method and Selected Writings,* trans. John Veitch (New York: Dutton, 1951), pp. 53-54.
15. LM, ch. 9, no. 1, p. 698.
16. *Op. cit.,* p. 134.
17. Gaston Bachelard, *L'eau et les rêves* (Paris: Corti, 1942), p. 13.
18. 2C 165, p. 495.
19. Sp, ch. 119, p. 1258.
20. Sp, ch. 118, p. 1256.
21. LM, ch. 8, no. 6, p. 692.
22. Sp. ch. 118, p. 1257.
23. 1C 80, p. 296.
24. Louis Beirnaert, "The Mythical Dimension in Christian Sacramentalism," in Cecily Hastings and Donald Nicholl (eds.), *Seclection I* (New York: Sheed & Ward, 1953), p. 67.
25. Bachelard, *L'eau et les rêves,* pp. 129-30.
26. Erhard W. Platzeck, *Das Sonnenlied des heiligen Franziskus von Assisi: Eine Untersuchung seiner Gestalt und seines inneren Gehaltes nebst einer deutschen Ubersetzung* (Munich: Hueber, 1957), p. 44.
27. Mircea Eliade, *Patterns in Comparative Religion,* trans. Rosemary Sheed (New York: Sheed & Ward, 1958), pp. 132-33.
28. Cf. introduction to *The Canticle of Brother Sun,* in *Omnibus,* pp. 127-29.

Chapter 2

A Hypothesis for Interpretation

1. Jean Lacroix, *art. cit.*
2. Paul Ricoeur, *The Conflict of Interpretations: Essays in Hermeneutics,* trans. various hands, ed. by Don Ihde (Evanston: Northwestern University Press, 1974), pp. 12-13.
3. Peter Lippert, *Bonté* (Paris: Aubier, 1946), p. 106.
4. Scheler, *op. cit.*, p. 93.
5. Ricoeur, *The Symbolism of Evil,* pp. 12-13.
6. Pierre Emmanuel, *Evangéliaire* (Parish: Editions du Seuil, 1961), p. 74.
7. Pierre Teilhard de Chardin, *Writings in Time of War,* trans. René Hague (New York: Harper & Row, 1968), p. 27.
8. Carl Gustav Jung, *L'âme et la vie,* trad. de l'allemand par R. Cahen et Y. Le Lay (Paris: Buchet-Chastel, 1963), p. 18.
9. Phil 2:6-9.
10. 3Let, p. 108.
11. St. Bonaventure, *The Journey of the Mind to God,* ch. 6, no. 7, and ch. 7, no. 1, trans. José de Vinck, in *The Works of Bonaventure* 1: *Mystical Opuscula* (Paterson: St. Anthony Guild Press, 1960), pp. 54-55.
12. *Op. cit.*, p. 56.

Chapter 3

The Impossible Praise

1. Apoc 4:11.
2. Lds, pp. 138-39.
3. 3Let, p. 108
4. Mircea Eliade, *The Sacred and the Profane,* trans. Willard R. Trask (New York: Harcourt, Brace, 1959), p. 118.
5. 1Reg, ch. 23, p. 51.
6. 2Adm, p. 79.
7. Friedrich Nietzsche, *Thus Spoke Zarathustra* [henceforth: *Zarathustra*], trans. Walter Kaufmann (New York: Vintage Books, 1954), Part 3, no. 4: "Before Sunrise," p. 164.
8. 1Reg, ch. 17, p. 44.
9. 19Adm, p. 84.
10. 3Let, p. 106.
11. Cf. 4Adm, p. 80; 13Adm, p. 83; 14Adm, p. 83; 15Adm, p. 83.
12. 2C 4, p. 364.
13. 3Let, p. 108.

Chapter 4

The Mediation of Creatures

1. Rainer Maria Rilke, *Selected Works* 2: *Poetry,* trans. J. B. Leishman, (New York: New Directions, 1960), p. 245.
2. 2C 165, p. 495.
3. 1C 80, p. 296.
4. 1C 81, p. 297.
5. Scheler, *op. cit.*, p. 88.
6. *Op. cit.*, p. 93.
7. *Op. cit.*, p. 92
8. *Ibid.*
9. Sp, ch. 118, p. 1257.
10. Teilhard de Chardin, *op. cit.*, p. 88.
11. Louis Lavelle, *L'erreur de Narcisse* (Paris: B. Grasset, 1939), p. 152.

Chapter 5

The Praise of the Sun

1. Nietzsche, *Zarathustra,* Part 1, no. 22: "On the Gift-Giving Virtue," p. 75.
2. Mircea Eliade, *Images and Symbols: Studies in Religious Symbolism,* trans. Philip Mairet (New York: Sheed & Ward, 1961), pp. 11, 20.
3. Sp, ch. 119, p. 1258.
4. *Ibid.*
5. Sp, ch. 119, pp. 1257-58.
6. Goethe, *Faust,* Part 2, Act 5, lines 11288-11303.
7. Cf. Eliade, *Patterns in Comparative Religion,* p. 132. Among some peoples the sun is a feminine and maternal symbol. "The symbolism of the sun is as multivalent as the reality of the sun is filled with contradictions" (*Dictionnaire des symboles,* ed. J. Chevalier [Paris: Laffont, 1969], p. 710). Thus, "among the Dogons of Mali, whose whole cosmogonic system is dominated by lunar symbolism, the sun is not male but female. It is described as a pot of earth that is white-hot and wrapped in a spiral strip of red leather which is wrapped around it eight times. It is thus the prototype of the maternal womb" (p. 712). "The sun is female (*mother sun*) and the moon male (*father moon*) in nomadic pastoral cultures. This is true of most of the Turko-Mongol tribes of central Asia" (p. 713). In German, of course, the noun for "sun," *die Sonne,* is feminine in gender, as it was in Celtic and all ancient Indo-European languages. It remains a fact, however that "among peoples possessing an astral mythology the sun is a symbol of the father, just as it is in children's drawings and adult dreams. In astrology, too, the sun has always been the symbol of the masculine generative principle and the authority principle, of which the father is, for the individual human being, the first embodiment" (p. 713).

8. Jean Daniélou, *Myth and Mystery,* trans. P. J. Hepburne-Scott (New York: Hawthorn, 1968), pp. 17-18.
9. Paul Claudel, *Oeuvre poétique* (Paris: La Pléiade, 1957), p. 110.
10. Gaston Bachelard, *The Poetics of Space,* trans. Marie Jolas (New York: Orion, 1964), p. xix.
11. Carl Gustav Jung, *Symbols of Transformation,* trans. R. F. C. Hull (Collected Works 5; New York: Pantheon, 1956), pp. 121-22.
12. Charles Baudouin, *De l'instinct à l'esprit* (Paris: Desclée De Brouwer, 1950), p. 287.
13. Text of the so-called Mithras Liturgy, published by Dietrich in 1910 and quoted by Jung, *op. cit.*, p. 87.
14. Eliade, *Patterns in Comparative Religion,* p. 138.
15. *Ibid.*
16. 1C 16, p. 242.
17. LP 43, pp. 1020-21; cf. 2C 213, pp. 532-33.
18. Jung, *L'âme et la vie,* p. 66.
19. LP 43, p. 1021.
20. Eliade *Patterns in Comparative Religion,* pp. 145-46.
21. Eliade, *op. cit.*, pp. 136-37.
22. Claudel, *Oeuvre poétique,* p. 244.
23. Carl Gustav Jung, *The Relations between the Ego and the Unconscious,* in *Two Essays in Analytical Psychology,* trans. R. F. C. Hull (Collected Works 7; New York: Pantheon, 1953), p. 236.
24. Carl Gustav Jung, *L'homme à la découverte de son âme,* trad. de l'allemand par R. Cahen (Paris: Buchet-Chastel, 1963), p. 335. [I could not locate this passage in the English translation, *Modern Man in Search of a Soul,* trans. W. S. Dell and Cary F. Baynes (New York: Harcourt and Brace, 1933). – Tr.]
26. Carl Gustav Jung, *Gut und Böse in der Psychotherapie* (Stuttgart: 1959), p. 37.
25. Carl Gustav Jung, *The Development of Personality,* trans. R. F. C. Hull (Collected Works 17; New York: Pantheon, 1954), p. 184.
27. Charles Baudouin, *L'oeuvre de Jung* (Paris: Payot, 1963), p. 228.
28. Paul Ricoeur, *The Symbolism of Evil,* p. 12.
29. Ricoeur, *op. cit.*, p. 13.
30. 2 Cor 4:6.
31. 1C 103, p. 318.

Chapter 6

The Lamps of Night

1. Test, p. 67. Cf. 2Let, p. 101: "a place that is properly prepared for it (*in loco pretioso*)"; 5Let, p. 113: "The [the clergy] should set the greatest value. . .on chalices. . . (*pretiosos habere debent*). . . .They should put It [the Body of Christ] somewhere that has been properly prepared for It (*in loco pretioso*)."

2. Eliade, *The Sacred and the Profane,* p. 157.
3. Eliade, *Patterns in Comparative Religion,* p. 184.
4. Eliade, *The Sacred and the Profane,* pp. 156-57.
5. *Sermo* 361; *De resurrectione* (PL 39:1605).
6. *Psychanalyse du symbole religieux,* p. 153.
7. Charles Péguy, *God Speaks: Religious Poetry,* trans. Julian Green (New York: Pantheon, 1945), p. 78.
8. *Op. cit.,* p. 80.
9. *Op. cit.,* p. 76.
10. *Op. cit.,* p. 77.
11. *Op. cit.,* p. 78.
12. Clemens Brentano: "Dunkelheit muss tief verschweigen / Alles Wehe, alle Lust; / Aber Mond und Sterne zeigen / Was mir wohnet in der Brust."
13. Goethe, *An den Mond:* "Lösest endlich auch einmal / Meine Seele ganz!"
14. Goethe, *An den Mond:* "Was im Menschen nicht gewusst / Oder nicht bedacht, / Durch das Layrinth der Brust / Wandelit in der Nacht."
15. Bachelard, *L'eau et les rêves,* p. 157.
16. Celano, *Vie de sainte Claire d'Assise,* French trans, by Damien Vorreux (Paris: Editions Franciscaines, 1953), p. 30. Italics added.
17. 1C 18, p. 244.
18. LM, ch. 12, no. 2, p. 722; Fior, ch. 16, pp. 1334-35.
19. Scheler, *op. cit.,* p. 93.
20. LP 43, pp. 1020-22; Sp, ch. 100, p. 1235. Cf. Arnaldo Fortini, *Nova Vita di San Francesco* (Assisi: Porziuncola, 1959), 2:471-543; and Raphael Brown, Appendix VIII in Englebert, *op. cit.,* pp. 441-58.
21. Sp, ch. 100, p. 1235; 2C 213, p. 532.
22. Jean Guitton, "Mythe et mystère de Marie," communication to the International Mariological Congress at Lisbon, 1967.
23. Novalis, *Hymns to the Night and Other Selected Writings,* trans. Charles E. Passage (Indianapolis: Bobbs-Merrill, 1960), pp. 3-4.
24. Ricoeur, *The Symbolism of Evil,* p. 13.
25. *Psychanalyse du symbole religieux,* p. 153.
26. *Patterns in Comparative Religion,* p. 147.
27. Nietzsche, *Zarathustra,* Part 2, no. 13: "On Those Who Are Sublime," p. 117.
28. *Op. cit.,* Part 3, no. 4: "Before Sunrise," p. 164.
29. *Op. cit.,* Part 2, no. 19: "The Night Song," pp. 105-6.
30. Ania Teillard, *Le symbolisme du rêve* (Paris: Stock, 1944), p. 202.
31. Rainer Maria Rilke, *The Book of Poverty and Death,* quoted in Gabriel Marcel, *Homo Viator: Introduction to a Metaphysics of Hope,* trans. Emma Craufurd (Chicago: Regnery, 1951), p. 236.
32. *Ibid.*

Chapter 7

The Song of Wind and Water

1. Gn 1:2.

2. Ex 14:21-22.
3. Ez 36:25-26.
4. Jn 3:5, 8.
5. "Seele des Menschen, / wie gleichst du dem Wasser! / Schicksal des Menschen, / wie gleichst du dem Wind!"
6. Paul Claudel, *Five Great Odes,* trans. Edward Lucie-Smith (Chester Springs, Pa.: Dufour, 1967), p. 30.
7. Gaston Bachelard, *L'air et les songes* (Paris: Corti, 1943), p. 21.
8. "Il y a quelqu'un / Dans le vent": Gillévic, *Terraqué,* p. 71, quoted in Bachelard, *op. cit.*, p. 262.
9. Rilke, *The Book of Poverty and Death,* quoted in Marcel, *op. cit.*, p. 236.
10. Louis Lavelle, *Four Saints,* trans. Dorothea O'Sullivan (New York: Pantheon, 1956; Notre Dame: Notres Dame University paperback, 1963), p. 47.
11. 2Reg, ch. 10, p. 63.
12. Cf. Beaudouin, *Psychanalyse du symbole religieux,* p. 248.
13. Emile Verhaeren, quoted in Bachelard, *op. cit.*, p. 267.
14. Ps 104:29-30.
15. LP 43, pp. 1020-21; 2C 213, pp. 532-33.
16. "Wind ist der Welle / lieblicher Bühler; / Wind mischt vom Grund aus / schäumende Wogen."
17. Trans. C. Day Lewis, in *Paul Valéry: Selected Writings,* by various translators (New York: New Directions, 1950), p. 49.
18. Francis Jacques, "Le moi, l'eau, et la parole," *Revue de Métaphysique et de Morale,* July-September, 1966, p. 341.
19. Ps 69:2-3.
20. Ps 88:17-18.
21. Bachelard, *L'eau et les rêves,* pp. 13-14.
22. Ez 47:1-12.
23. Jn 4:11
24. Fragment no. 10.
25. Martin Heidegger, *Approche de Hölderlin,* translated from German by H. Corbin et al. (Paris: Gallimard, 1962), p. 98.
26. Carl Gustav Jung, unpublished seminar on Nietzsche's *Thus Spoke Zarathustra* (1937), cited by Aniela Jaffé in C. G. Jung, *Ma Vie,* translated from German by R. Cahen and Y. Le Lay (Paris: Chastel, 1966), p. 452.
27. 1Let, p. 96.
28. LP 43, pp. 1020-21; cf. 2 C 213, pp. 532-33.

Chapter 8

Brother Fire

1. Sp 116, p. 1255.
2. 2C 166, p. 496.
3. *Op. cit.*, p. 137.
4. 2C 166, p. 496.
5. Sp 116, p. 1255.

6. *Ibid.*
7. 2C 165, p. 495.
8. *Ibid.*
9. 2C 166, p. 496.
10. Sp 118, p. 1257.
11. Pierre Teilhard de Chardin, "The Mass on the World," in *Hymn of the Universe*, trans. Simon Bartholomew (New York: Harper & Row, 1965), p. 21.
12. Gaston Bachelard, *The Psychoanalysis of Fire*, trans. Alan C. M. Ross (Boston: Beacon, 1964), chapter 3.
13. Gaston Bachelard, *La flamme d'une chandelle* (3rd ed.; Paris: Presses Universitaires de France, 1964), p. 3.
14. *Op. cit.*, p. 59.
15. Ps 29:7.
16. Ps 97:3.
17. Jer 23:29.
18. Lk 12:49.
19. Rv 1:14-16.
20. *Symbols of Transformation*, p. 89.
21. In *Père voici que l'Homme* (Paris: Editions du Seuil, 1955).
22. Paul Claudel, *L'oeil écoute*, quoted in Bachelard, *op. cit.*, p. 59.
23. Carl Gustav Jung, *Psychology and Religion*, chapter 2, in *Collected Works*, vol. 11 (New York: Pantheon, 1958), pp. 36-37.
24. Empedocles, *Le Livre de l'Occident* (Geneva, 1965).
25. Jb 41:11, 13.
26. Rv 12:3; 9:17-18.
27. Rv 20:12.
28. Is 66:24.
29. Scheler, *op. cit.*, p. 93.
30. Lippert, *op. cit.*, pp. 108, 109, 113.
31. LM, ch. 9, no. 4, p. 700.
32. LM, ch. 1, no. 1, p. 636.
33. 2C 6, p. 365.
34. 2C 6, pp. 365-66.
35. LM, ch. 1, no. 2, p. 637.
36. 2C 6, p. 366.
37. 2C 7, p. 366.
38. *Saint François d'Assise* (Paris: Bloud et Gay, 1964), p. 15.
39. Scheler, *op. cit.*, p. 92.
40. *Missa sine nomine*, French trans. Jacques Martin (Paris: Calman-Levy, 1953), p. 98.
41. 2C 166, p. 496.
42. Fior 24, pp. 1354-55.
43. Fior 15, p. 1333.
44. Cf. Chesterton, *op. cit.*, p. 166: "It would be hard to find a more imaginative image, for some sort of utterly pure and disembodied passion, than that red halo round the unconscious figures on the hill; a flame feeding on nothing and setting the very air on fire."
45. 3Let, p. 108.

46. Lippert, *op. cit.*, p. 116.
47. 1C 47, pp. 268-69.
48. *Metamorphoses*, Book 2.
49. The Latin text is from the critical edition: *Legendae S. Francisci Assisiensis saeculis XIII et XIV conscriptae* (Quaracchi: Collegio di S. Bonaventura, 1926-41). The works of Celano in this edition were also published separately in 1926; in the latter, the text of our story is on p. 52.
50. *Interior Castle,* trans. E. Allison Peers (New York: Sheed & Ward, 1944; Doubleday Image Books, 1961), Seventh Mansions, chapter 2, p. 216.
51. Jung, *Symbols of Transformation*, p. 97.
52. LM, ch. 4, no. 4, p. 656.
53. LM, ch. 9, no. 1, p. 698.

CHAPTER 9

Sister Earth, Our Mother

1. Eliade, *Patterns in Comparative Religion*, p. 245.
2. Francis attached a good deal of importance to grass and flowers. In each house, the gardener was to leave a border around the kitchen-garden for grass and flowers, so that these in their season might show how beautiful the Father of all things must be; cf. 2C 165, p. 495.
3. Bachelard, *L'eau et les rêves*, p. 1.
4. 1 C 71, p. 288.
5. Bachelard, *La terre et les rêveries du repos* (Paris: Corti, 1948), p. 209.
6. Jung, *Symbols of Transformation*, p. 388.
7. *Op. cit.*, p. 302.
8. Bachelard, *La terre et les rêveries du repos*, p. 204.
9. 1C 6-7, pp. 234-35.
10. Ricoeur, *The Symbolism of Evil*, p. 13.
11. 1C 10–11, pp. 237-38.
12. Mircea Eliade, *Myth and Reality*, trans. Willard R. Trask (New York: Harper & Row, 1963), p. 81.
13. Chesterton, *op. cit.*, p. 121.
14. Sp 119, p. 1257.
15. LP 43, pp. 1020-21; cf. 2C 213, pp. 532-33.
16. 1C 85, p. 300.
17. 1C 86, p. 301.
18. LM, ch. 10, no. 7, p. 711.
19. 2C 35, p. 392.
20. Jung, *Symbols of Transformation*, p. 303.
21. Eph 4:9-10.
22. 3Let, p. 106.
23. 1C 33, p. 256.
24. Eliade, *The Sacred and the Profane*, pp. 148-50.
25. Mircea Eliade, *Naissances mystiques* (Paris: Gallimard, 1959), p. 49.

26. Cf. *Symbols of Transformation*, p. 233.
27. Jung, *op. cit.*, pp. 245-46.
28. Dan 4:7-8.
29. Dan 4:17-19.
30. P. 196.
31. 1C 217, p. 536.
32. *Ibid.*
33. 1 C 214, p. 524.
34. 1C 217, p. 536.
35. LM, ch. 14, no. 4, p. 739.
36. Elaide, *The Sacred and the Profane*, pp. 142-43. Eliade is quoting Marcel Granet, "Le dépôt de l'enfant sur le sol," *Revue archéologique*, 1922, reprinted in his *Etudes sociologiques sur la Chine* (Paris, 1953), pp. 192-94.
37. P. Teilhard de Chardin, "The Mass on the World," in his *Hymn of the Universe*, pp. 31-32.
38. 2C 214, p. 534.
39. *The Brothers Karamazov*, trans. David Magarschack (Baltimore: Penguin, 1958), 1:334.
40. *Op. cit.*, 2:426-27. [The interior quotations, except the last, are allusions to statements of Zossima in the section, "From the Discourses and Sermons of the Elder Zossima," 1:368-81.]
41. P. Ricoeur, *The Symbolism of Evil*, p. 167.
42. *Ibid.*
43. Mikel Dufrenne and Paul Ricoeur, *Karl Jaspers et la philosophie de l'existence* (Paris: Editions du Seuil, 1947), p. 393.
44. Paul Ricoeur, *Freedom and Nature: The Voluntary and the Involuntary*, trans. Erzaim V. Kohák (Evanston: Northwestern University Press, 1966), p. 481.

Chapter 10

Pardon and Peace

1. Cf. *Omnibus*, pp. 128-29.
2. 1C 2, p. 230; cf. LM, ch. 1, no. 1, pp. 635-36.
3. Lippert, *op. cit.*, p. 119.
4. Test, p. 68.
5. 2C 172, p. 500.
5. *Ibid.*
7. 4Let, p. 110.
8. 1C 50, p. 271; cf. 7Let, p. 119.
9. Cf. 2C 165, p. 495: "He embraced all things with a rapture of unheard of devotion."
10. LM, ch. 9, no. 1, p. 698.
11. *Symbols of Transformation*, p. 226
12. Lavelle, *Four Saints*, p. 46.

Chapter 11

Sister Death

1. 2C 217, p. 536.
2. Ricoeur, *Freedom and Nature,* p. 456.
3. Ricoeur, *op. cit.*, p. 458.
4. Ricoeur, *op. cit.*, p. 471.
5. Ricoeur, *op. cit.*, p. 481.
6. 3Let, p. 106.
7. Lavelle, *op. cit.*, p. 41.
8. *Op. cit.*, pp. 240-41.
9. 1Let, p. 98.
10. *Ibid.*
11. *Op. cit.*, pp. 241-42.
12. PLeo, p. 126.
13. Emmanuel, *op. cit.*, p. 252.
14. Lavelle, *op. cit.*, p. 50.
15. LP 43, pp. 1020–21.
16. Rilke, *Sonnets to Orpheus,* Part I, Sonnet 3, in *Selected Works* 2: *Poetry,* translated by J. B. Leishman (New York: New Directions, 1960), p. 254.
17. *Op. cit.*, Part I, Sonnet 7, p. 256.
18. *Duino Elegies,* Elegy 7, p. 239.
19. *Sonnets to Orpheus,* Part I, Sonnet 9, p. 257.
20. *Op. cit.*, Part I, Sonnet 6, p. 255.
21. LP 43, pp. 1020-21.
22. *The Book of Poverty and Death,* in Marcel, *op. cit.*, p. 237.
23. Part I, Sonnet 5, p. 255.

Chapter 12

The Sun and the Cross

1. Cf., e.g., G. Bianquis' preface to his French translation, *Ainsi parlait Zarathoustra* (Paris: Aubier, 1946), p. 37.
2. *Zarathustra,* "Zarathustra's Prologue," p. 10.
3. *Zarathustra,* Part III, no. 13: "On Old and New Tablets," p. 198.
4. *Zarathustra,* Part I, no. 1: "On the Three Metamorphoses," p. 27.
5. Cf. chapter 2, above.
6. *Zarathustra,* Part II, no. 6: "On the Rabble," p. 99.
7. *Zarathustra,* Part III, no. 4: "Before Sunrise," p. 165.
8. Bachelard, *op. cit.*, p. 147.
9. *Ibid.*
10. *Op. cit.*, p. 149.
11. *Ecce Homo, suivi de poésies,* French trans. by H. Albert (Paris: Denoël-Gonthier, 1971), p. 144.
12. Bachelard, *op. cit.*, p. 150.
13. *Zarathustra,* Part II, no. 15: "On Immaculate Perception," p. 124 (ital-

ics added).
14. *Zarathustra,* Part III, no. 4: "Before Sunrise," p. 164.
15. *Ibid.*
16. *Ibid.*
17. *Zarathustra,* Part III, no. 4: "Before Sunrise," p. 165.
18. *The Gay Science,* trans. by Walter Kaufmann, Book 5, no. 371 (New York: Random House, 1974), p. 332.
19. Bachelard, *op. cit.*, p. 147.
20. *Ecce Homo, suivi de poèsies,* p. 245.
21. *Zarathustra,* Part III, no. 4: "Before sunrise," pp. 164-65.
22. *Zarathustra,* Part II, no. 6: "On the Rabble," pp. 98-99.
23. Mansuy, *op. cit.*, p. 337.
24. *Zarathustra,* Part I, no. 8: "On the Tree on the Mountainside," p. 42.
25. Poem quoted in Bachelard, *op. cit.*, p. 165.
26. Bachelard, *op. cit.*, pp. 165-66.
27. *Zarathustra,* Part III, no. 11: "On the Spirit of Gravity," p. 192.
28. *Zarathustra,* Part I, no. 7: "On Reading and Writing," p. 41.
29. Bachelard, *op. cit.*, p. 168.
30. *Op. cit.*, p. 158.
31. *Zarathustra,* Part III, no. 1: "The Wanderer," p. 154.
32. *Zarathustra,* Part III, no. 16: "The Seven Seals," p. 231.
33. *Freedom and Nature,* p. 477.
34. *Zarathustra,* Part II, no. 9: "The Night Song," p. 106.
35. *Le chemin de campagne,* French trans. by A. Préau, in *Questions III* (Paris: Gallimard, 1966), p. 11.
36. André Malraux, *Le musée imaginaire de la sculpture mondiale* 3: *Le monde chrétien* (Paris: Gallimard, 1954), p. 79.
37. 1C 115, p. 329.
38. Leonce de Grandmaison, *Jesus Christ: His Person—His Message—His Credentials,* trans. Basil Whelan and Ada Lane (New York: Sheed & Ward, 1935), 2:225.
39. Friedrich Hölderlin, quoted by Martin Heidegge in his *Approche de Hölderlin,* French trans. Corbin (Paris: Gallimard, 1962), p. 41.
40. St. Bonaventure, *Collationes in Hexaemeron,* XIII, 12, in *Opera Omnia* 5 (Quaracchi: Collegio S. Bonaventura, 1891), pp. 389-90: ". . .Mundus, etsi servit homini quantum ad *corpus,* potissime tamen quantum ad *animam;* etsi servit quantum ad *vitam,* potissime quantum ad *sapientiam.*"
41. Jn 9:6-7.
42. Beirnaert, *op. cit.*, p. 67.
43. Eph 2:15.
44. Paul Claudel, *The Tidings Brought to Mary,* trans. Louise Morgan Sill (New Haven: Yale University Press, 1916), Act 3, Scene 3, pp. 101-102.

Chapter 13

Man Redeemed

1. LP 43, pp. 1020-21; 2C 213, pp. 532-33.

2. Claudel, *The Tidings Brought to Mary*, p. 8.
3. Scheler, *op. cit.*, p. 91.
4. *Op. cit.*, pp. 90-91.
5. Rudolf Bultmann, *Jesus Christ and Mythology* (New York: Scribner's, 1958), p. 84.
6. Cf. our book, *Wisdom of the Poverello*, trans. M. L. Johnson, (Chicago: Franciscan Herald Press, 1961).
7. 1Vesp, p. 147.
8. LP 43, p. 1021.
9. *Op. cit.*, p. 196.

Conclusion

1. Jean Jaurès, *Histoire socialiste de la revolution française*, revised by A. Mathiez (Paris: Editions de la Librairie de l'Humanité, 1922 ff.), Introduction.
2. Rilke, *Sonnets to Orpheus*, Part I, Sonnet 3, in *op. cit.*, p. 256.
3. Sp 100, p. 1236.
4. Sp 101, p. 1238.
5. Dante, *The Divine Comedy* 3: *Paradise*, Canto XI, lines 46-54, trans. Dorothy L. Sayers and Barbara Reynolds (Baltimore: Penguin, 1963), p. 150. Italian text: "Di questa costa là dov'ella frange / piu sua rattezza, nacque al mondo un sole / . . . / Però chi d'esso loco fa parole / non dica Ascesi, che direbbe corto, / ma Oriente, se proprio dir vuole."
6. Heidegger, *Le chemin de compagne*, p. 11.
7. Cf. SV, pp. 132-33.
8. *Freedom and Nature*, p. 477.
9. Ricoeur, *Freud and Philosophy*, p. 551.
10. Rilke, *Duino Elegies*, Eighth Elegy, in *op. cit.*, p. 242.
11. *Les âges de la vie*, (Paris: Editions du Cerf, 1957), p. 81.
12. Cf. 4Adm, p. 8; 13Adm, p. 83; 14Adm, p. 83.
13. Cf. 11Adm, p. 82; 15Adm, p. 83; 27Adm, p. 86; 2Reg, ch. 7, p. 62; 1Reg, ch. 7, p. 38.
14. SV, p. 132.
15. Herbert Marcuse, *One-Dimensional Man: Studies on the Ideology of Advanced Industrial Society* (Boston: Beacon, 1964), p. 240.
16. Dostoyevsky, *The Brothers Karamazov*, 2:426.

Epilogue

1. One of the five Franciscans.
2. *Zarathustra*, Zarathustra's Prologue, no. 5, p. 17.
3. Rilke, *The Book of Poverty and Death*, in Marcel, *op. cit.*, p. 237.
4. *Ibid.*

Canticum Solis

1. Cf. Damien Vorreux, *Opuscules de saint François d'Assise*, Latin text and French translation (Paris: Editions Franciscaines, 1956), pp. 309-310: "We give here, as the original text, the oldest written version of the *Canticle of Creatures.* It is contained, with the other works of the Saint, in ms 388 of the Municipal Library of Assisi (originally in the Sacro Convento San Francesco), which dates from 1279."

Bibliography

Bibliography
1. Texts and Documents

Analecta Franciscana, volumes 1-10. Quaracchi, 1885-1941.
Analekten zur Geschichte des Franziskus von Assisi, edited by H. Boehmer and F. Wiegand. 3rd ed. Tübingen, 1961.
Opuscula sancti Patris Francisci Assisiensis. Quaracchi, 1904. 2nd ed., 1948.
St. Francis of Assisi: Writings and Early Biographies. English Omnibus of the Sources for the Life of St. Francis, edited by M. A. Habig. Chicago, 1973.

2. Studies
(in chronological order)

Benedetto, L. F. *Il Cantico di frate Sole.* Florence, 1941. Cf. review in *Archivum Franciscanum Historicum* (*AFH*) 34 (1941), 236-42.
Pagliaro, A. "Il Cantico di frate Sole," in *Quaderni di Roma* 1 (1947), 218-35, and in *Saggi di critica semantica* (Messina—Florence, 1953), pp. 201 ff.
Branca, V. "Il Cantico di frate Sole," *AFH* 41 (1948), 3-87. Published separately, Florence, 1950.
De Robertis, G. "Il Cantico delle Creature," in *Studi* (2nd ed.; Florence, 1952), pp. 17 ff.
Vicinelli, A. "Il Cantico di frate Sole," in *Tutti gli scritti di San Francesco e i Fioretti* (Milan, 1955), pp. 219-52.
Fortini, A. "Di alcuni questioni reguardanti la composizione del Cantico del Sole," *in Santa Chiara: Studie Cronaca del VII centenario* (Assisi, 1954), pp. 275-98.
Getto, G. *San Francesco d'Assisi e il Cantico di frate Sole.* Turin, 1956.
Platzeck, E. W. *Das Sonnenlied des Heiligen Franziskus von Assisi.* Munich, 1957.
Sabatelli, G. "Studi recenti sul Cantico di frate Sole," *AFH* 51 (1958), 3-24.
Fortini, A. *Nova Vita di San Francesco.* Assisi, 1959. Cf. 2:471-543, and volume 3. Cf. also review in *AFH* 53 (1960), 324-26.
Englebert, O. *Saint Francis of Assisi: A Biography.* New trans. by E. M. Cooper, 2nd Eng. ed. rev. and aug. by I. Brady and R. Brown, Chicago, 1965. Cf. Appendix VII, pp. 441-58, Cf. review in *AFH* 61 (1968), 234-37.
De Beer, Fr. *La conversion de saint François selon Thomas de Celano.* Paris, 1963.

3. Works Cited in This Book

Bachelard, G. *L'air et les songes.* Paris, 1943.
———. *L'eau et les rêves.* Parish, 1942.
———. *La flamme d'une chandelle.* 3rd ed. Paris, 1964.
———. *The Poetics of Reverie,* trans. D. Russell. New York, 1969.
———. *The Poetics of Space,* trans. M. Jolas. New York, 1964.
———. *The Psychoanalysis of Fire,* trans. A. C. M. Ross. New York, 1964.
———. *La terre et les rêveries du repos.* Paris, 1948.
———. *La terre et les rêveries de la volonté.* Paris, 1948.
Baudouin, Ch. *De l'instinct à l'esprit.* Paris, 1950.
———. *L'oeuvre de Jung.* Paris, 1963.
———. *Psychanalyse du symbole religieux.* Paris, 1957.
Beirnaert, L. "The Mythical Dimension in Christian Sacramentalism," in C. Hastings and D. Nicholl (eds.), *Selection I.* New York, 1953.
Bonaventure, St. *Collationes in Hexaemeron.* Opera omnia 5. Quaracchi, 1891.
———. *The Journey of the Mind of God,* trans. J. de Vinck, in *The Works of Bonaventure* 1: *Mystical Opuscula.* Paterson, 1960.
Bultmann, R. *Jesus Christ and Mythology.* New York, 1958.
Chesterton, G. K. *St. Francis of Assisi.* New York, 1924.
Chevalier, J., and Gheerbrant, A. (eds.). *Dictionnaire des symboles.* Paris, 1969.
Claudel, P. *Oeuvre poétique.* Paris, 1957.
———. *The Tidings Brought to Mary,* trans. L. M. Sill. New Haven, 1916.
Dufrenne, M., and Ricoeur, P. *Karl Jaspers et la philosophie de l'existence.* Paris, 1947.
Eliade, M. *Images and Symbols: Studies in Religious Symbolism,* trans. P. Mairet. New York, 1961.
———. *Myth and Reality,* trans. W. R. Trask. New York, 1963.
———. *The Myth of the Eternal Return,* trans. W. R. Trask. New York, 1954.
———. *Naissances mystiques: Essais sur le symbolisme magico-religieux.* Paris, 1952.
———. *Patterns in Comparative Religion,* trans. R. Sheed. New York, 1958.
———. *The Sacred and the Profane,* trans. W. R. Trask. New York, 1959.
Emmanuel, P. *Evangéliaire.* Paris, 1961.
———. *Le goût de l'Un.* Paris, 1963.
Guardini, R. *Les âges de la vie.* Paris, 1957.
Heidegger, M. *Approche de Hölderlin.* Paris, 1962.
———. "Le chemin de compagne," in *Questions III.* Paris, 1966.
Jung, C. G. *L'âme et la vie.* Paris, 1963.
———. *The Development of Personality,* trans. R. F. C. Hull. Collected Works 17. New York, 1954.
———. *L'homme à la découverte de son âme.* Paris, 1963.
———. *Gut und Böse in der Psychotherapie.* Stuttgart, 1959.
———. *Psychology and Religion.* New Haven, 1938. Reprinted in Collected works 11.
———. *Symbols of Transformation,* trans. R. F. C. Hull. Collected Works 5. New York, 1956.
———. "The Relations between the Ego and the Unconscious," in *Two Essays in Analytical Psychology,* trans. R. F. C. Hull. Collected Works 7. New York, 1953.

______. Unpublished seminar on Nietzsche's *Thus Spoke Zarathustra.* (1937).
Lavelle, L. *L'erreur de Narcisse.* Paris, 1939.
______. *Four Saints,* trans. D. O'Sullivan. New York, 1956; paperback, Notre Dame, 1963.
Lippert, P. *Bonté.* Paris, 1946.
Malraux, A. *Le musée imaginaire de la sculpture mondiale* 3: *Le monde chrétien.* Paris, 1954.
Mansuy, M. *Gaston Bachelard et les éléments.* Paris, 1967.
Marcuse, H. *One-Dimensional Man: Studies in the Ideology of Advanced Industrial Society.* Boston, 1964.
Nietzsche, F. *Beyond Good and Evil: Prelude to a Philosophy of the Future,* trans. W. Kaufmann. New York, 1966.
______. *Ecco homo, suivi de poésies.* Paris, 1971.
______. *The Gay Science,* trans. W. Kaufmann, New York, 1974.
______. *Thus Spoke Zarathustra,* trans. W. Kaufmann. New York, 1954.
Novalis, F. *Hymns to the Night and Other Selected Writings,* trans. C. E. Passage. Indianapolis, 1960.
Péguy, Ch. *God Speaks: Religious Poetry,* trans. J. Green, New York, 1945.
Ricoeur, P. *The Conflict of Interpretations: Essays in Hermeneutics,* ed. by D. Ihde. Evanston, 1974.
______. *Freedom and Nature: The Voluntary and the Involuntary,* trans. E. V. Kohak. Evanston, 1966.
______. *Freud and Philosophy: An Essay on Interpretation,* trans. D. Savage. New Haven, 1970.
______. *The Symbolism of Evil,* trans. E. Buchanan. New York, 1967.
Rilke, R. M. *The Book of Poverty and Death,* selections translated in G. Marcel, *Homo Viator: Introduction to a Metaphysics of Hope,* trans. E. Craufurd.
______. *Duino Elegies* and *Sonnets to Orpheus,* trans. J. B. Leishman, in *Selected Works* 2: *Poetry.* New York, 1960.
Scheler, M. *The Nature of Sympathy,* trans. P. Heath. New Haven, 1954.
Teilhard de Chardin, P. "The Mass on the World," in *Hymn of the Universe,* trans. S. Bartholomew. New York, 1965.
______. *Writings in Time of War,* trans. R. Hague. New York, 1968.
Teillard, A. *Le symbolisme du rêve.* Paris, 1944.
Valéry, P. *Selected Writings,* trans. various hands. New York, 1950.
Vorreux, D. *Saint François d'Assise.* Paris, 1964.